1982

.B38
621
HT

D1255433

1982
.838
621
HT

Memories of class

International Library of Sociology

Founded by Karl Mannheim
Editor: John Rex, University of Aston in Birmingham

Arbor Scientiae

Arbor Vitae

A catalogue of the books available in the International Library
of Sociology and other series of Social Science books published
by Routledge & Kegan Paul will be found at the end of this
volume.

Memories of class

The pre-history and after-life of class

Zygmunt Bauman

012565

LIBRARY
SOUTHWEST CENTER, SAUJD
800 Quintana Road
San Antonio, Texas 78221

Routledge & Kegan Paul
London, Boston, Melbourne and Henley

ST. PHILIP'S COLLEGE LIBRARY

First published in 1982
by Routledge & Kegan Paul Ltd
39 Store Street, London WC1E 7DD,
9 Park Street, Boston, Mass. 02108, USA,
296 Beaconsfield Parade, Middle Park,
Melbourne, 3206, Australia and
Broadway House, Newtown Road,
Henley-on-Thames, Oxon RG9 1EN
Printed in Great Britain by
The Thetford Press Ltd, Norfolk
© Zygmunt Bauman 1982
No part of this book may be reproduced in
any form without permission from the
publisher, except for the quotation of brief
passages in criticism

Library of Congress Cataloging in Publication Data

Bauman, Zygmunt.

Memories of class.
(International library of sociology)
Bibliograhy: p.
Includes index.
1. Social classes--History. I. Title. II. Series.
HT621.B38 1982   305.5'09   82-9828

ISBN 0-7100-9196-6   AACR 2

Contents

Acknowledgments

I am deeply grateful to Philip Abrams, Reinhard Bendix, Thomas Bottomore, Anthony Giddens, Ralph Miliband and Dennis Warwick, who read various parts of this work at various stages of its production, offered their insightful criticism and invaluable advice and greatly contributed to the ultimate maturation of the project. I wish I could make a better use of the inspiring ideas I owe them.

Z.B., Leeds

1 Class: before and after. A preview

Memory is the after-life of history. It is through memory that history continues to live in the hopes, the ends, and the expectations of men and women as they seek to make sense of the business of life, to find a pattern in chaos, to construe familiar solutions to unfamiliar worries. Remembered history is the stuff of which these hopes, objectives and insights are made; in turn, the latter are the repositories where images of the past are rescued from oblivion. Memory is history-in-action. Remembered history is the logic which the actors inject into their strivings and which they employ to invest credibility into their hopes. In its after-life, history reincarnates as a Utopia which guides, and is guided by, the struggles of the present.

Remembered history seldom agrees with the history of the historians. This does not mean that historians, great or small, are immune to the group practice which shapes historical memory; neither does this mean that the work of the historians exerts no influence on the way the memory of the group selects and transforms its objects. By and large, however, remembered history and the history (histories?) of the historians follow their own respective courses. They are propelled by different needs, guided by different logic, and subject to different validity tests. There is little point, therefore, in asking whether the beliefs in which remembered history may be verbalised are true or false, by the standards set by professional historical inquiry. The 'materiality' of remembered history, its effectivity, indeed, its historical potential - do not rest on its truth so understood.

For a sociologist trying to grasp the springs of group practices, remembered history (or historical memory) is not a competitive account of something which can be presented by another, perhaps better, narrative; it is not an object of critique, a text called upon to hold out its credentials, and dismissed once it fails to do so. Sociology is neither a rival, nor the judge of historical memory. The failure of the latter to pass the professional truth-test is therefore of no relevance to the question of its sociological importance.

The phenomenon of historical memory presents, however, problems more complex than this of the choice between the attitude of critique and the attitude of description and explanation. Before such a choice is made, remembered history must first be 'constructed'. Unlike the history of the historians, remembered

1

history cannot be 'referentially defined' by pointing to so many
books where its content has been duly and fully recorded. Worse
still, it cannot always be gauged by extending inquiry to a new
type of potentially objective evidence – say, the sales or library
demand for some rather than other historical books, the intensity of the contemporary interest in or neglect of various types
of historical literature, etc.; this latter method, if effective,
is naturally limited to the 'historical memory' of the educated,
the literate, the articulate. But not all historical actors belong
to this category. In the case of those who do not (who neither
write the books nor read them), one would search in vain for
the direct or indirect articulations of history as they 'remembered' it. Also, the recently developing methods of 'oral history'
would shed only oblique light on the issue; the problem with
'remembered history' of virtually all groups except the educated
elite is not merely that it has not been recorded in writing, but
that it rarely, if ever, surfaces to the level of verbal communication, written or oral. The historical memory of a group
which has been ploughed into its collective actions, which
finds its expression in the group's proclivities to some rather
than other behavioural responses, is not necessarily recognised
by the group as a particular concept of the past. The authority
of the past, and the ensuing need to possess some clear knowledge of the past in order to select right patterns of present
conduct, is a philosophers' issue, read into the collective
actions by the interpreters, and not an organic factor of the
action itself. The existential mode of historical memory is not
unlike that of grammar. For the interpreter, the observed
behaviour is incomprehensible unless its presence is assumed,
and remains unexplained as long as its guiding rules remain
inarticulate. But the actors themselves need not have the
consciousness of the rules in order to follow them properly;
and it is not they whom the interpreter would wish to inter-
rogate in his search for the consistent formulation of the rules.

It is in this sense that the remembered history must be 'constructed'. The reconstruction is, essentially, the task of the
interpreter, a task which is indispensable for the understanding of group action, though not for its accomplishment.
In the process of construction, recorded opinions of the actors
are not seen by the interpreter as accounts, complete or partial, of the living history which merely need to be assembled
into a cohesive totality through hypothesising the possible forms
of the missing links and employing analogy to postulate affini-
ties: they are not treated as incomplete or imperfect theories
of tradition which ought to be implemented and at times cor-
rected. Such opinions, together with non-verbalised actions,
are seen rather as elements of behaviour which is to be understood in its totality, by reference to the antecedent experiences
of the group, and to the challenge the new situation of the
group presents if perceived against this background. The
interpreter's view of remembered, or living history emerges in

the course of his effort to understand group reactions to the
changing circumstances of life.

The procedure may be considered legitimate only if some
assumptions are tacitly made. First, that - by and large -
people prefer repetitive patterns of conduct, these being more
economical and less unnerving than designing a response ad
hoc, without being able to calculate the chance of success in
advance. Second, that for this reason effective patterns prac-
tised in the past tend to be reinforced; the more they are
habitualised, as it were, the more they are economical. Third,
that it is precisely because of this propensity to learn that
people experience a rapid change of circumstances as a threat;
they resent the invalidation of the once trustworthy life wisdom.
Fourth, when faced with such a change, people would be
inclined either to refute the legitimacy of the new, or to try
to force it into the familiar patterns; most often, they will
attempt to do both things at the same time.

Projected upon our theme, these assumption generate the
notion of remembered history as a residue of historical learning,
which 'makes sense' of the group reactions to the change in
the circumstances in which their business of life is conducted.
What the notion implies is that these reactions are best understood as backward-looking. Even when articulated in a vocabulary of future, as-yet-unachieved states, and however profound the alteration of social realities they bring about as a
consequence, the group actions derive their meaning from
tradition. Historical action - human existence as such, as it
were - is, to borrow Heidegger's expression, a constant recapi-
tulation of tradition: in other words, it is a process of constant
negotiation between learned proclivities and new dependencies,
marked by the resistance of the traditional language to resign
its authority over perception of reality and the normative regulation of group behaviour. This account of the role of historical
memory in historical action does not necessarily imply that a
conservative bias is built into historical interpretation. What it
does inevitably imply is the need for the interpreter to untangle
the subtle dialectical interaction between the future orientation
and the past determination, Utopia and tradition, the emergence
of new structures of action and the language which had shaped,
and was shaped by, the old.

To put it differently, the concept of historical memory does
not imply the idea of well-formed, consciously appropriated
and consulted visions of tradition, resilient to change and
suggesting, by this very resilience, a 'natural preference' for
traditionalism. Even less does the concept imply a version of
the 'plus ça change, plus c'est la même chose' historiosophy.
The concept refers simply to the fact that at the foundation of
any historical transformation lies the growing inadequacy of
the learned pattern of expectation and behaviour to the circumstances in which the business of life is conducted. The likely
reaction to such inadequacy is initially an attempt to bring the

ST. PHILIP'S COLLEGE LIBRARY

circumstances back into accordance with the pattern of learned
behaviour. If this fails (and it normally does), a situation of
crisis follows, marked by a high degree of disorganisation and
reflected, on the one hand, in the prophecies of imminent doom,
and on the other in the proliferation of revolutionary Utopias.
Apathy coupled with growing ineffectivity of social institutions,
or radical vigour leading to political, social and cultural re-
alignments are both possible outcomes. Neither is predetermined
by the sheer configuration of inadequacy and guaranteed in
advance. The choice between possible outcomes cannot be pre-
dicted; its mechanism can be only described retrospectively.

The essays collected in this book attempt to do just this.

The two hypotheses followed in this book are concerned with
the origins and the later crisis of a society articulated as a
configuration of social classes characterised by opposed interests and preoccupied with rendering the distribution of social
product to their advantage. According to the first hypothesis,
the articulation of class society was an almost century-long
process which culminated in the first part of the nineteenth
century. It was an essentially unintended and unanticipated
effect of a struggle to restore social institutions guaranteeing
group status and individual security in a historical configuration which these institutions could not effectively serve: its
mature product institutionalised the memory of this struggle
as well as divisions and alliances which crystallised in its
course. According to the second hypothesis, the current multi-
faceted crisis of class society (economic crisis: falling growth,
falling rate of profit, growing unemployment; political crisis:
'blocked' corporatist state and a schizophrenic mixture of
excessive expectations aimed at government with almost universal disapproval of the expansion of its activities; cultural
crisis: the ever more evident ineffectuality of work-and-
achievement ethics and the gradual substitution of the 'power
of disruption' for the 'contribution to communal welfare' in
the rhetoric of distributive struggle) is a symptom of the
incapacity of the institutions of class society to guarantee
group status and individual security in an essentially transformed social organisation. Either side can gain little, if anything at all, from the strategy of distributive class warfare.
Nevertheless, it is the memorised class strategies which provide
cognitive and normative patterns to deal with the crisis. In
this sense, the present period rehashes the situation of the
early nineteenth century: the rhetoric of restitution, restoration, defence of ancient rights and ancient justice actuated
processes with effects which cannot be deduced from their
conscious articulations, however strongly they depend on them.

The argument supporting the first hypothesis can be out-
lined in several points:

1 The factor mainly responsible for the crisis (an interruption
in the gradual, accremental change when the extant institutions
absorb new conditions, modifying in the process in a fashion not

sudden enough to be perceived as revolutionary) in Western
Europe which was to lead eventually to the articulation of
class society was the demographic explosion of the eighteenth
century. A rapid growth in population is by itself merely a
statistical phenomenon. Its sociological significance, and its
role as a factor of historical change, cannot be deduced from
the numbers (though many interpretations, skipping the whole
area of socio-cultural mediations, try to do just this, from
Malthus on); they derive instead from the inability of available
institutions to assimilate the growing numbers of people and
meet their status and security needs in keeping with the established standards. No population, however large, is super-
numerary or superfluous because of its sheer numbers; 'superfluity' itself is a notion which cannot be defined with sense
without reference to concrete socio-cultural patterns. The
problem with the eighteenth-century demographic upsurge was
that it exceeded the absorptive capacity of the then available
social institutions. As Barrington Moore Jr succintly put it,
'it was surplus to that particular social order and that particular
level of technical development at that specific stage of historical
development. Later in the nineteenth century there was a much
bigger increase in population without serious social strains.'[1]
     For the overwhelming majority of the pre-modern population,
the tasks of status definition and maintenance, as well as the
provision of life security, were performed on the local level and
grounded in local institutions – parishes, village and town
councils, craft guilds. The parish and the guild were not
specialised organisations, assigned clearly defined jobs; for
most of the people they were total worlds, in which the expectation of work and insurance against poverty – indeed, the guarantee of the place in society – was naturally inscribed. It is
not that the parish and the guild performed the task better than
alternative institutions and were for this reason preferred;
simply, there were no alternative institutions fit for the task.
The failure of the parish or the guild to deliver according to the
time-sanctioned expectations took the bottom out of the entire
mode of life.
     It is worth emphasising that England, where the modern
class society, as well as the new industrial system which under-
lay it, were theoretically and institutionally articulated earlier
than elsewhere in Europe, had had an intricate network of
social relief, and the concomitant notion of the state responsibility for the subsistence of all its subjects, well entrenched
for several centuries before the dramatic take-off of the late
eighteenth century. In Harold Perkin's words, what made
English history so different from that of continental Europe
was the 'defeat of the peasants and their transformation into
large commercial rent-paying farmers on the one hand and a
larger body of landless labourers on the other', which, among
other things, accounted 'for the unique English system of poor
relief...not needed in peasant societies where the holding

supports everybody, or when famine comes they all starve together'.[2] Writing in 1764, Richard Burn listed some twenty-five different legislative acts spelling out the duties of towns, villages, parishes in providing for the survival of 'impotent poor' and for the employment of the able-bodied.[3] The equally profuse legislation which conceptualised the phenomenon of vagrancy and called for an exceptionally harsh treatment of 'unauthorised' beggars and vagabonds, tied the poor even more firmly to their native parishes, thus reinforcing the bond of the locally inscribed duties and rights. The centuries of such legally fortified structure bore heavily on the kind of historical memory which proved to be instrumental in the articulation of class society.

2 The demographic bulge of the late eighteenth century, while providing the fuel for industrial take-off, stretched the locally based institutions of social security to the point of breakdown. The old system was slow to recognise its imminent bankruptcy, as testified by the abortive Speenhamland effort to maintain the old principles in the face of changed circumstances. But it had to declare its insolvency under the double pressure of the rapidly growing numbers of propertyless families and individuals, and the manufacturers keen to untie the local bonds which limited both the mobility and the pliancy of potential labourers. When the local network of the status and security allocation finally gave way, the crucial 'second period' in the history of social services began, 'brief on the Continent, but more prolonged in England', when the state in Ernest Barker's words, had to take some responsibility for the 'mass of uprooted country-workers employed in the factories of the towns or in mining centres'.[4] With the benefit of hindsight, these times, marked by the despair, suffering, sometimes fury of the 'uprooted', appear as an intermediate stage between two successive systems through which society catered for status allocation and security needs; even as a period of 'site clearing' for the erection of the new, arguably more comprehensive and universal network of institutions. Obviously, this was not the way in which the contemporaries could perceive their turbulent times, when the old centre did not hold any more while the new could be at best conceived as a noble vision of social dreamers. The dearth of foresight was not the sole reason for alarm. The natural limits of historical imagination apart, the times were indeed institutionally under-provided, and the vanishing laws and ancient customs left a gaping hole where before (as historical memory suggested) spread the solid ground of secure existence.

No retrospective wisdom, however, can justify the dismissal of diagnoses and demands of the era as errors of historical judgment or product of sluggish imagination; still less can they be disposed of as retrograde, backward-looking ideas, slackening the pace of progress. If later history invalidated most of the diagnoses and took the steam off most of the demands, it

did so precisely thanks to the shape these diagnoses and
demands took, moulded as they were by historical memory. Far
from being spokes in the wheel of history, these diagnoses
and demands, and the 'living history' which gave them shape
and vigour, set historical change in motion and pushed the
vehicle of society to its qualitatively new mode of equilibrium.

3 What made the period in question an era of sharp conflicts,
shifting alliances, consolidation of new divisions and, on the
whole, an accelerating social change, was ultimately (to borrow
Barrington Moore's cogent term) the sense of 'outraged justice'
on the part of those who justly felt their status withdrawn and
the grounds of their security undermined. Paradoxically, the
most profound re-articulation of society in human history
derived its momentum from the hostility to change which spurred the impaired and the threatened into defensive (to wit,
subjectively conservative) action. The intensity of militancy
did not reflect the absolute level of destitution, but the distance
between expectations and reality. Penury correlated but feebly
with social protest. The rebels were sometimes paupers - but
more often than not they acted to stave off the spectre of indigence; invariably they took to the warpath when the rung of
the social ladder on which they stood just started to feel slip-
pery. Habitual rights withdrawn accomplished what a habitualised privation never would have done.

In his recent survey of the seminal half century of European
history, Olwen H. Hufton explored the consequences of the
rapid increase of population for the insecurity of habitual ways
and means of existence. The effect of the demographic upsurge
of 1760s was in all parts of the West 'an uncomfortable imbalance
between population and economic performance. Even in years
of normal harvests the number of those unable to make their
resources stretch without recourse to begging was rapidly
growing.' The remarkable result of the widespread insecurity
was, as Hufton documented country by country, that 'the poor
themselves were not protesters but the same could not be said
for those fighting to remain on the right side of the line mark-
ing sufficiency from destitution'.[5] Insecurity as such made a
miserable condition; but it was the withdrawal of security which
kindled the fire of social protest.

The rapid erosion of protective institutions was a major
(perhaps the major) immediate cause of discontent. The gradual
disassembly of the legal foundation of state-enforced paternalism
was particularly painfully felt by the groups which grew
accustomed to the permanence of their, however humble, privileges of status. Since Brentano, historians have tended to
underline the crucial role of certain parliamentary acts, like
the repeal of the apprenticeship clause of the 1563 Statute of
Artificers and Apprentices (5 Elizabeth) in 1814, as milestones
in the re-alignment of social and political forces - as, indeed,
crucial factors in the formation of labourers into a working
class. In his seminal 'The Making of the English Working Class',

E.P. Thompson profusely documented the role of the 'deep-rooted folk memory', which expressed itself not only in the natural longing for stable foundations of individual security, but also, more specifically, in the nostalgia for traditional patterns of work and leisure. Thompson's conclusion was that 'these years appear at times to display, not a revolutionary challenge, but a resistance movement, in which both the Romantics and the Radical craftsmen opposed the annunciation of Acquisitive Man'.[6] The abolition of 5 Elizabeth meant not only the withdrawal of status for labourers used to expect, with reason, the custom-prescribed advancement in their trade position. It changed as well, and changed beyond recognition, the very character of apprenticeship as an initiation into a totality of patterned existence of the closely-knit trade community. The repeal of the limited access to apprenticeship meant in practice the denial of access to this community: the craftsmen's resistance against the withdrawal of legal protection of apprenticeship (the first protest movement of the disprivileged as producers, rather than consumers), was a struggle for the restoration of such a community. In John Rule's recent summary, 'the protest of the manufacturing poor was conservative in its appeal to custom, paternalistic legislation and in its seeking to reinforce traditional usage'.[7]

4 The dissipation of locally based paternalistic institutions giving way under the overwhelming pressure of demographic bulge resulted in a massive production of paupers and beggars. This was the aspect of change most easily sighted by both intellectual reformers and the governments worried with the anticipated threat to the public order; the end of the eighteenth century is the time of a most fervent, at times panic-stricken, legislative bustle aimed at the containment and confinement of vagrants and vagabonds and sweeping the beggars out of the streets and highways. It is, in Michel Foucault's apt summary, the 'age of prison' - the time when legislatures, manufacturers, doctors and psychiatrists co-operated in using enclosure as a main method of separating order from disorder, the speakable from the unspeakable, the visible from the unseen. And yet, as Barrington Moore concludes in the wake of a scrupulous comparative research of the origins of the modern revolt against injustice, 'those who are the worst off are generally the last to organise and make their voices heard'. The voice of protest rises to its pitch just above the destitution line and fades off once the line is crossed. It was the guild masters of the suddenly overcrowded German towns of the early nineteenth century who stood fast: they wanted 'much greater power in the state, measures to preserve their social and moral role as well as the economic one - a harking back to the pre-capitalist situation with a certain amount of idealised window-dressing - and measures to restrict the number of apprentices and tighten up access to the guilds.'[8]

The spectre of pauperisation undeniably added a sense of

urgency to the defensive action, and subconscious fears to its passion. But the objectives of struggle were fixed by historical memory, and this was not the experience of poverty and lack of subsistence. The 'harking back' was towards the recollection of trade as property of the craftsman, as against the new-fangled idea, and practice, of labour (and, for all practical intents and purposes, the labourer himself) as commodity. Karl Polanyi, in his daringly synthetic 'Great Transformation', dwelt at length on the inconclusive, and in the end abortive, struggle of the expanding market system to absorb labour and dissolve it in the uniform mass of commodities dependent for their price on the free play of offer and demand: and on the intrinsic indivisible unity between economic and social facets of labour as the natural barrier between the reality of capitalist society and its idealised projection in the form of the perfect market. The barrier could be neither knocked down nor leapt over, however strong were the legally backed market pressures. Unlike other commodities, labour could not be separated from its former owner after the act of purchase; the way in which it was used or abused reflected back on the well-being of the owner, ineradicably present at the act of its consumption. The consumption of labour as commodity was in practice indistinguishable from the management of the condition of the labourer as a social being (looking from the market side of the coin, Ricardo was perhaps first to articulate this subsumption of the social category of labourers under the economic category of labour). Reduction of labour relations to a purely commodity transaction, the detachment of contract from all and any 'social strings' unrelated to the consumption of effort as an abstract value, could not but be experienced from the other side of the coin as an attack on the social standing of the labourer, an attempt to transform the labourer himself into a commodity. One can interpret in retrospect the resistance of the craftsmen against unhampered market play as, above all, the defence of labour as a property of those who labour; more generally and perhaps more abstractly than contemporary consciousness would have it - as the defence of the activity of labour as an integral part and parcel of social bonds, against its reduction to a merely economic transaction.

This interpretation goes some way towards the explanation of the remarkable loyalty to the customary privileges of the trade as a whole, and acceptance of the hierarchy of power within the trade, which throughout most of the epoch of the great transformation united masters and their apprentices against the landowner's interests, grain merchants, financiers, entrepreneurs, and the governments which lent their support to their destructive practices. The self-defence of labourers which left lasting sediment in the form of trade unions was originally seldom aimed at the masters; when it was, the intention was to bring the masters back into line with the custombound expectation of 'fairness'. As John Rule found out,[9]

within a trade horizontal fissures arose because the component levels did not live up to reciprocal expectations. Thus
some masters might be seen as acting in an *unmasterlike*
manner, or at *some* time masters in general might forget their
obligations sufficiently to act solely in their own interest.
This would produce temporary conflict along horizontal lines
implying perceived separation of interest.

The conflict, though, was to remain, for some time, temporary.
The dominant tendency was the defence of the essential unity
of the trade: more generally, the defence of the principle of
labour as inscribed in the framework of inviolable social relations and thereby exempt from the heavy-handed, rough and
callous 'justice' of the market.
   It was ultimately the failure of this strategy of defence which
led to the fateful re-alignment of solidarities and antagonisms
known as the emergence of class society.
   5 The conservative rebellion can be seen also in another
way: as the last tremors of the long earthquake which shook
the foundations of the old social power thus clearing the
ground for the new one. The process took several centuries
to accomplish, but its last stages made a particularly dramatic
spectacle, as the process was compressed and accelerated with
the advent of the factory system. The passage from the old to
the new power was a corollary of the seminal change in the
management of the surplus product. Up to the beginnings of
the industrial society, this product was extracted from the producers mostly as an element of redistribution - as a levy, a
tithe, a rent which the producer had to deduct from his output
at the completion of his productive cycle. With the spread of
hired labour, and in particular with the emergence of the
factory system, the surplus product was extracted 'at the root';
it was now the right of the producer to a share of output which
had become an outcome of redistribution.
   The two distinct ways in which the surplus product was
managed and divided could be only serviced by two entirely
different types of social power. This first was a power which
intervened in the life of the producer only on occasion; its
sole function was to assure the periodical transfer of the product of labour - not the administration of labour itself. This
power could therefore manifest its externality and operate,
as its major resources, the twin terrors of physical punishment
and spiritual damnation; but it had no concern with the administration of the producer's body, which was left largely to the
logic of nature and habit. The second type of power, however,
had to descend to the level with which the former type had no
need to concern itself. Its task was to organise the productive
process itself. It remained external only in the sense that the
productive effort itself came to be external to the 'natural'
logic of the producer's life. Otherwise it penetrated actions
and functions left before to the discretion of the producer. The

latter had to be forced now to subject himself to a daily and hourly rhythm which bore no evident relation to the logical order of his own life. The new power could not, therefore, limit its appearance to the annual tax collection and ceremonial reminders of its unchallengeable potency and super-human sanctions. It had to be a daily and an hourly power, permeating the totality of the producer's life and deploying constant surveillance and 'garrisons in conquered cities' (Freud's metaphor for the conscience sedimenting from repression) as its paramount weapon. Not the products of labour, but the producer himself, his body and thought, now had to become the objects of power. If not for the old power, the surplus product would not be split to maintain an unproductive elite; if not for the new power, the surplus would not be produced at all.

The new power was therefore directed at the bodies of producers, aspired to mould the totality of their life process, and displayed an unprecedented volume of repression. Large sections of ordinary behaviour were set aside as passion-ridden (in opposition to the ones classified as rational), bound to be confined and best of all suppressed altogether. The new power was mostly a disciplining force. It was set to reshape the behaviour of producers according to a pattern which, by definition almost, they would not choose if the matter was left to their discretion. Since the entire pattern of life was involved, the matter could not be solved by sheer compulsion or an occasional display of superior force. The new power had to be constant and ubiquitous. Through its numerous institutions it had to chart the entire territory of life. It had to come into the direct and permanent contact with the body of the producer.

It was in the factory system that the concerns and the ambitions of the new type of power attained their fullest and most vivid manifestation. For obvious reasons, factories were from the outset the first line of the power struggle. Labour bought by the factory owners could be brought to the machines only together with the labourers; and it could not be extracted otherwise than by forcing the labourers to apply their force and skill, continually and according to the pace set by machinery in motion. To prise their labour free, the labourers had to be, therefore, deprived of freedom. E.P. Thompson documented in a brilliant essay the tortuous process of drilling the factory workers into obedience to the clock.[10] The process was repeated everywhere and each time people brought up in a pre-industrial way of life had to be transformed into factory operatives.[11]

The factory order, whatever its impact upon the standard of living measured by the quantity of commodities bought and consumed, had to appear to the producers as a superimposition of a coercive, other-controlled order on what seemed by contrast a self-regulated, autonomous existence. For this very reason the system had to arouse resentment, particularly among yesterday's craftsmen or cottage producers. When confronted with the new order, historical memory painted the picture of bliss and tranquillity destroyed by the 'satanic mills'. To the impersonal, enforced individuality of a factory hand, it juxtaposed the image of sociability and mutual esteem of independent producers. To the factory hands, the new order revealed itself first and foremost as the loss of freedom; its repressive impact arose mainly from its other-directedness. This order came supported by naked force but no meaning. In Weber's words:[12]

> The Puritan wanted to work in a calling; we are forced to do so....In Baxter's view the care for external goods should only lie on the shoulders of the 'saint like a light cloak, which can be thrown aside at any moment'. But fate decreed that the cloak should become an iron cage.

Factory hands were the first to experience this irony of fate. To them, the order which determined 'the lives of all the individuals who are born into this mechanism, not only those directly concerned with economic acquisition, with irresistible force', was an iron cage from the start. And, for a long time yet, its iron bars were not to be hidden behind the glittering prizes of the supermarkets.

6 In the pre-industrial order, the producer was forced to share his product with his social superiors. But until the moment the levy was collected, the product was his. The producer was in control of tools and materials which, when subject to the process of labour, resulted in the final product. Tools, work and the rights to the product of labour belonged 'naturally' together. Industrial society, on the other hand, 'requires that wealth be directly in the hands, not of its owners, but of those whose labour, by putting that wealth to work, enables the profit to be made from it'.[13] The advent of industrial society brought, therefore, an ambiguous situation, poorly articulated by historical precedent. It made the re-definition of rights and duties inevitable, a matter of open contest and power struggle.

Never since the collapse of slave societies was such a formidable wealth entrusted to the care of people who had no stakes in its integrity. From the point of view of the owners, this situation meant taking enormous risk and called for constant vigilance; Bentham's 'Panopticon' encapsulated the dream of the all-penetrating supervisory gaze, of a surveillance unconstrained by walls of privacy and piercing through most sheltered niches of individual autonomy. The practice which 'Panopticon' idealised was one of the mixture of physical drill and moral preaching, aimed at the reversal of the traditional relation between things and their users. Through discipline and punishment the unity of capital, work and product was to be 'denaturalised' and dismembered. This could be achieved only by an uncompromising suppression of producers' autonomy; by transforming yesterday's subjects of rights into objects of control.

From the point of view of the producers, however, the new situation presented an entirely different picture. It was seen as a sinister departure from the natural principle of the producer's control over the entirety of his work, including the tangible results of labour. Long before economists made their discovery of labour as the source of wealth, the intimate link between work and its product was too evident for the producer to call for reflection.

It seems strange, therefore, that most renderings of the origins of industrial conflict interpret the appearance of the demand of the 'whole product of labour' as the result of the socialist reading of Ricardo's economic vision. It has been accepted almost without further questioning that the idea of the right to the whole product was injected into inchoate associations of workers by their intellectual advisors and preachers, having been first distilled from abstract analysis of the structure of market economy. This idea is commonly seen, in other words, as the outcome of pushing the logic of market economy to its radical conclusions; or, alternatively, as the consequence of a value judgment applied to the structure of capitalist economy. In both cases, the producers' demand for the whole product of their labour is interpreted as a phenomenon born of the distinctive character of the capitalist society; sometimes - particularly within the Marxist tradition - it is presented as a fateful step beyond ('forward from') the capitalist organisation of the productive process. Most authors agree that the 'right to the whole product of labour' can and should be traced back to Ricardian socialists, who had the courage and the imagination to gaze beyond the confines of bourgeois self-interest which blinded Ricardo's vision, but who made their observation with both feet firmly put on the territory of bourgeois society, as charted by Ricardo's theory.

Contrary to the prevalent opinion, the 'right to the whole product of labour' seems much more at home in the historical memory of the individual producer, than in advanced Utopias of the forward-looking critics of the capitalist management of surplus value. Economic theory was hardly necessary for the producers to guard the remembered 'natural' link between labour and its product and - in the name of this memory of 'natural' order - resist the concentrated efforts of new industrial powers to break it. What had been articulated as the demand of the right to the whole product was, indeed, a call to restore the old order. Not that in past history the producers ever enjoyed and consumed the totality of their output without sharing it with the dominant and idle, or weak and impoverished groups; but the old order, when confronted with the factory system, did appear to place the producer in a position of control over the whole of his product and its later destination. In practice, therefore, the demand for the whole product of labour was a part of power struggle which the attack launched by the factory system against the self-

management of the producer had set in motion. The images and
the vocabulary dictated by 'remembered history' articulated the
producers' defence against the new 'discipline power'.
   This interpretation requires a qualification. It is meant to
capture the meaning bestowed upon the demand by factory
workers in the early power struggles of the new system. It
was, at least obliquely, confirmed by the fact that for many
decades, practically until the introduction of 'skilful', advanced
technology in the later part of the nineteenth century, the
factory owners failed to extend the unified pattern of factory
discipline over skilled labour. Throughout most of the nineteenth century the skilled workers, organised for their self-
defence in trade unions, retained considerable autonomy within
the factory and to a large extent controlled their own part
in the production process; it was the weak and unorganised
labour, mainly women and children, to whom the discipline and
surveillance of the new power were applied in full (it was the
very inability of these groups, with no historical memory to
fall back on, to resist the encroachment of the new power that
made them the natural objects of the defensive legislation by
the state). But in the intellectual debate of the era, and particularly in its socialist section, 'the right to the whole product
of labour' tended to acquire a rather straightforward economic
interpretation. There, it was translated into the language of
the market discourse and decoded as the demand of the repay-
ment of the full value of expended labour. In the classic version, later summed up by Anton Menger, this reading of the
right to the whole product of labour founded it on self-
interest.[14]
   Menger's analysis, however, itself remained within the market
discourse within which other analysed interpretations were
enclosed. A longer view, embracing the historical context of
the era when the intellectual debate on the right to the whole
product was launched, reveals a somewhat different meaning
of the economic readings of the 'right'. Rather than referring
to the individual or group self-interest, the concept of 'the
right to the whole product' appears to partake of the power
discourse on global-societal level; it represents an alternative
notion of the management of the socially produced surplus.
Contrary to what Menger suggested ('under such a system
every one works for himself alone, while under present conditions he works partly for himself and partly for another's
unearned income'), the intellectual interpretations of the
'right' never implied the abolition of a social re-distribution
of surplus; hardly ever, even in case of most radically
syndicalist solutions, did they intimate a possibility of the
product being appropriated (not to mention consumed) in its
entirety by its immediate producer. The emphasis in the economic interpretations of the right was always a negative one; in
a sense, they attacked what the workers' concept of the right
defended: the association of the right to dispose of the final

product with the investment of factors which led to its creation.
In the concrete circumstances of capitalist industry, these
interpretations were aimed at the dissociation of the management of surplus from the ownership of capital, thereby allowing
for a relatively narrow common ground on which the two (social
and economic) interpretations of the right to the whole product
could meet and even be mistakenly seen as identical. They met
in so far as they pointed, for the time being, to the same
adversary. Their tactical alliance could not, however, outlive
the attainment of the right in either of the two versions. Realisation of any of the two versions was bound to reveal their
long-run discordance. The economic version did not by necessity imply granting of the right postulated by the social one.
The issues articulated in the social version could well retain
all their topicality even with the postulates of the economic one
met in full. On the other hand, were the demands of the social
version ever fulfilled, this would not bring the redistribution
of power implied by the economic version any nearer.

7 The social version of 'the right to the whole product of
labour' derived its initial impetus from the producers' resentment of the discipline power represented by the factory system
– resentment given shape by the 'memorised past' of the craftsman's workshop. It was at this stage a part of the power struggle for the control over the process of labour, a manifestation
of the defiance of the externally imposed, alien order aspiring
to a full control over the substance and the form of producers'
actions. This power struggle was to be lost by the workers.
The discipline power was, in the end, triumphant; its base
extended far beyond the factory walls, and the factory floor
was not a battlefield on which a successful war against the
new type of power could be waged. With the advance made by
the new order, the workers' version of 'the right to the whole
product' did undergo a gradual, but seminal, change of meaning. It came closer to Menger's interpretation. As Offe and
Wiesenthal recently commented:[15]

> workers can neither fully submit to the logic of the market
> (first of all, because what they 'sell' on the market is not
> a 'genuine' commodity), nor can they escape from the mar-
> ket (because they are forced to participate, for the sake
> of their subsistence).

Once the defensive and delaying action failed to halt the
advancement of the new power, the second aspect of the
workers' situation, having become for all practical intents and
purposes a necessity, began to generate a constant pressure,
pushing labour to the never fully attainable 'commodity' pattern. Short of a drastic alteration of the 'discipline power'
pattern, the only way of attending to their situation open to
the workers was to behave as if labour was a commodity, while
simultaneously exploiting the fact that it is not, and cannot be,

a commodity tout court ('the capitalist cannot buy labour itself
- a certain quantity of activity, as it were. Instead, he has
to apply incentives, force, etc. to the *bearers* of labour power
- that is, the workers - in order to get them to work and to
keep them working[16]). The liminal notion of the 'whole product
of labour' turns, therefore, into a legitimating formula for
bargaining in the name of increased incentives. The link
between the practice of bargaining and the logic of its original
legitimation tends to become, however, increasingly tenuous.
Little is left of either the economic or social ambitions that
the formula once implied. Contrary to what the economic view
of labour-commodity would make us expect, the limits of bargaining power are weakly correlated with the value of the
'whole product'. They depend instead on the 'negative value'
of distortion in the power pattern that a particular category
of labourers may create through its refusal to expend its
labour force. What really counts in the distribution of the
'whole product' is not 'how much do we contribute to the
creation of the product', but 'how much harm we can cause
by refusing to contribute'. This practice creates the visibility
of a typically market-oriented behaviour, but only if all its
highly specific contextual determinants and complex inner
springs are ignored.

Thus Menger's 'self-interest', allegedly underlying the
demand of 'the whole product of labour', at no stage seems to
give justice to the complexity of workers' behaviour. It could
be used to construct working models of such behaviour only at
a later stage; at the time when the vindication of the 'right
to the whole product', which, according to Menger, it was
meant to explain, has already receded into the background to
be invoked, if at all, on rare, ceremonial occasions.

At this later stage the chances of various categories of
labour depend on their capacity to disrupt the production of
surplus value - directly or indirectly (i.e. by undermining
some of the 'meta-conditions' of such production). This means
that the chances are unequal. It is then that the defence of
the relative status of certain sectors of employed labour
becomes in principle dissociated from the power struggle, aimed
at the securing of existence of the non-capital-owners in
general. The general notion of the 'labour versus capital'
struggle is still held in the collective memory of the origins,
but it now covers an essentially fragmented pursuit of gains.
The fate of the two objectives is guided by two largely autonomous sets of factors. It becomes possible, therefore, that a
success in one direction may have an adverse effect on the
other.

It is time to recapitulate the argument.

The conflict between workers and the owners of capital is
not similar to the immediately preceding conflict between producers of surplus and its non-producing consumers (inasmuch
as the production of surplus in the industrial society is not

similar to its production in the past). It arose from the struggle over the control over production of surplus, and not merely
its distribution. The advent of industrial society meant that
the external management of surplus, previously limited to its
division, spread over its very production. This tendency meant
not just depriving the producer of a part of his labour's product, but a total control over his body and soul; taking away
the right to manage the application of his working capacity. The
conflict between workers and the factory owners emerged as
a resistance of the objects of such control against a new system
of power which implied it. The organisation of workers into a
class hostile to the rule of capital owners was an outcome of
this resistance.

The odds in this defensive struggle were, and remain, decisively against the workers. One obvious disadvantage derived
from the backing the other side received from the liquidity of
'dead labour' (their possession of tools, premises, raw materials)
as against the incurable 'non-liquidity' of the live one; unlike
the capitalists, workers depend for their livelihood on the
other side's willingness to employ it; not being able to store
their labour force or stock it for more propitious occasions,
they are bound to lose it once they decide to opt out from the
physical submission which selling it entails. Another disadvantage (as Offe and Wiesenthal recently indicated, often overlooked by political scientists who 'equate the unequal' and
dissolve the uniqueness of workers' situation in the indis-
criminating notion of 'interest groups'[17]) stems from the fact
that the power of each and any capitalist is assured automatically by his legally guaranteed property rights; ultimately,
the right of property means the right to control its use (and
prevent its 'abuse', understood as such use as does not conform with the intention of the owner), which, in the case under
discussion, amounts to the control over action, body and soul
of the individuals employed to accomplish this 'use'. An individual worker, on the contrary, except for an unlikely case of
possessing unique and irreplaceable skills indispensable for
the use of a capitalist's possessions (the standardisation of
machines renders such cases increasingly improbable), has no
assets with which to counter and confine the capitalist's control; by himself he is not a 'source of uncertainty' which may
confound the capitalist's calculation, and for this reason he is
unambiguously an object of power, and not a side in the power
game. In order to achieve what the capitalist attains as an
individual, without surrendering virtually any of his personal
autonomy, the worker has to associate with others: with other
workers employed by the same capitalist, to make the replacement of his skills somewhat more costly; and, preferably, with
all workers possessing the same skill or potentially employable
by the same industry, in order to remove fully the power
disadvantage arising from replaceability.

It is, in other words, the resistance to the new power's bid

for the total control over body and soul of the producer which
forces the workers to act in unison, to form associations, to
surrender the individuality to the logic of group action - in
short, to form a class rather than a loose aggregate of individuals of mostly statistical existence.

Regardless of their political persuasion, most economists and
social scientists agree that the tendency of the workers to
organise is best explicable in terms of the rational pursuit of
gain. The science of economics, with relatively few exceptions,
conceives of the worker (as, for this matter, of any other
individual within the orbit of the market) as above all a 'maximising' entity; it is this inherent proclivity to maximise which
bestows rationality upon joining of forces. Marxist sociologists
and political scientists supplant a wider perspective and add
the evaluation, but agree with the essence of the proposition:
the workers unite to regain the possession of the surplus
value expropriated by the capitalist. In both cases the interpreters view the class organisations of the workers as a form
of adjustment to the logic of the market exchange, and particularly to the situation where labour itself is turned into a
marketable commodity.

It is against this interpretation that our argument is aimed.
The contention elaborated in this book is that the class of
industrial workers came into existence in the course of the
producers' resistance against the new system of power; this
was a battle for control over body and soul of the producer,
and not for the division of surplus value; much less for the
right to manage the surplus. It was not the new form of
surplus-management, as such, but its impact upon the autonomy of the producer, which generated the sense of outraged
justice and led the producer to seek the restoration of the
power balance through unification of their forces. The objective
of a take-over of the surplus itself was never a factor in the
formation of workers into a class (though, as will be seen later,
it was imputed subsequently to the formed working class by
sides participating in another power struggle).

It is a further contention of this book that the battle for
control which sedimented and continues to sediment organised
forms of resistance among its objects (consider the spreading
of 'industrial action' to the work settings in which no surplus
is produced, and hence no division of surplus may be disputed),
if not exactly lost by the producers, was not won either.
Instead it has led to a stalemate, within which both sides have
the means and the willingness to draw and re-draw the limits
to the other side's prerogatives or autonomy. It is within the
framework of this tension-generating and tension-supported
precarious balance of control that the wage-battle led by
workers' unions is best understood. This battle is not just a
manifestation of the alleged 'maximising tendency' of the market-
oriented individuals. Still less is it an act of war against the
current system of surplus-management. It is rather one of the

few available ways in which the controlled may assert and
manifest their not-yet-entirely-forlorn autonomy. It is not so
much the ultimate monetary effects of the struggle which
count, as the display of force which led to their attainment.
This is, perhaps, the deepest reason of the workers' unions'
resentment against all forms of wage control, and of their
attachment to the principle of free collective bargaining. This
attitude is unlikely to change even if it has been proved that
the 'free bargaining' does not protect the real wages better
than a well-administered and balanced incomes policy. It is
unlikely to change precisely because the comparative virtues
of the two forms of wage determination are measured not by
their 'maximising' effects, but by their impact on the power
relations built into the work situation.

If industrial society is above all about control reaching where
other power systems did not reach and had no need of reaching, then the wider, unintended meaning of the wage battle as
well as of other forms of asserting producers' autonomy is their
continuous resentment of industrial society; it is not, contrary
to what is frequently implied, a resentment against the specifically capitalist form of dividing surplus value in line with the
property rights (not, in other words, the fight for the 'right
to the whole product of labour' in the economic sense). This
wider meaning applies to the management as such, rather than
management legitimising its prerogatives by reference to legal
ownership. Employees of nationalised, not privately owned,
institutions go out of their way to establish the same principles
of wage bargaining as in private industry, as if to manifest
the irrelevance of the 'whole product' argument and the supreme
importance of the issue of control. If, in consequence of the
pressure exerted on wages, capitalist property rights are also
affected and their exercise is limited, it happens because of
the fact that these rights in their capitalist form cannot be
deployed without a concomitant assault on the personal autonomy of producers. To put the issue still more sharply, the
formation of workers into a class was a response to the advent
of industrial society; only obliquely, because of the circumstances of the time and place, can this formation be portrayed
as a reaction to the capitalist form of industrial society.

Manual workers were the first to be subjected to the new
work discipline of industrial society; above all, they were first
to be condemned to such a discipline for life - the first for
whom the work regime was to become the total form of life.
Other parts of the population were to enjoy for some time yet
the status of economic independence. They remained connected
with the rest of the society, including its dominant groups -
through the traditional link of distribution, while retaining
self-control in the sphere of production. For the time being,
therefore, they found themselves among the beneficiaries of
industrial society. This situation, however, was bound to end
soon. By now the fully documented transformation of the

'middle classes' from self-employed and self-managing individuals into an army of employees reduced the manual workers
to a constantly shrinking sector of those confronted with the
same threat which the manual workers had faced from the outset of industrial society. The staging of the process, however,
left manual workers for almost a century alone on the battlefield. This fact made it somewhat easier to depict their struggle
as related to the issue conspicuously distinctive from the form
of their productive activity: as related, in other words, to
the control over the finished, tangible, product of labour,
rather than over the bodies and souls of its producers.

The lapse of time between the beginning and the final stage
of control expansion rendered such an interpretation plausible.
But it can hardly be seen as its causal explanation.

The more likely cause of the interpretation was the natural
tendency of the interpreters to view visible antagonisms of the
society as manifestations of the conflict in which they themselves were engaged. This other conflict was indeed about the
control over socially produced surplus. This conflict was not
resolved by the ascent of industrialists. The many lurid intellectual pictures of the new society portraying the capitalist
as in sole and full control of the surplus reflected the reality
of industrial society at no stage of its history. They captured
the true trends of development as much as they displayed,
consciously or inadvertently, concerns and ambitions of the
interpreters; more often than not they were sounds of alarm
and declarations of continuing war over the control over surplus. In short, they are best understood as the texts of the
ongoing struggle for power.

Many followers and readers of Marx were embarrassed or
puzzled by the apparent incongruity of his list of historical
contenders in the perpetual class struggle. Obviously, the
landowners and the bourgeois were engaged in a different kind
of war from slaves and slave-owners, or capitalists and proletarians. The blunder of comparing the incomparable, committed by an otherwise superbly logical mind, is somewhat less
bewildering once it is seen against the overall tendency to
collapse - indeed, to identify - the two separate strands of
conflict intertwined in the dynamics of industrial society.
Once the two strands have been twisted into a single continuous
thread of class warfare, the struggle of the labourers to retain
control over their labour could be presented as a further stage
of the bourgeois struggle to acquire control over surplus; if
the labourers were reluctant to conform to the logic of the
latter struggle, they could be always charged with the sin, or
the weakness, of false consciousness or opportunism.

In his critique of the capitalist society Marx was at pains to
distinguish the phenomenon of expanding surplus labour,
which the capitalist form of acquisition boosted, and the transformation of surplus labour into capitalist profit. The first
advanced the productive potential of mankind and hence

served the objective of human emancipation; the modern division of labour, with its careful planning of partial tasks,
meticulous administration and supervision of productive functions, was to be seen in the long run as a powerful stride
away from the realm of natural necessity. Like Adam Smith
in his famous eulogy of the pin factory, Marx was deeply impressed by the possibility of well-nigh unlimited increase of surplus
product which the factory system has created. To a large
extent Marx shared an almost aesthetic admiration of the planned, rhythmical, co-ordinated effort brought about by industrial technology. Implicitly, he revealed it in the metaphor of
the symphonic orchestra and its conductor who blends dis-
parate sounds into a pleasing tune. The one point which Marx
stressed over and over again throughout the three volumes of
'Capital' was that the quality of orchestral performance did
not depend on the conductor being the owner of the instruments. Indeed, all the ills of the capitalist society Marx traced
to this latter circumstance. There was nothing wrong with the
unprecedented increase of surplus product attained through
the new organisation of the productive process; everything,
however, was wrong with the acquisition of this surplus product as the profit of the capital owner.

The ills of the capitalist form of the management of surplus
product which Marx (and other, both radical and not-so-
radical critics) condemned, were two-fold. First, the personal
union between management of productive process and profit-
making resulted in the tendency to a ruthless exploitation of
labour force. Rationality of technology was surrendered to the
logic of gain. Hence the moral turpitude of the capitalist-
managed factory, which could be cured only by the breaking
of the unholy (and contingent) alliance between the administration of the productive process and the ownership of the means
of production. Second, what appeared to the workers as a
planned, tightly organised, purposeful system, was in its
higher regions an anarchy. The blending of control and ownership enthroned the confusion of universal competition where
the planned use of resources should rule, and thus drowned the
potential of organised production in the sea of massive irrationality. Both evils of the capitalist system require, therefore,
the same medicine. One has to salvage the new form of production, which capitalism pioneered, from the capitalist system of
acquisition and management of the surplus product. The surplus product ought to be distributed as rationally as it is
produced.

Marx was by no means alone in tracing the moral abomination
of industrial regime to the anarchy in the distribution of social
product. The two themes of critique and the intimate bond
between them remained a major characteristic of intellectual
debate from the outset of the new power. The general tendency
of this debate was the presentation of the issue of repression
as subsidiary to the question of the management of surplus.

The need of discipline, management, and organised control over the productive process (i.e. the producers) was questioned by nobody but the anarcho-syndicalist margins who were dismissed by dominant opinion, whether conservative, liberal, or socialist, as Utopian or retrograde. What invited widely shared condemnation was the 'excess of repression', allegedly uncalled for by the logic of production, and caused solely by the competitive pressure of a disorderly market. By this reasoning, people who suffered most from the repressive factory regime were naturally interested in changing the rules according to which the surplus was appropriated and divided; hence the tendency to present such a change of rules (depicted, with varying degrees of radicalism, as state intervention, nationalisation, or abolition of private property) as the ultimate horizon of working-class interests and the substance of its class consciousness.

This latter belief was most pronounced, of course, among radical participants of the debate. It appeared mostly as a hoped-for substitute for the missing, or inaccessible, levers of effective political action within the extant structure of power. Other participants of the debate, sufficiently close to the centres of authority, had less need of a messianic surrogate. They could instead bid realistically for a decisive influence on existing administrative agents. All participants, however, with minor exceptions only, shared in the condemnation of the irredeemable irrationality of the market anarchy. They demanded that the 'invisible hand' be guided by conscious advice of reason. J.S. Mill made the distinctiveness of the two themes explicit: production of commodities is subject to objective laws which ought to be learned and respected; distribution, however, is a matter of policy, dependent on man-made laws, and ought to be a matter of conscious care and well-informed choice.

It seems, in other words, that the intellectual critique of the capitalist market cannot be interpreted as a reflection of the same conflict which – as I suggested earlier – led to the formation of factory labour into the working class. In the intellectual critique, the focus of workers' concerns and discontents had been markedly displaced, as if moving under the force of gravity of another powerful conflict. As to the nature of this additional conflict the intellectual debate itself kept remarkably quiet, betraying its presence only obliquely, through its persistent concerns and steady shift of emphasis.

Marx's litany of 'historic classes', in which the conflict between capitalists and proletarians followed the conflict between feudal landlords and the bourgeois, ceases to puzzle once the actuality of the other conflict is admitted. Like the struggle waged by the bourgeois against the rights of land property, this new conflict is mainly about the administration of surplus product, to wit, about the ultimate foundation of political power. The question is, who, in this other conflict, represents the true adversary of the capitalist – or, more generally, of the right to the whole product attached to the ownership of capital.

The question is by no means new. It has been asked many times before, and a number of answers are already on offer, some backed by a tradition long enough to render the author-ship forgotten or debatable. Some of the answers are fairly well-known and already receive their share of popularity and counter-argument.

The answer which stirred perhaps the widest, and probably the longest commotion was the one associated with James Burnham (though Burnham's originality has been seriously questioned by Daniel Bell, who defended the ownership rights to Burnham's ideas of writers publishing long before the spectacular bestseller success of the 'Managerial Revolution' - like Rizzi, Trotsky, or even Emil Lederer, who sensed the ascent of Privatangestellten as far back as 1912[18]). This answer favours managers of privately and publicly owned firms as the next 'ruling class', eager to take over control over surplus from its titular owners. According to Burnham, the detachment of control from ownership was already well under way in the whole of the industrialised world and a virtual 'managerial revolution' was taking place, or was imminent, in a violent (Soviet or German) or quiet and hardly perceptible (American) form. Few authors adopted Burnham's historiosophic assertion in its shockingly radical version, but its milder variant - of the growing separation of control from ownership - had acquired enthusiastic supporters in quarters which Burnham perhaps did not expect to inspire. The thesis of the real power moving slowly but steadily into the laps of the hired managers acquired in the post-war decades wide popularity among economists and political scientists keen to disprove the persistence of the capitalist features of the current society and by so doing to prove that the charges once made by the critics incensed by the immorality of capitalist exploitation, had lost most of their force. The temporary popularity of the attenuated Burnham's thesis was well geared to the brief, but exuberant period of managerial optimism - when it seemed to many that the zeal of the 'rationalisers' of the market economy would not be brought to a halt by entrenched powers inimical to the 'scientifically modelled' society. The popularity faded together with the hope.

The Burnhamian episode was both preceded and followed by another proposition, which never reached the heights of Burnhamian short-lived success, but which is likely to outlive the latter's memory thanks to the amazing survival-and-resurrection capacity it has demonstrated to date. According to this second proposition, the society ruled by competition and private appropriation is to be replaced by a society domin-ated and ruled by men of knowledge - variously described as intellectuals, scientists and technologists. The first formulation of this idea is sometimes ascribed to a Polish rebellious com-

munist, Machajski (pen-name A. Wolski), who accused the
intellectuals of exploiting the struggle of the workers to pave
the way to their own rule and yet harsher repression of the
proletariat. Even if Machajski did not succeed in originating
an alternative, 'intellectual-free' proletarian movement, his
indictment was to remain just below the level of consciousness
of all left-wing movements claiming proletarian credentials, and
surfaced time and again in spite of all exorcisms and the concentrated effort of repression. Quite recently the idea reap-
peared, with vengeance, this time at some distance from political
battlefields, in the mainstream of sociological discourse. It
immediately captured 'sociological imagination', thanks, at least
in part, to the blunt, deliberately provocative way in which it
was brought to public attention by its major proponents.

If I am not mistaken, the first major contribution to the recent
renaissance came from the then doyen of American political
science, Harold D. Lasswell.[19] In direct reference to Machajski,
Lasswell explored the developmental tendencies of the mature
industrial society only to find out that they can be logically
depicted as a 'permanent revolution of modernising intellectuals'.
It was mostly the intellectuals themselves, wrote Lasswell, who
failed to notice that they moved steadily towards the strategic
positions of power; a curious case of the 'temporary "false
consciousness" on the part of intellectuals who nevertheless
served the power interests of the rising intellectual class. By
deceiving themselves they were better able to deceive others'.
Like most ruling classes, the intellectuals are preoccupied with
internecine squabbles to the point of overlooking a class unity
which underlies all arguments and divisions. They are, in fact,
a distinct entity, and one which already dominates the industrial
world. The fact will decide the shape of the world to come:

> In characterising the outcomes and effects of an intel-
> lectually dominated world, it is possible to offer at least
> one major generalisation: the trend of policy will express
> a balance of power favourable to more and more intellectual
> activity, supported by more and more utilisation of social
> resources.

At the time Lasswell's study appeared the intellectuals were
too neatly integrated in the mechanisms of power in both parts
of the industrial world to need an exercise in self-consciousness.
Lasswell's shot was fired before the ranks thought of a battle.
Hence two books which did not significantly depart from
Lasswell's main contention, but appeared a little more than a
decade later, seem to have made from the start a much stronger
impact. The first of the two, by George Konrad and Ivan
Szelenyi,[20] set openly on the unmasking course. Lasswell's
'false consciousness' was replaced by a merciless pursuit of
group interests:

it has been the common aspiration of the intellectuals of
every age to represent their particular interests in each
context as the general interests of mankind. The definition of universal, eternal, supreme (and hence immutable)
knowledge displays a remarkable variability over the ages,
but in every age the intellectuals define as such whatever
knowledge best serves the particular interests connected
with their social role.

Where Lasswell spoke of the late industrial society, Konrad
and Szelenyi speak of 'every age'. Where Lasswell pondered
the domination of the intellectuals as the outcome of technological transformation in modern society, Konrad and Szelenyi
practically reverse the causal order of things: it was the
perpetual thrust of intellectuals to class power which finally
led to whatever technological, or any other, transformation is
currently taking place. The present class ideal of the intellectuals, which (if realised) would finally place them at the
helm, is one of 'rational redistribution'. Thus far, the ideal
came closest to fulfilment in the communist states, where 'it
is the rationality of the planning process, not the decisions of
owners of capital, which redistributes the retained surplus
product, whose size cannot be effectively regulated by the
market'. 'Under rational redistribution it is above all technical
knowledge, intellectual knowledge, which legitimises the right
to dispose over the surplus product. That is what justifies the
superior position of the redistributors and provides the ideological basis for the formation of the intelligentsia into a class.'
Almost simultaneously with the English translation of Konrad
and Szelenyi's statement, Alvin Gouldner's book appeared,[21]
which in its very first words proclaimed that

in all countries that have in the twentieth century become
part of the emerging world socio-economic order, a New
Class composed of intellectuals and technical intelligentsia -
not the same - enter into contention with the groups already
in control of the society's economy, whether these are
businessmen or party leaders.

It soon becomes clear that in Gouldner's view the New Class is
best understood as a next link in the historical chain of dominant classes; its collective behaviour is to be interpreted in
terms of a tendency, and an aspiration, to class domination in
the historically established sense of the word: that of the control over surplus product, conducted in the controllors' own
interest.

The New Class is elitist and self-seeking and uses its special
knowledge to advance its own interests and power, and to
control its own work situation. Yet the New Class may also
be the best card that history has presently given us to

play. The power of the New Class is growing. It is substantially more powerful and independent than Chomsky
suggests, while still much less powerful than is suggested
by Galbraith who seems to conflate present reality with
future possibility. The power of this morally ambiguous
New Class is on the ascendent and it holds a mortgage on
at least *one* historical future.

Gouldner makes it explicit that he uses the term 'class' in its
Marxist sense, constituted by the idea of 'certain communality'
uniting members of a given group, particularly in regard to
'the same relationship to the means of production'. Even the
type of means of production the New Class is related to, is
analogous to the kind commanded by the preceding and currently rival dominant class: it is capital, though a distinct form
of it, made to the measure of the ascending class power:
'cultural' or 'human' capital. It is the latter capital which
becomes decisive for the effective possession of the mode of
production, as distinct from its legal ownership.
    The third answer to our question belongs to a somewhat dif-
ferent category. It has become, so to speak, a folklore of the
thinking public brought up in the world conceptualised as a
wrestling match between contradictory class interests. There
is a constant feedback movement between this diffuse folklore
and the articulated public or academic opinion; thanks, however, to its broad folkloristic base, the third answer does not
require such a systematic theoretical elaboration as the other
two. More often than not it is offered in the guise of the 'facts
of life', a statistics which takes its meaningfulness for granted,
a press report referring to the established community of meaning, academic propositions starting from 'as we know' - this
sacramental incantation of paradigmatical consensus too universal to need legitimation.
    Obviously, a belief which invokes folklore as its paramount
authority must be lacking in precision. The third answer
assumes, indeed, numerous verbalisations, which are not
always easy to correlate. One reads of 'the government', 'the
politicians', 'the bureaucrats' - various groups of rather
unclear mutual relations, but always 'power greedy' and
attempting with varying degree of success, to wrestle power,
control and initiative from 'private industry'. The mental
image behind these verbalisations, seldom articulated with the
cohesion of a theoretical model, is of two integrated and powerful groups, pitted against each other in a continuing struggle
for the control over economy. The image is of a zero-sum
game; whatever 'politicians' or 'bureaucrats' manage to cream
off from the profits made by 'private industry', detracts from
the possessions, and the power, of the latter; the more freedom 'private industry' retains in the disposal of its product,
the weaker 'the bureaucrats' become. For all practical intents
and purposes, this is an image of class struggle, of an on-

going battle between two entrenched groups guided mostly
by their respective interests, each aspiring to overpower and
dominate the other.

The three apparently different answers have one crucial
attribute in common. They are all determined by a tacit acceptance of the extant interpretative model, which identifies the
task of explanation of socio-political processes with the need
to locate a group which benefits from these processes; and
which assumes that such a group could be imputed with an
intuitive tendency, and in the long run also with a deliberate
effort, to promote the said processes for this very reason.
All three answers derive, therefore, their ultimate authority
from common sense - this world image which projects on to the
large screen of society the interpretative habits daily reinforced
by micro-social individual experience. In unison with commonsensical predisposition, these answers anticipate a purposeful
agent behind every event, self-interest behind every change
or its prevention, an individual or collective culprit behind
every guilt.

But this universal tendency of common sense, determined by
the very structure of the life-world, has been given the currently specific shape by historical memory. It is in this form,
mediated by 'living history', that common sense informs the
three answers under discussion. To the constant, commonsensical search for a self-interested agent, historical memory
contributed the belief that the point around which collective
interests crystallise and integrate is the command over the
'whole product of labour', variously named 'control of economy',
'ownership of means of production', or 'right to profit' -
depending on theoretical allegiance or political denomination.
In other words, the historical memory which inspires and
constrains all three answers is one of class conflict, but a class
conflict interpreted in the course of the nineteenth century,
in terms suggested by the idealisation of the capitalist market,
as a conflict about the management of the surplus product,
rather than about the regimentation of the body and the soul
of its producer. It was this theoretical interpretation, rendered
plausible and steadily reinforced by the growing commoditisa-
tion of life conditions, which has sedimented as the historical
memory of our times. In this capacity, it supplies the chisels
with which to carve the self-portrait of the era.

The way in which the problems are verbalised determines
the range of possible solutions. All three answers are contained
within the same set of assumptions. They all arise out of the
search for the 'next dominant class'. No wonder all of them
find one. Whatever class is found, it is defined in the same
way: the way dictated by historical memory of a specific historical form of class domination. It is thus defined as a collection of people so situated in the network of social dependencies
that they must, and often wish to, pursue a total control over
social product and particularly over its distribution. Each

answer locates the discovery in a different part of society; but each proclaims the discovery of the same thing.

All in all, the three answers, together with the orthodox Marxist view which insists that things have not changed since the 'Communist Manifesto', and that the labour versus capital struggle remains the main class conflict, are on the side of the essential immutability of the springs of historical change. They all in the end agree that now, as much as in the time of bourgeois revolution, the moving force of history is the thrust of a new class to take over the management of the social surplus which previous rulers are not able to administer properly. And much in the spirit of the bourgeois propaganda against the retrograde land property, they describe the bid, and the chances of the challenger, in terms of efficiency and effectiveness of the management it is capable of providing.

The second of the two main hypotheses of this book contends that all the answers discussed thus far have little but historical memory to justify their claims; while historical memory, this pool of metaphors and analogies necessary to make sense of the present, fails in its task once the new realities refuse to be stretched or pressed so as to fit the moulds of historical tradition. If this happens, historical memory may well prevent the insight into the genuine levers of societal dynamics. It is the contention of this book that historical memory of class and class struggle plays at present such a 'holding back' role.

This second contention is argued along the following lines:

1 Late industrial society at its present stage is held together by systemic, rather than social, dependencies (thus, it is neither the 'segmental' nor the 'class' society of Durkheim's two-part division). Accordingly, the phenomena which tend to be identified as 'problems' of this society, or the dearth of available solutions to these problems, identified as its 'crisis', arise from endemic structural incongruities and contradictions of the system, rather than from structural location and ensuing policies of one particular class of people occupying a commanding position within the society. Though the consequences of each problem are distributed between various groups unevenly, they are in the end afflictions of the system as a whole and tend to accumulate and reinforce each other, so deepening the chasm between the volume of conflicts and the number of available solutions.

2 The management of surplus product (of its production as well as allocation) is now a function of the system; no single group, identified by a specific legal ownership status, or access to special sources of authority, or by any other unique property, can either do, or aspire to do, it alone. No group is free in a 'homo-oeconomicus' type tendency to the acquisition of surplus; no group's condition can be lastingly enhanced by pursuing the economic model of 'maximisation of goals'. The 'right to the whole product', allegedly the focus of crystallisation of the class-type conflict, is not, therefore, at issue.

In a sense, the satisfaction of any group's interests depends
on the systemic curb imposed on maximisation tendencies, in as
far as these continue to be prompted by the market-mediated
consumption.

   3 Correspondingly, no single group can be identified as the
'historical class' of the late industrial society; i.e. as a class
whose 'group interests' are identical with the 'interests of the
society as a whole', and which for this reason cannot serve its
own interests without simultaneously promoting social interests
in general; or (according to the inspired vision of Marx) a class
oppressed in such a way that the removal of its particular
oppression would mean the end to social oppression in general.
It was an integral belief of the class vision, and a major source
of its intellectual attractiveness, that the passage to the next,
improved form of the society is therefore assured, and in the
long run inevitable, thanks to this structural identity of the
particular and the universal. If this sociological concretisation
of Hegel's dialectical law of reason ever approximated the
realities of industrial society, it certainly does not apply to
its late version. The intricate network of systemic inter-
dependencies precludes the possibility of reducing the dynamics
of the whole system to this of one of its sectors. The interests
of no single group, however carefully scanned and veridically
articulated, may be seen as representing the interests of 'the
system as a whole'.

   4 The other facet of the same is that no group pressure, or
a group programme legitimising this pressure, is likely to
provide a solution to the system's problems. Expectations,
or promises, to the contrary, are ultimately based on an
assumption that the system 'can be made to work', which is
counter-factual. It seems rather that the difficulty of the
system in coping with conflicting demands are endemic, and
that promotion of no one of the contradictory interests will
remove it, or even visibly alleviate it. The endemic nature of
the system's problem has been traced by Jürgen Habermas to
the impossibility of reproducing commodity relations without
simultaneously weakening the motives and the predispositions
(like work ethic or family privatism) which are indispensable
for their effectivity;[22] by James O'Connor, to the ineradicable
tendency of the systemic outputs to outrace the inputs, and
worse still, to deplete their sources;[23] by Claus Offe, to the
inherent proclivity of the state to neglect the weak or inarticulate parts of the system and hence to allow the gestation of
problems beyond the capacity of systemic control.[24] What follows
from all these analyses is that, far from carrying the promise
of a solution to systemic crisis, all group interests, demands,
and pressures contribute to its aggravation. The crisis is not
traceable to the interests of policies of any group in particular,
but rather to the way in which these interests and policies
relate to each other and influence each other's chances. In
effect, the results of apparently purposeful, intentionally

rational actions, have all the bearings of 'natural catastrophes'.
Policy mistakes or groups' ill-will may perhaps account for the
particular shape such catastrophes assume; certainly not,
however, for their appearance and persistence.

5 One central feature of the system, which class vision on
the whole relegated to a subsidiary role, is the function played
in the production and distribution of social surplus by the
state. In fact, the role of the state was from the outset of
industrial society much larger than most political scientists or
economists of the time were prepared to admit. If the economic
significance of the state's defence of the internal and conquer-
ing of the external markets, protecting rights of ownership,
and providing services which market interests were unwilling
to support have been all universally acknowledged, one powerful factor in continuous expansion of the state, particularly
in its earliest period, has been noticed on but a few occasions,
namely, the function of the state consisting in 'legislating
morals'[25] – in guarding sexual ethics, teaching thrift, tutoring
good manners, fighting display of passion in all possible forms,
separating the public sphere from the private. However wary
of an expanding and costly state, the bourgeois never objected
to the state's tendency to redefine an ever-widening range of
morally contentious behaviour as criminal activity, requiring
intervention of state organs. The support for the new forms
of control over body and spirit was perhaps the single most
important factor of growth in the first stage of state expansion.
More directly economic tasks joined later, when the tendency
of the market to generate crises which it was ill-prepared to
solve on its own became evident, and when growing costs of
reproducing labour and controlling its carriers made it less and
less possible for the capitalists to meet these costs in full from
the surplus product they directly administered due to their
ownership rights. The combined effect of all these needs (and
many others) is a state occupying the position of the main
'throughput' of the system and best understood as neither a
'parasite' feeding on the output of social production, nor
source of authoritative command, but as a link within the communication network, without which no integrated existence of
the system is further possible.

6 The unique location of the state within the totality of the
system makes it, however, more socially visible than other units
may be. This circumstance breeds the illusion of the centrality
and the causal role of politics which the latter does not possess.
Another illusion is the conscious character of political process,
and in particular a causal connection between motives or
purposes of the politicians and economic and social effects of
the system. Perhaps the illusion most formidable in its consequences is that of the extensive power potential of the state.
The form in which politics presents itself to public view suggests a rational nature of economic and social processes; one
which can be, with due care, subordinated to the rules of

argument and the test of truth. Hence the malfunctionings of
the system appear as flaws in the rationality of state decisions,
which can be rectified by the substitution of better policies.
It is for this reason that most group demands and grievances
assume a political form and tend to be articulated as postulates
of changes in state policies, while systemic roots of problems
tend to escape attention. As a result the state is chronically
overloaded with demands, while simultaneously serving as a
lightning rod absorbing tensions arising from systemically
diffused agencies of power and control.

7 Under these circumstances, the state moves steadily into
the focus of group divisions and alliances. The society, when
seen as an aggregate of state subjects, is a pool of potential
tensions which articulate into definite forces in response to
the action (or the lack of action) on the part of the state.
Groups integrate, enter alliances, set programmes in relation
to the state. Their dimension, absorptive capacity, and possible scale of expansion are determined not so much by the
attributes the group members possess individually or conjointly,
as by the potential of common action defined by the state-
originated issue. The boundaries of groups are, therefore,
'ad hoc' and shifting. Alterations of policy lead to successive
re-alignments of divisions. Due partly to the varying degree
of institutionalisation, some divisions are more lasting in comparison with others; one could plot the groupings along a
scale ranging from such as are defined by more or less permanent organisations which determine the selection of issues
and attitudes, up to one-issue, campaign-like, loosely integrated
and short-lived movements. But no division seems to occupy
an 'over-determining' position in relation to others; one to
which all other divisions could be related as its manifestations
or modifications. Hence, as Alain Touraine repeatedly stated
in a series of recent works,[26] political action becomes an ever
more important, and all-powerful, determinant of group divisions. Action is ill-understood if interpreted as a reflection of
underlying economic interests; it is, rather, the politically
prompted action which tends to articulate the identity of the
group in the dominant vocabulary of economic gains or losses.

8 While it is true that groups and movements constitute themselves around demands addressed to the state, the impact of
state policies does not only differentiate between groups; it
has also an ambiguous effect on individual interests, further
complicating the chart of the field of social forces. The widening scope of activity of the state as the principal agent of
transfer, the growing proportion of social surplus directly
administered by the state, favours some and harms some other
aspects of individual interests, prompting truly schizophrenic
attitudes towards the role of the state. Though the degree to
which the expansion of social expenses of the state, or, alternatively, the confinement of its fiscal claims, is regarded as
'being in the group's interests', varies from one part of popu-

LIBRARY
SOUTHWEST CENTER, SAUJO
800 Quintana Road
San Antonio, Texas 78221 012565

lation to another – a proportion of both attitudes is present
in each category. Moreover, the balance between the two is
shifting in a nearly cyclical way, producing the notorious
'see-saw' movement of public mood. One can conclude that
the 'through-put' role of the state in the social system does
not split the society into opposing classes; it is not presently
an object of class contention. More importantly still, the present
location of the state within the system has passed the threshold line beyond which it acquires a self-perpetuating, and
perhaps also a self-reinforcing, capacity. Under these conditions, even self-consciously anti-etatist demands and pressures
lead in their practical consequences to the further enhancement of the strategic potency of the state and increase the
dependency of the system on state activity. A good recent
example is the monetarist adventure. As if to provide a text-
book example of 'false consciousness', it led to the state reaching never yet attained commanding positions regarding economy,
social and cultural life, while preaching the virtues of private
initiative and the need to free the individual from bureaucratic
control.

It is not the task of these essays to speculate about the possible scenarios of the future. Still less do they claim to articulate an unambiguous policy advice. The much more modest
aim which I set for myself is to encourage a debate with 'ground-
clearing' objectives only. These essays are, in the end, another
contribution to the ongoing effort to discard the categories
which do not help any more to understand the present crisis,
and to construct a conceptual framework better fitted for its
interpretation.

It is one of the suggestions this book promotes that such an
interpretative framework should contain, as one of its major
constructive blocks, the proper concept of social power able to
replace the discipline power which once supported the spectacular success of industrial society, but which undergoes
a crisis similar to this experienced by the sovereign power a
couple of centuries ago, once industrial society is nearing its
dead end, having succeeded in an almost complete translation
of its control conflicts into conflicts over the share in the
division of surplus. The economisation of social conflicts, which
for many decades successfully defused the tensions arising
from the bid to control the producers, led finally to the endemic
excess of distributive demands over the productive potential,
and hence becomes increasingly inadequate as a makeshift
solution to the problem of social integration, and through it,
of the reproduction of society. The present crisis can therefore hardly be resolved by another shuffle among the traditionally principal actors or a new, ingenious way of performing
the old task of re-dividing the surplus in favour of the loudest
and potentially most noxious claimant. All future attempts at
its resolution can claim adequacy to the problem only to the
degree to which they come to grips with the essential issue of

'discipline power' which serves as a constant source and boost
of distributive pressures. They can hardly hope for success
if they seek the impossible feat of meeting the ever higher
targets of consumer satisfaction which the removal of the issue
of control from the public agenda is bound to render ever less
manageable.

In other words, it is one of the main arguments of this book
that the mechanism of social reproduction which for a time
assured the flourishing of industrial society is now near the
exhaustion of its historic potential and that the crisis we experience is not 'more of the same' problems, but a qualitatively
new stage in history which can be passed only with a change in
the type of social power as seminal as the one which took place
in the times preceding the advent of the industrial system.

2 From rank to class

At the end of his most thorough research of the birth of class, E.P. Thompson found a puzzle: 'By 1840 most people were "better off" than their forerunners had been 50 years before, but they had suffered and continued to suffer this slight improvement as a catastrophic experience.'

Few people would disagree that the contradiction Thompson so pointedly phrased was real; that the coincidence of improving standards on the one hand, and the experience of suffering and deterioration of life, is at least 'unnatural', and in any case calls for explanation. Indeed, the coincidence was seen by many as such a contradiction when found, with astonishing regularity, in so many places other than Britain and so many times other than the first decades of the nineteenth century. Both the coincidence itself, and its perception as a logical puzzle, defying the common wisdom of social psychology, was and still is so ubiquitous that long ago sociologists thought it necessary to hypothesise a general law which would explain away the regularity with which social reactions to change apparently depart from the otherwise simple relation between 'rising incomes' and 'rising happiness'. This auxiliary hypothesis came to be known under the name of the 'revolution of rising expectations'. As the popular version of the 'law' has it, once standards of life start to improve, anticipations of improvement accelerate still faster; and it is in the gap between overambitious expectations and the somewhat slower progress of actual conditions, that discontent gestates into an overt rebellion. As most auxiliary hypotheses attempt to do, this one endorses the validity of the general law (of the causal link between, roughly, level of income and the degree of satisfaction and acceptance), through applying it also to the numerous cases when the social attitudes seem to develop in a direction opposite to the one which a more straightforward version of the main law would suggest.

I do not think that E.P. Thompson would conceive of the 'law of rising expectations', or of any other general 'sociological laws', as the right solution to the particular riddle he revealed. What, however, seems to me more important than the disagreements about such solutions, is the broad consensus which made the puzzlement unproblematic; which led both sides to agree that the synchrony of rising wages and swelling discontent was contrary to some basic truths about human nature and hence had to be explained by reference to some special circumstances.

Generally speaking, there is no problem without explicit or tacit assumptions about reality which must first be accepted before they can be challenged. Something is a problem only in so far as its reality comes into conflict with an idea (often inarticulate) of what should be the case. The coincidence which E.P. Thompson pointed out so cogently is seen, immediately and without further argument, as a contradiction because of the widely shared assumptions about the substance of social conflicts and objects of social revolutions. The shared assumptions of the utmost importance for the perception in question are all related, even if only obliquely, to the essentially economic articulation of human needs and motives. Within such an articulation, social manifestations of disaffection and dissent are in advance defined as reflections of material hardship or frustrated hope for material progress. The dramatic, seminal struggles of the first half century of the capitalist era are then referred to the concentrated assault of the budding entrepreneurs on the material standards of the people: in other words, to the growing intensity of economic exploitation. If and when meticulous comparisons of wages show that the 'standard of living' measured in real income and purchasing power was in fact going up rather than down, a puzzle results which normally inspires explanations as economically biased as the reasoning which was originally responsible for the appearance of the puzzle. More often than not, such explanations point to the narrowness and insufficiency of the applied measures of living standards. In their positive suggestions, however, they rarely step beyond the realm of economic motives and interests, whenever the visible intensification of social tension and unrest is to be accounted for. The principle of capitalist exploitation as the cause and substance of the class-formation process is not a subject of the argument; for all practical intents and purposes, it is left unexamined.

In other words, both Marxist and non-Marxist interpretations of the conflict normally take for granted its essentially economic nature. If the interpretations conceived in the spirit of liberal economics confine themselves on the whole to the constant tendency of every individual to maximise his/her gains, 'to get more for less', their Marxist counterparts place emphasis rather on the institutional arrangement which gives some players a stronger hand and permanently better chances of maximisation. Both interpretations find it difficult to account for the phenomenon which Thompson described. Fortunately, there is always this residual category (i.e. 'underdetermined factor'), like politics or ideology, to which one can resort whenever either the conduct of market players, or the actual distribution of chances, depart from ideal-typical anticipations.

The interpretative controversy is of crucial importance to our theme, as Thompson's paradox seems to contain the key to the factors responsible for the formation of class society. An

inadequate interpretation may well result not only in an insufficient understanding of the process, but also - more importantly - in missing the chance of revealing the springs of class
formation and class conflict which the paradox offers.

Thompson's paradox refers to the same period in which the
well-nigh common agreement of contemporary historians locates
the emergence of 'class society' in this country. It was during
this period that differing categories of people came to be
defined and see themselves as 'classes', rather than orders
or ranks. Above all, however, this period was prominent for
a dramatic change in the alignment and the shifting of the foci
of integration of major social forces.

In his seminal study of the language of class in early nineteenth-century Britain, Asa Briggs traced the gradual replacement of the language of the 'chain of connection' (Cobbett),
or 'bonds of attachment' (Southey) by the vocabulary of
class. The old language referred to an image of a society constituted mainly by a string of unequal rights and obligations;
to the gentleness and smoothness of social gradation, whereby
each rank was intimately close to its neighbour; and to a permanent association between rank, duty, and dependence. It
was an image of society with vertical only connections, at no
stage interrupted drastically enough to warrant horizontal
alignments. The concept of rank served far more than a mere
object-identification function. It had philosophical, moral, often
religious meanings. The new concept, destined to convey a new
social experience and to preside over the crystallisation of new
social alliances (and also deep divisions), this of class, was,
in Briggs's opinion, 'a more indefinite word than "rank" and
this may have been among the reasons for its introduction'.[1]

The word 'class' was around for a long time before its adop-
tion as a resource of the new social practice. The participants
of the public debate had grown accustomed to its most indiscriminate and always imprecise use. The primary meaning of
class was a unit in any distribution of traits (classification);
in its applications, the meaning varied, therefore, depending
on the point of view or the objective of the classification. The
appearance of the word in the text conveyed little, if any,
information, about the author's political or moral intentions.
The discourse of class did not necessarily signify a commitment
to the class vision of society as it came to be understood later.
For a considerable time such a signification was an exception
rather than the rule. As Harold Perkin convincingly demonstrated, 'down to the end of the eighteenth-century and
beyond the word ['class'] was still used interchangeably with
the traditional concepts, "ranks", "degrees", and "orders",
and without its 19th century overtones of social strife and
antagonism'.[2] Even when such overtones did become more frequent, the traditional vagueness of its connotations remained.
In the 1820s still:[3]

contemporaries often talked of the higher, middle and lower
or working *classes*, each in the plural, and this was more
than a hangover from the pluralistic ranks and orders of
the old society. It reflected the vagueness of the social
facts, the existence of the numerous layers and sections
within the three major classes which only time and the
experience of class conflict would hammer into something
like compact entities.

In one article, published in 1831, addressed explicitly to the
'labouring classes' and therefore accepting the new vocabulary
complete with its semantic associations, one could find refer-
ences to the 'landlords' class' and 'all the producing classes',
but also to the 'class of writers who are loudest in their opposition to the corn law' and the 'class of Irish workers'.[4]
To add further complication: as its popularity grew, the
word 'class' came to be hotly contested and frantic efforts
were made to appropriate it for mutually contradictory social
perspectives. The political literature of the early nineteenth
century is replete with inventories of classes which in no
conceivable way could be plotted on the same chart. To offer
only a few examples: In 1818, Cobbett wrote of upper classes,
'middling classes' ('the active, working journey men of cor-
ruption'), 'productive classes' (who 'by their labour increase
the funds of the community'), 'unproductive classes' (lawyers,
parsons, aristocrats) and a class 'of paupers and public
creditors'. In 1831, William Carpenter appealed to the spokesmen of the 'labouring classes': 'I most confidently state, that
the middle classes of 1831...are not only *not* a class of persons
having interest, different from your own: but that *they are*
not a different class from your own. They are the *same* class;
they are, generally speaking, *working* and *labouring* men'.[5]
Most commonly, the dichotomy 'productive-unproductive',
arguably not the most felicitous of Adam Smith's many conceptual distinctions, was employed to secure the compliance
of the workers with the capitalist formula of the anti-aristocratic
alliance, and to gloss over its internal contradictions. On the
other hand, the term 'class' was incorporated into another
dichotomy of opposite political consequences; the latter was
most tersely expressed by Cobbett in 1825: 'Working men combine to effect a rise in wages. The masters combine against
them.... So that there is one class of society united to oppose
another class.'[6]
These words of Cobbett strike the modern reader as particularly akin to the contemporary semantic intuition. They
anticipate, in a sense, the meaning of class which was to become
dominant and render its competitors archaic. Two features of
the emergent meaning deserve particular attention. First,
Cobbett selects as the major class-formative factor the confrontation in the battle of interests; a group unites into a class to
confront another group and force it to surrender or compromise;

conflict, so to speak, precedes class. Second, the nature of
the conflict responsible for class formation is, in Cobbett's
view, unambiguously economic: it is, to be precise, about
wages, which the masters want to keep low, but workers wish
to increase. Cobbett's version of the conflict, therefore, had
been already refracted through the prism of the market economy. It still speaks of masters and their apprentices, but it
recognises already that both sides are entangled in the web of
market exchange and that the price of their services is about
all one needs to characterise their mutual expectations. In
these two respects Cobbett's statement anticipated the idea of
class which was to emerge in the end from the protracted
semantic confusion.

These two respects are also crucial for our theme. On the one
hand, we need to comprehend the true nature of the conflict
which disrupted the old rank order and led to the formation of
a class society. This means penetrating contemporary (and
particularly the retrospective) articulations of the conflict to
its inner core: to the situation which people experienced as
hardship and which they consequently resisted. One has to
separate again what in the course of time has become inextricably mingled: the cause of discontent and unrest, and the
objectives (more often than not portrayed as motives) politically
imputed to resulting actions. On the other hand, we need to
discover the sequence of events and the configuration of social
forces responsible for the ultimate prevalence of one political
imputation, which articulated the emergent conflict as economically motivated. This is what we propose to do in this chapter.

FROM THE MANAGEMENT OF SURPLUS TO THE MANAGEMENT OF PEOPLE

Class was born of social conflict. Perception of class as the
ultimate human reality was born of the discourse of conflict. One
should be grateful to R.J. Morris for his timely reminder of
the dangers threatening a historian settling for a merely philo-
logical analysis of the origins of class:[7]

> Comparing the language of rank and orders with the lan-
> guage of class as used by Carlyle, Cobden, Hetherington
> and the Political Unions and Chartists is not to compare like
> with like. It is a comparison of 18th century discussion of
> status groups with the 19th century discussion of conflict
> groups or classes. The real comparison must be with the
> language of 'gentlemen', 'the people', and 'the mob', for
> this was the 18th century language of social conflict.

It was not the language of class which displaced and eventually
replaced the language of rank; it was, rather, a society articulated by conflict which replaced one which could still define

itself in terms of lasting dependencies rather than the challenge
to them. Besides – and this seems to be a factor of crucial
importance – the society about to be replaced, the rank society,
had also its language of conflict. Its self-description was not
full without setting aside categories like 'mob', 'riff-raff', 'the
scum', or, for this matter, 'vagabonds' or 'dangerous classes'.
All these terms belonged to the language of conflict. They differed from the later vocabulary of classes in that they all
denoted departures from the norm, failures of order, the margins which refused to be meaningfully attached to the 'chain
of connection', the categories which stuck out from the web
of duties and obligations in which other, 'normal', 'orderly'
categories were tightly enmeshed. The discourse of class society
would move the conflict from the murky, shadowy and threatening margins of the social order into the very centre of society;
from the scrap heap to the main building site of social order.

It is the later, already thoroughly 'economised', vision of class
conflict which suggests an intimate link between the birth of
class with the establishment of capitalist industry, with the factory and the prevalence of hired labour. Indeed, it was only in
the wake of the industrial organisation of social production that
society came to acknowledge the permanence and 'naturalness'
of conflict and absorbed the vocabulary of conflict for its self-
definition. However true the suggestion is, it is a part of the
truth. The other part, which the 'economised' vision of class
does not help to reveal, is that what was absorbed into the
self-image of class society was the assortment of conflicts and
tensions which emerged long before the beginnings of capitalist
industry; which, in a sense, can be best seen as the condition
of capitalism, rather than its product.

This assortment of conflicts and tensions which preceded
capitalism and forged the instruments with which the modern
industry could be built was simultaneously a stimulus and a
creation of the new forms of social power which crystallised
in the course of the seventeenth and eighteenth centuries. In
the vivid language of Michel Foucault, what slowly, though
dramatically, came into being during this period, was a 'capillary
form' of power, power which 'reaches into the very grain of
individuals', a 'synaptic regime of power, a regime of its exercise
its exercise *within* the social body, rather than *from above*
it'.[8]

Why this new regime of power had emerged, is a fascinating
question to which no simple answer comes to mind. The question
lies, however, outside the scope of this study. It is the consequences, not the roots, of the new regime, which bear direct
and crucial relevance to our topic. Partly by necessity and
partly by choice, we will confine ourselves to some broad hints
only regarding the social and cultural transformation which
could be suspected of being instrumental in the process.

The old regime of power, the 'sovereign' power, the royal
or princely power, was the characteristic feature of the pre-

dominantly agricultural, in most of Europe feudal, society,
where administration of surplus was secured through the institution of land property and tenure, vassalage and serfdom.
In such a society, surplus product was typically extracted
from the producers, so to speak, in leaps and bounds; say,
once or several times during the annual cycle of the essentially
agricultural production, in the form of rent, or tax, or a levy,
or a tribute, or a tithe. The one function of power was to
force the producer to part, of will or of fear, or of both, with
a fraction of his product. Once he had done that, he could be
(and should be, if the production was to continue) left to his
own resources. It was largely irrelevant for the circulation
of surplus how he went about his daily business, how he
administered and deployed his bodily and spiritual powers. The
one thing which mattered for the 'sovereign' power - the availability of suplus - was quite adequately taken care of by the
double pressure of natural cycle and the threat of what Ernest
Gellner, this supreme master of the metaphor, once called
'the dentistry state' - a state specialising in extraction by
torture. The sovereign power could remain distant from the
body of the average producer, towering majestically at the far
horizon of his life cycle. Its remoteness, not-of-this-worldness
was heavily underlined by the sacralisation of the royal reign,
which ceremonially, in a timelessly repetitive fashion, symbolised
the eternal order of social supremacy. In practice, this supremacy boiled down to the upward flow of agricultural surplus.
In Georges Duby's words, the whole system of feudal power
could well be portrayed as a method of keeping the stomachs
of the barons and their retainers full.[9] Otherwise, the customs
and habits which ruled the daily life of the food suppliers were
no concern of power. This era of merciless exploitation, of the
organised universal theft of the surplus product, was also a
time of rich and robust folk culture, which the church, so exacting and meticulous in its defence of the divine rights of secular
powers, was quite happy to leave to its natural logic.

And then, from the seventeenth century onwards, an all-out
assault, and a virtual destruction of the popular culture were
launched. They entailed a cruel repression of popular cultural
autonomy, of traditional conduct now redefined as immoral,
heretical, criminal or mad, brutal or animal-like, suppression
of popular festivals and carnivals, of heterodox beliefs and
of 'witchcraft' - a process, for example, brilliantly and profusely documented for France by Robert Muchembled.[10]

The frontal attack against the popular culture, this stronghold of popular autonomy, was in no sense an isolated phenomenon which could be referred to one cause - be it growing
ambition of churches, moral revivalism of urban middle classes,
or absolutist inclinations of supreme rulers. It was just one
aspect of the general redeployment of social power; which
entailed both the restructuring of authority and a drastic shift
in the scope of power and the method of its exercise. Power

moved from the distant horizon into the very centre of daily
life. Its object, previously the goods possessed or produced
by the subject, was now the subject himself, his daily rhythm,
his time, his bodily actions, his mode of life. The power
reached now towards the body and the soul of its subjects. It
wished to regulate, to legislate, to tell the right from the
wrong, the norm from deviance, the ought from the is. It
wanted to impose one ubiquitous pattern of normality and eliminate everything and everybody which the pattern could not
fit. Unlike the sovereign power which required only a ceremonial reminder of the timeless limits to autonomy, the emergent
power could be maintained only by a dense web of interlocking
authorities in constant communication with the subject and in
a physical proximity to the subject which permitted a perpetual
surveillance of, possibly, the totality of his life process. Old
forms were transformed into such authorities, while new
authorities were brought to life to serve the fields old authorities were incapable of reaching. Thus families and sexual
functions of the body are deployed in a new role; churches
become teachers of business virtue, hard work and abstemious-
ness - and if old churches fail to hammer the lesson home,
sects or dissident churches emerge to do the job; workhouses
and poorhouses join forces in instilling the habit of continuous,
repetitive, routine effort; idiosyncrasy and, indeed, any
non-rhythmical, erratic behaviour is stigmatised, criminalised,
medicalised or psychiatrised; individualised training by
apprenticeship or personal service is replaced with a uniform
system of education aimed at instilling universal skills and,
above all, universal discipline - through, among other means,
culling the individual qua individual from the guidance and
authority of his group of origin and subjecting him to an external source of authority superior to this group and free from
its control.[11] No one of these many powers is now total, like
that of the absolute monarch claimed to be. But together they
reach a kind of totality which no power dreamed of reaching
before. Between themselves they legislate for well-nigh totality
of human life, though the legislation is often exercised surrepti-
tiously by developing within the individual a tendency to a
specifically patterned conduct and blocks against departing
from the pattern: in other words, by installing the Freudian
'garrison in the conquered city'.

    The dramatic extension of social control over areas previously
ruled autonomously by community-supervised tradition was
intellectually articulated in new dichotomies which were to provide the axis for moral philosophy and, indeed, for the new
rational, scientific culture: the dichotomies of reason and
passion, civilisation and brutality, true needs and wanton or
ignorant, but always reprehensible, wants. Through the joint
efforts of religious reformers, administrators of the emerging
absolutist or centralised states and court philosophers, the
freshly articulated duality of human nature came to be seen as

an object of concern and a task for social control. The two
antagonistic constituents of the self came to be seen as stages
in a process, the first stubbornly persistent through its own
inertia, but nevertheless destined to be eventually eliminated
and replaced by the second. Most importantly, the replacement
was not expected to come of itself – the process was not seen
as developing from natural causes; it called for hard work and
constant vigilance. The new attitude viewed man as an unfin-
ished product, raw and crude stuff bound to be shaped and
moulded into a human form by external agents; as an object of
activity, variously called culture, civilisation, Bildung, refinement – all these nouns, as Lucien Febvre convincingly demonstrated,[12] meaning a transitive activity long before they came
to denote achieved states.

Thus the old coexistence of forms of life, blind and tolerant
to differences and reconciled to their permanence, gave place
to a reforming-teaching-punishing urge. The abominable duality
of human nature was projected upon the relations between
groups and categories within society, or between societies,
which turned the result into the relations of superiority-
inferiority, teaching and learning duties, policing and crimin-
ality or insanity. These applied to adults and children, men
and women, sane and mad, the civilised and the barbarians,
gentlemen and plebs, *l'honnête homme* and the mob. It was the
duty of the first to assist the triumph of reason over passion
and to help 'human nature' to emancipate itself from the fetters
of animality. The task made the second into objects of control,
entitled to the master's instruction, but bound to be forced
into submission in case the instruction falls on to a barren soil.
The moral stance associated with the deployment of new powers
was a mixture of condescension and intolerance.

The intimate connection between the new concept of human
nature and destiny on one hand, and the ascent of the new
bourgeois regime on the other, has by now become a rarely
disputed assumption of social-scientific common sense. And yet,
as so many other uncontrolled assumptions, it ill stands either
historical scrutiny or immanent logical analysis. Two arguments
in particular cast serious doubt on its soundness. First, while
retrospectively one can show the usefulness of the new 'synaptic', 'discipline' powers for the capitalist economy, it is much
more difficult to prove the logical necessity of various forms
which the new powers took for the proper functioning of this
economy; with a little effort one could even show that quite
opposite attitudes towards, say, sexuality or madness, would
have been equally, if not more, functional for the needs of the
factory system. Second, the new tools and mechanisms of control and the conquest of human body and soul preceded the
establishment of the factory system by roughly two centuries.
If they later came to perform a vitally functional role in the
creation and the entrenchment of the factory system, their
anticipated usefulness for an order hardly foreseen at the time

cannot be seriously viewed as a factor operative in their
development. The opinion recently expressed by Foucault seems
to dispose radically of these difficulties confronting the dominant
assumption. Foucault reverses the common order of reasoning:
the mechanisms of power emerged first for reasons of their own
– but their availability made the emergence of the capitalist
order plausible, as the means of control and surveillance which
such an order required were already at hand:[13]

> These mechanisms of power, at a given moment, in a precise
> conjuncture and by means of a certain number of transform-
> ations, have begun to become economically advantageous and
> politically useful....What the bourgeoisie needed, or that
> in which its system discovered its real interests, was not
> the exclusion of the mad or the surveillance and prohibition
> of infantile masturbation,...but rather, the techniques and
> procedures themselves of such an exclusion....What in fact
> happened...was that the mechanisms of the exclusion of
> madness, and of the surveillance of infantile sexuality,
> began from a particular point in time...to reveal their poli-
> tical usefulness and to lend themselves to economic profit,
> and that as a natural consequence, all of a sudden, they
> came to be colonised and maintained by global mechanisms
> and the entire State system.

The assumption of a causal connection between the emerging
bourgeois economic interests and the deployment of new power
made all further exploration of the origins of the latter superfluous. Once the assumption is put in doubt, the sudden eruption of controlling ambitions appears as a mystery which only
thorough historical research, neglected until recently, may
eventually solve. As I have already admitted, such research
has not been undertaken for the sake of this study – as the
causes of both new forms of social power and their intellectual
correlates bear only oblique relevance to the major topic of
this book. It seems, however, that one hypothesis can be
risked: rather than being a more or less conscious application
of the bourgeois dominance project, the new powers and their
philosophies arose from the crisis and disintegration of the old
regime. Not that new forces launched an offensive with the
view of evicting the present occupants of the centre of the
social order, and occupying it themselves; it was, rather, that
the old centre could not hold any more.
   The old social order did disintegrate long before the ascending capitalist order delivered its political coup de grâce. The
old order was organised around the institutional principle of
perpetuity of bonds and obligations; it offered security in
exchange for freedom. The order was all-embracing – it included
those of high rank and the poor alike; locked in the reciprocal
obligations, they were hardly imaginable unless complemented
by their counterparts. The mighty were not conceivable without

their duty of paternal care and charity; the poor were unthinkable without the service they rendered to the powerful and the
fatherly - stern but benevolent - support they received in
exchange. What tied the ranks together appeared to outweigh
everything that set them apart. Within the perspective of
patronage, the poor belonged to the rich; they were the rich's
natural extension, like the land which the rich owned and which
the poor had no right, or no practical resources, to abandon.
The poor could not, by custom and by law, expect or demand
any assistance (or, indeed, work) outside the boundaries of
their native parishes. The law drew a sharp dividing line
between the relative security of the inherited space and the
terrifying inhospitality of the rest. The poor could venture
to explore the chances offered by faraway places only at their
own risk - and the risk was enormous. Even if the poor man
dared to move outside his 'natural' space, he would, more often
than not, be returned 'home' by force. Were he allowed to
remain in the new place long enough to establish his rights of
settlement, he would sooner or later claim assistance when
losing his job and falling into a destitute state - a prospect
which the local authorities, in absence of the land-based bond,
could see only as an unnatural and unwarranted financial
burden which was to be prevented by barring the 'alien' poor
from staying around. The poor were, by what could be seen
as a universal conspiracy of parishes, forced into the arms of
the local patrons to whom they belonged by birth. In eighteenth-century Britain,[14]

> the fact that a man could legally claim relief only from that
> parish where he was settled deprived all but the most cap-
> able and energetic of any incentive to go in search of
> work....By providing maintenance on the one hand and the
> threat of physical violence on the other, the law ensured
> that the rural labourer, at least, should become not unlike
> the shell-fish, which cling to the rocks and let the drifting
> tide bring them their daily food.

This condemnation, spelled out by Dorothy Marshall, reflected
the bourgeois opinion of the day, which was whole-heartedly
in favour of unhampered mobility of labour seeking in the wide
world its chancy employment and natural price. But beneath
the evaluations there was the hard reality of the 'glebae
adscripti' system on which social control in the old regime was
grounded. The shellfish metaphor fits well the order based,
first and foremost, on control-through-space. This principle
was dramatically symbolised by the prevalence of land property
over fluid, mobile, space-independent capital which was to
become dominant later.

It was this system of control-through-space which began to
disintegrate throughout Western Europe starting from the
seventeenth century. Elaborate Elizabethan laws classifying,

dividing, and segregating the growing population of beggars
and vagabonds and legally enforcing rules of charity earlier
left to the autonomous social mechanisms, testified that in
England the disintegration moved further than on the continent;
this was due to the early defeat of English peasantry and the
transformation of land-holders into tenants and farm-hands.
But with a somewhat different speed and in different forms,
similar processes also took place elsewhere. Alexis de Tocqueville
wrote of the French Revolution and its allegedly crucial role
in the transformation of social patterns, that

> though it took the world by surprise, it was the inevitable
> outcome of a long period of gestation, the abrupt and vio-
> lent conclusion of a process in which six generations had
> played an intermittent part. Even if it had not taken place,
> the old social structure would nonetheless have been shat-
> tered everywhere sooner or later. The only difference
> would have been that instead of collapsing with such brutal
> suddenness it would have crumbled bit by bit.

The main reason for the collapse de Tocqueville saw in the fact
that 'the lord no longer felt bound by his natural obligations.
And no local authority, no poor relief committee or parish
council had taken them over.[15] De Tocqueville laid the ultimate
blame for the disintegration at the door of the absolutist
monarchy whose centralising zeal divested the lords of their
traditional authority and therefore left its 'other side', the
patronage duties, unsupported. Whatever the true order of
causes and effects, though, the paramount fact is the increasingly evident insufficiency of the control-through-space as the
principal instrument of social order.
    Space was a powerful and sufficient means of control in so far
as locality remained the seat of comprehensive obligations and
equally comprehensive, and also realistic, rights, which between
themselves catered for the fullness of human life. The web of
place-tied obligations and rights could be, indeed, so complete,
that it might allow the owner of the land, the holder of power,
not to be concerned with control of time. The latter, in a predominantly agricultural society, could be left almost entirely to
the rhythm of nature, processed, and symbolically reinforced,
by the seemingly equally natural rhythm of community life. (De
Tocqueville noted the telling coincidence between the disintegration of manorial authority and the sudden appearance of state-
sponsored pamphlets on agricultural, and laws on artisans',
methods - both attempting to regulate activities which previously
hardly needed to be regulated from outside.) The crucial point,
however, was - that given the permanence of place and a negligible ratio of territorial mobility, human behaviour in its
totality was so clearly visible that keeping it on the customary
course did not call for an organised, separately institutionalised
surveillance. However all-penetrating and effective it was,

the communal surveillance could well be unobtrusive to the point of not being noticed and articulated as a phenomenon in its own right. In stable and familiar surroundings, such community vigil could well appear to its objects as what Erasmus called 'social probability': an almost unthinking certainty that everybody else will follow a specific pattern of conduct and that no one will seriously attempt to break it. An effective social probability renders the 'legal probability' (a conscious obedience based on the calculation that a certain pattern will be enforced by a specialised institution and that no one, therefore, will be allowed to get away with breaking it) unnecessary. Instead of confronting the object as an outside force, communal surveillance may well be seen as the 'art of life', or 'life wisdom', or the 'natural course' of life. Social historians who in recent years have thrown new light on the early modern history of the family have shown the remarkable openness of family life towards the community. In particular, Norbert Elias and Philippe Ariés have demonstrated in different ways the virtual absence of family privacy. The family home, as a rule not divided into private and public regions, stayed permanently open to visitors, while most family business, including the aspects which are seen today as thoroughly intimate, was conducted in the open. When the kitchen was not the family sanctuary, when adults and children slept in one bed, when sexual intercourse was not kept too carefully from public gaze, when families strolled naked to the communal bath, there was little chance for surveillance to emerge as an external and specialised agency responsible for the maintenance of the 'pattern of conduct' as separate from the 'way of life'.

Now both the sufficiency of control-through-space and the concomitant superfluity (or, depending on interpretation, invisibility) of control-through-time could not survive the disintegration of this tight web of rights and obligations which was the small township or a village community. As was noted before, such a disintegration, for whatever reasons, did take place in the course of the seventeenth and eighteenth centuries. Rapidly swelling cities, these seats of 'universal otherhood' where stranger lived among strangers, were the prime products of the disintegration. At the same time, they were the very places where the old type of social power, with its instruments of control-through-space, revealed its limitations.

The old power simply could not cope with the masses of anonymous strangers congested in a relatively constrained space in such a way that the conduct of each could not but affect the plight of everyone else. Besides – and perhaps more importantly – the old power was geared to the task of creaming off the surplus product; it was never confronted, at least on an important scale or fot prolonged periods, with the need to organise the production itself; it had little occasion, therefore, to develop effective means of managing the activities of the producers: it was, so to speak, ill-adjusted to the control of

human bodies and any but few aspects of human spirits. But
urban life required exactly this kind of control. Urban crowds
were not producers of surplus - at least not producers above
all else. It was not the need to expropriate their produce which
defined the problem of the urban crowd to the rich and the
powerful. In a much more immediate and straightforward way
the anonymous crowd of the urban poor appeared to the bourgeois, and to the agencies of the state to which he looked for
protection, as an unruly, obstreperous, rowdy and rebellious
mob, which was bound to remain a constant source of danger
as long as its conduct was not forced into regular, predictable
patterns. To perform this task, a power was needed able to
administer human bodies, and not merely the goods which their
labour might turn out.

The picture emerging from the recent comparative study of
eighteenth-century Europe by Olwen H. Hufton is one of the
'towns as places of refuge for the extreme poor, sometimes
the hopeless and helpless: towns as monuments to rural
poverty....The urbanisation of poverty, a poverty born in
the countryside but which manifested itself in the town, created
problems of public order, menaced public health and placed
a strain on traditional patterns of provisioning'.[16] There was
no rhythm of nature punctuated by the communal ritual to
guide the conduct of rural refugees; and no communal guarantee
of basic security to provide succour in times of distress or to
make destitution bearable. But the still fresh collective memory
suggested that such guarantees are the duty of the high and
mighty. When the help was slow in coming, the outbursts of
popular anger, recorded as food riots, were a violent and erratic reaction. From the upper rungs of the social ladder, the
very spontaneity, irregularity, unpatterned nature of such
outbursts was the proof of the endemic savagery of the passion-
ridden mob.

It seems a plausible hypothesis that at the roots of the
vehement, often hysterical onslaught against passions (i.e. self-
management of human bodies) was the great terror among the
'established' (to employ Norbert Elias's terms) faced with
the influx of unstructured crowds of the 'outsiders'. This great
terror was among the main factors which added urgency and
attraction to the missionary zeal of the Enlightenment. It was
the highest priest of Reason, after all, who described the
masses as 'les bêtes féroces, furieux, imbéciles, fous, aveugles'.
It was Voltaire himself who recorded in his notebook the final
indictment: 'The people will always be composed of brutes';
'The people is between man and beast.'[17] The 'philosophes' joined
whole-heartedly the outcry against the 'mendiants' and the
'vagabonds'. In Alan Forrest's recent summary of the mood of
the era, 'the erstwhile children of Jesus had by the middle of
the eighteenth century assumed a less beatific countenance and
were generally depicted as violent, drunken, and menacing'. One
Guillaume Le Trosne in a popular and widely read pamphlet,

published in 1764, described 'mendiants' as standing outside
civilised society, a breed apart from the community amongst
whom they lived, a race both undisciplined and dangerous:
theirs was 'une rébellion sourde et continuelle'.[18] The public
debate of the Enlightenment praised the unlimited potential of
human reason and proclaimed the principle of perfectibility of
man. But it also split mankind into those who are called to
perform the job of perfecting and those – the multitude – who
can and should do no more than serve as the objects of enlightened efforts. The acute awareness of the presence of 'dangerous classes' rendered the appeals to reason that much more
convincing; the 'universal human nature', which Enlightenment
declared, served most immediately as strategic formula for the
concentrated offensive against the unruly mob. As Witt Bowden
observed, for pre-industrial eighteenth-century England, the
wretchedness of the labouring poor arose essentially from the
keen, condensed efforts to extend a new, more comprehensive
than ever, control over their lives; the poor were not credited
with an innate ability to partake of universal human reason.
'The "public" of that time was to be sure not very comprehensive, for the masses, the "vulgar and common sorts" of people,
were not included. Their welfare was believed to consist in
poverty-bred ignorance and subjection.'[19]
    If this hypothesis is true (as I believe it is), then the deploy-
ment of the new 'discipline' power, the power aimed at the
management of human bodies, rather than of the surplus of
human labour, was in no way a result – or even a functional
correlate – of the capitalist industrialisation. It was instead a
product (however indirect) of the disintegration of the social
organisation characterised by the overlapping of the institutions of surplus distribution, social dominance and social welfare. A most significant aspect of this disintegration was the
appearance of a growing stratum of people who were not (at
least not primarily) producers of surplus; the problem they
presented was therefore not one of the continuing compliance
with the demand to part with the surplus they produced, but
one of refraining from the rebellion against the order which
had no use for their labour, but which also failed to observe
the traditional guarantee of welfare. The new scope and the
new ambitions of social power were made to measure for this
new problem. New forms and methods of control were forged in
'dépôts de mendicité', parish workhouses, prisons, hospitals,
madhouses. The dark, satanic mills, when they appeared,
found them ready-made. The late arrivals merely employed
the existing resources of body-management and time control
and put them to a new use.
    The bourgeois society has been often described as one which
invented, entrenched, and philosophically legitimised the right
to privacy as well as the privacy itself. What is more often than
not overlooked, however, is that the same society invented and
did its best to enforce the principle of transparency – this

founding stone of power which consists in the total and perpetual supervision of human action. Bentham's 'Panopticon' can
be seen as a most spectacular embodiment of this principle - an
extreme expression of what was a general concern of the era.
Foucault reminded us recently that Bentham himself admitted
his debt to older architectural attempts, the intentions of which
'Panopticon' had merely brought to a radical perfection; in
particular, Bentham pointed out the role of the report which
his brother gave him about the dormitories of l'Ecole Militaire
of Paris, built already in 1751. These implemented the principle
of 'isolating visibility': the cadets slept in glass cells, which
opened them to the watchful gaze of the superior, but barred
all visual contact between equals. The idea of 'Panopticon'
identified power with observation, submission with visibility:
power as such, any power, social order in general, the universal principle of social organisation with infinite applications.
In Foucault's words:[20]

> the very word 'Panopticon' seems crucial here, as designat-
> ing the principle of a system. Thus Bentham didn't merely
> imagine an architectural design calculated to solve a specific
> problem, such as that of a prison, a school or a hospital.
> He proclaimed it as a veritable discovery, saying of it him-
> self that it was 'Christopher Columbus's egg'. And indeed
> what Bentham proposed to the doctors, penologists, indus-
> trialists and educators was just what they had been looking
> for. He invented a technology of power designed to solve the
> problem of surveillance. One important point should be
> noted: Bentham thought and said that his optical system
> was *the* great innovation needed for the easy and effective
> exercise of power. It has in fact been widely employed
> since the end of the eighteenth century.

'Dangerous classes' and 'dark districts' of the towns must
have had something to do with the obsessive fear of darkness,
invisibility, opacity; and the overwhelming wish to pierce the
mist enveloping crowded new cities, to place the people in a
space so organised that whatever they did was immediately visible, and visible so clearly that the people themselves were
aware of their openness to public gaze, and would therefore
refrain from performing acts which they would not enjoy being
seen to do. What had been accomplished matter-of-factly in a
village community or in a small market township had to be an
object of conscious effort and administrative vigilance in a
crowded city. Early socialists still dreamed of the diffuse,
'democratic' gaze of the community as a whole - Fourier hoped
that harmony could be restored if the community succeeded in
combining the passions of its members.[21] Less Utopian versions
of socialism shared, however, the dominant conviction that
the universal, dispersed gaze was not a realistic solution to a
highly condensed society, and that any social order, whatever

its moral objectives, would require from now on surveillance as
a specialised function, as an institutionalised occupation of
power. Power was to consist in an inspecting gaze - in Foucault's words again, 'a gaze which each individual under its
weight will end by interiorising to the point that he is his own
overseer, each individual thus exercising this surveillance over,
and against, himself'.[22]

The thrust of the new power, which Bentham's 'Panopticon'
dramatically brought into relief, but by no means invented,
stemmed from the fear which resulted in the mood of universal
distrust: people cannot be left unattended, the free roaming
of unattached people is in itself a danger, people must be kept
in place in order that their time might be subject to reassuring,
because repetitive, patterns. The other, closely related, consequence of distrust was the intense urge to classify, categorise,
stereotype the motley unattached crowd no longer defined in
the 'vegetable' way, by the bonds of local community. Perhaps
the most devoted of Bentham's disciples and followers, and
certainly the one who more than anyone else dedicated his life
to the implementation of the master's ideas, Sir Edwin Chadwick,[23]

> held strongly that the destitute should be divided into dis-
> tinct classes. He would have built industrial schools for the
> children of the workless; the aged he would have housed
> in almhouses; the insane he would have housed in proper
> asylums under scientific medical care; the sick he would
> have placed in hospitals.

Chadwick, as his biographer Marston testifies, was obsessed
with what he himself called the 'Sanitary Idea', the breath-
taking vision of society where every 'problem' finds its own
place and its own, proper, specially designed care which
together procure both control and containment. The 'Sanitary
Idea', if put into operation, would have solved 'problems' so
wide apart as unhealthy lives, children growing up ignorant,
the prevalence of immorality or cholera epidemics. Again,
Chadwick was a radical like his teacher and not many contemporaries were ready to follow him all the way, particularly when
embarrassed by his notorious blunt and irreverent fashion of
expressing his ideas. Still, Chadwick was second to none in
capturing the spirit of his era, the direction in which social
powers developed. It was indeed a new, but already dominant,
view of social power as an equivalent of medicine in its relation to human body. The task and the duty of politics was to
diagnose the 'social disease', segregate the ill as they have
been segregated for many years now in the hospitals, attach
to their places labels with the name of their infirmity and pres-
cribe to each the drug which suits his own category of ailment.

Time routine, isolation, classification, surveillance - these
were power resources developed well before the ascent of the

factory system and clearly not in response to the needs of this
system, which was still not in existence. Rather than arising
from the capitalist industry, they proved to be indispensable
and fertile, though not sufficient, conditions of its development.

THE BIRTH OF THE FACTORY

The disintegration of the old regime affected different strata of
the poor differently.

In rural areas of Britain the traditions of land tenancy were
almost obliterated from collective memory. The two successive
waves of enclosures transformed former peasants into farm-
hands thoroughly divested of all control over their subsistence
and, above all, their productive activities. Farm-hands worked
under the constant control of the bailiffs and minor supervisors and followed their commands. They had little chance to
exercise any but their physical faculties. Their productive
effort was controlled and patterned by others. In a sense,
agricultural workers were the first to be subject - mostly
piecemeal and without evident resistance - to the new regime
of power, aimed at production itself instead of its products.
But only in a sense; agriculture could never fully emancipate
itself from the cyclical rhythm of nature, and the latter set
unencroachable limits on the routines designed artificially, and
barred some routines which could be, theoretically, better
geared to the task of maintaining the order of subordination
and leave the supervisors in full command of the subordinates'
situation. Second, however penetrating the impact of the market
spirit and the concomitant callousness to the plight of hired
labour might be, social relations in agricultural areas remained
infused with a - however tenuous - memory of patronage; this
drew another limit to deployment of the new regime of power,
which must be truly impersonal to become fully effective. The
lord of the manor was, if more in theory than in practice, the
protector and the guardian of the poor. As long as the theory,
animated by cyclical rituals, retained some of its grip on the
conduct of both sides of the relation, control over the bodies
of agricultural producers could remain somewhat less than complete. Third, beyond the limits of time spent in production
proper, life could still be regulated effectively by communal
control. Enforcement of mindless discipline at work did not,
therefore, have to be supplemented by the diffuse network of
surveillance aimed at the totality of life functions.

It was entirely different with the masses of surplus population, whom the shrinking employment potential of the increasingly efficient agriculture, coupled with demographic growth,
transformed into dependants of parish workhouses or, alternatively, homeless vagabonds, doomed to make their living by
begging or stealing, at least in the intervals between casual
jobs. These were the people to whose measure the 'synaptic',

'discipline' power was cut; and it was, expectedly, on their
backs that the full weight of the new power first fell. It was
these people in the first place who were meant by the most common, and popular slogan of the time: 'policing the poor'. It was
accepted by the powers-that-be, that as far as this category was
concerned, the art of politics (as the Hammonds put it) 'was
the art of preserving discipline among a vast population destitute of the traditions and restraints of a settled and conservative society, dissatisfied with its inevitable lot and ready
for disorder and blind violence'.[24]

The task was shared between political authorities and private
entrepreneurs. The first played into the hands of the others;
having defined rootlessness as crime, and put every able-bodied
person before a choice between accepting paid employment on
any terms the employer may deem proper, and the confinement
in a poor-house, 'l'hôpital' (which popular folklore quickly
renamed 'mouroirs'), or prison - the legal code of most European
countries literally forced the homeless 'vagabonds' to submit to
the employer's power. In England, since Elizabethan times it
was a duty of local parishes to direct the poor needing assistance to such employers as the parish could find. With the ranks
of the poor growing rapidly, the old rule led to massive transportation of children of unemployed parents to the mills. It can
be seen that the availability of large quantities of unskilled,
defenceless and legally incapacitated labour was a crucial factor
among the conditions which made the birth of modern industry
possible in the peculiar form in which it occurred. The spectacular growth of production accomplished by early capitalist
industry had not been achieved through a significant rationalisation in the technology of factory work; this did not come
before the late nineteenth century. The first gigantic strides
towards a new, unprecedented scale of factory output were
due entirely to the few mechanical inventions which shifted to
the machine the skills and the experience previously required
of producers themselves. This development enabled the entrepreneurs to turn out large quantities of quality products while
employing primitive, unskilled and virtually untrained labour:
nothing but sheer physical exertion and unfailing attention
over long periods of time. Thus the ready acceptance of initial
mechanical invention was in no small degree due to the very
fact of the availability of huge masses of the poor which authorities could - and were willing to - dispose of by handing them
over to the willing employers.

The first to be so disposed of were the sections of the poor
least likely to offer resistance, women, and above all children.
In his once famous account of his childhood experience, William
Dodd remembered that the contracting of children from poor-
houses to cotton manufacturers was understood at the time and
talked about by both sides as entering 'servitude' or 'bondage'.
Forty children were packed in one wagon while driven to their
place of employment; en route the grated doors were securely

locked, and a child who still managed to escape was hunted by local authorities and promptly delivered to the employer for punishment. The only introduction children were given to their industrial jobs was the mixture of threats and moral preaching, like the speech of certain Messrs Lamberts, Dodd's employers, who[25]

> exhorted them to behave with proper humility and decorum; to pay the most prompt and submissive respect to the orders of those who would be appointed to instruct and superintend them at the mills; and to be diligent and careful, each one to execute his or her task, and thereby avoid the punishment and disgrace which awaited idleness, insolence, and disobedience.

Not before 1816 did the parliament of Britain think it necessary to interfere with the massive transportation of children by the parishes. By this time, however, factories had moved closer to the towns, thanks to the introduction of steam engines, and the supply of child labour could be kept on the required level with the resigned co-operation of unemployed, or otherwise impoverished, parents.

With the kind of labour the early factories employed, the resources needed to render it effective were not apprenticeships in skills and arousal of personal interest in work, but continuous surveillance and coercion. It was in these latter fields that the early entrepreneurs were most keen and inventive. According to another important document of the era, factory children were 'harassed to the brink of death by excesses of labour....They were flogged, fettered, and tortured in the most exquisite refinement of cruelty....They were, in many cases, starved to the bone while flogged to their work.... Their happiest moments had been passed in the garb and coercion of a workhouse.'[26] It was on the backs of the children that the code of factory labour, the code of unlimited control over human body and time, was engraved. In the Hammonds' view, the massive employment of children in early factories supplied the link of continuity connecting the supervisory patterns developed in relation to African slaves with the early entrepreneurs' tempers and their treatment of factory labour.[27]

The fresh experience of the slave trade and slave plantations of West Indies could have played its role in the formation of factory patterns in Britain. It offered handy examples of effective surveillance, and basic outlines of a regime successful in squeezing the maximum of useful effort out of the assumedly idle, uncommitted and unco-operative labour force. It was particularly welcome since the task they confronted was seen by the early entrepreneurs as quite similar to the one faced by plantation owners. If, however, there was an important continuity between the treatment of labour in early factories and some patterns of domination developed in pre-industrial times, it was

above all with the disciplinary powers deployed against 'dangerous classes'; early factories were indeed direct descendants
(or perhaps siblings) of workhouses or 'dépôts de mendicité'.
As Alan Forrest observed, *'classes dangereuses* there were in
France, but they were not a neat, distinct social category, but
groups which overlapped with and could often be confused
with the *classes laborieuses'*.[28] Such was the situation throughout most of Western Europe. Everywhere[29]

> the demographic upsurge had by the sixties produced an
> uncomfortable imbalance between population and economic
> performance. Even in years of normal harvests the number
> of those unable to make their resources stretch without
> recourse to begging was rapidly growing - a phenomenon
> remarkable even in Britain where the best balance between
> population and supply had been struck....France in 1767
> saw the most stringent attempts ever made to stem the ris-
> ing tide of vagrancy by penal legislation, increasing the
> police force

concluded Hufton from his comparative survey of conditions
in major West European states.
    In the Europe of the second half of the eighteenth century,
the overriding category set as the target of urgent social policy
was 'the poor' - a term used, for all practical intents and
purposes, interchangeably with 'vagabonds' or 'the idle'.
Labour was seen as a sub-category of the poor; a unit set
apart from the rest not so much by special traits of those who
labour, but by a particular policy applied, or thought appropriate, to this part of the 'problem of the poor'. The problem
was not, first and foremost, economic. It was not the question
of putting unemployed resources to a socially more beneficial
use. Instead, it was the problem of keeping dangerous classes,
desperate because destitute, out of mischief. Workhouses and
factories were the means of achieving exactly this purpose:
they claimed and enjoyed the support of the state and the
enlightened opinion as predominantly moral institutions, and
instruments of maintaining social order, long before they were
cast in the role of vehicles of economic progress and guarantees
of national wealth. Early factories and parish poorhouses, or
'les mouroirs', were branches of the same tree. All were conceived as alternative means for the containment of the poor:
able-bodied in the first case; crippled, infirm, or old in the
second.
    It might be true that pure economic greed induced the mas-
ters of early factories to install the stern and merciless regime
for which these factories were famous. But such a regime was
to be expected whatever the personal motives of the factory
owners. People who operated machines were part and parcel of
the poor, a category already fully stereotyped by previous
social practices as incapable of managing its own life, provide

for its own needs, judge rightly its own interests; guided by
passions rather than reason; and, above all, inclined to rebel
and riot and hence potentially dangerous. The severe conditions, which left no room or time for the exercise of any faculties but the purely physical (and these in a thoroughly routinised and supervised way), were exactly what was needed for
their own interest and for the safety of the society at large.
There were no legal or conscientious limits to the power of
factory bosses at the time when the workers were seen as simply
a sub-division of the poor, and the poor in general stereotyped
as naturally idle and profligate; one would legitimately expect
industry to be regarded, in the Hammonds' words, 'as a system
that saved men by ruling them'; 'The view of the new system
as a beneficient mechanism which the mass of men must serve
with a blind and unquestioning obedience was firmly rooted in
the temper of the time'.[30] The road from socially coined concepts to industrial practice was made all the easier by the fact
that the 'men' of whom the Hammonds wrote were mainly, almost
solely, women and children.
   Before they reached the gates of factories, these women and
children had only the experience of the prison-like regime of
parish poor-houses or the precarious life of a person dependent
on alms meted out only together with a humiliating inquisition
aimed at detecting profligacy and moral depravity behind the
poverty. Naturally, they did not expect to find inside the
factory anything essentially different from the regime they
were subject to. There was no disappointment, no frustration,
no sense of outraged justice. Just a smooth, virtually imperceptible passage from one unit of control to another. These
women and children were not the stuff of which rebels were
made. This seems to be the explanation of the otherwise puzzl-
ing regularity noted by Hufton: 'The poor themselves were not
protesters',[31] or Barrington Moore Jr:[32]

> Those who are the worst off are generally the last to organ-
> ise and make their voices heard. Those at the bottom of the
> heap are generally the last ones to hear the news that there
> has been a change in the capacity of human society to cope
> with the miseries of human existence.

It was only when the early factory regime, itself a mere
variant of the power resources developed in response to the
challenge of 'dangerous classes', was to be stretched to encom-
pass the heretofore independent producers, now ruined by
the new method of employing unskilled labour and hence about
to become poor and 'dangerous' themselves, that the thread of
continuity snapped. Paradoxically, the factory regime descended
from the treatment of those whom the dominant powers considered dangerous, but who in practice proved to be pliant and
malleable; when it was extended to the categories of population
which it inadvertently - through competition - helped to

generate, it produced truly 'dangerous classes' out of groups
previously rightly viewed as the mainstay of social order.

In William H. Sewell Jr's splendid summary of the almost
unanimous opinion emerging from the most recent historical
research:[33]

> skilled artisans, not workers in the new factory industries,
> dominated labour movements during the first decades of
> industrialisation. Whether in France, England, Germany,
> or the United States; whether in strikes, political move-
> ments, or incidents of collective violence, one finds over
> and over again the same familiar trades: carpenters, tailors,
> bakers, cabinetmakers, shoemakers, stonemasons, printers,
> locksmiths, joiners, and the like. The nineteenth-century
> labour movement was born in the craft workshop, not in the
> dark, satanic mill.

From the vantage point of the dominant order, violence was
violence, and there was clear continuity and categorial identity
between the food riots of the desperate poor when European
governments one after another lifted the restrictions on grain
trade (and particularly the custom of fixing grain prices and
markets) and the rebellion of 'respectable trades' against the
factory system which sapped the grounds of their security and
status. This flattening of perspective was not without influence
on informed historical opinion, both contemporary and retrospective. It was not immediately evident that the two series of
social protest can be understood best, both in their origins
and their consequences, as belonging to sociologically distinct
categories.

To the craftsmen and artisans the growing ambitions of the
factory system meant, above anything else, the threat of the
loss of independence; more specifically, of the control over their
own labour which they theoretically, and to an extent also
practically, had maintained since mediaeval times. This independence was not articulated by the guild regulations as their
conscious perspective; it was noticed as valuable, and as a
possession to be defended, only when put in question by the
spread of the new regime of labour, tightly controlled, meticulously supervised, and fully regimented by external authorities. Unlike the village poor, and certainly unlike destitute
women and children, skilled artisans grew to expect a different
order of life. They had already developed life and work habits
which the factory regime had no use for, and which it was set
to destroy. Everything in the social position and cultural tradition of craftsmen pitted them against the advancing factory
and rendered the factory system their natural enemy.

The original conflict of craftsmen with the capitalist factory
was only indirectly economic. Most of the craftsmen were not
employees of capitalist entrepreneurs, and thus, if they were
exploited, the nature of this exploitation was not immediately

evident and easy to discover. The connection much easier to
make was one between falling profits of craftsmen and massive
mechanisation of labour in factories. An excellent example of
such a link has been supplied by John Foster, who closely
documented the deteriorating economic standards of hand-loom
weavers caused by the complete mechanisation of cotton spin-
ning and the resulting pressure of continental weaving on the
income of English weavers.[34] The conflict was not one between
exploited and their exploiters, but between competitors, some
of whom protested against conditions which they saw as unfair,
since they undermined their traditional market monopoly.

Even this indirect form of the clash of economic interests
was (at least originally) relegated to a second place in the
inventory of craftsmen's complaints against the factory system.
The pride of place on the list of grievances belonged to the
outrage caused by the legislative measures like dissolution of
guilds in France or the repeal by English parliament, in 1814,
of the apprenticeship clause of the 1563 Statute of Artificers
and Apprentices (5 Elizabeth). This dramatic change aimed at
the very heart of the craftsmen's mode of life. Removing all
limitations traditionally imposed on the numbers of newcomers
to the trade, it exploded the principle of task-continuity which
made every journeyman (in theory, if not always in practice)
a master-hopeful, and allowed the glossing over of the economic
conflicts within the workshop by 'binding the worker into the
larger household of the employer and then asserting the moral
priority of the overall group'.[35] The unlimited number of apprentices barred the journeyman from viewing their current dis-
comforts with the philosophical quietude derived from the sense
of their temporary character. Submission was not any more a
temporary station in life, with its rough edges considerably
blunted by the anticipation of future independence. Moreover,
the repeal of 5 Elizabeth (or, in other countries, abolition or
weakening of guild statuses in general) made the journeyman
expendable and easily replaceable, which all but destroyed his
capacity to resist the masters' bid for total control over their
labour and wages.

If the economic grievance discussed before served in many
cases as the device to preserve the unity of the trade by shifting the blame for deteriorating standards of life on external
factors (mechanised factories, and the government which supported their collusion with foreign competitors), the resistance
against the repeal of 5 Elizabeth split the trade in the middle.
It pointed to another collusion, this time between the government and the masters; and it laid the blame squarely on the
shoulders of the masters. It underlined the distinctiveness of
the journeymen's interest as against the interests of their
masters. It can be seen, for these reasons, as the first struggle with a class-formative potential. The conclusion reached
by Barrington Moore Jr, that the 'main popular group among
which Marxist and other radical notions took hold was the

journeymen',[36] comes as no surprise.

As will be shown in more detail in the next chapter, the
movements which arose from the conflicts discussed here and
which happened to play the crucial role in the process of
class formation, were predominantly backward-looking. They
did not seek accommodation inside the factory and in the framework of the capitalist structure of domination; they were set
in motion by the intense resentment of both, and the desire
to arrest their ascendance and to restore the old order. Unlike
the uprooted migrants from the overcrowded and inhospitable
countryside, who filled the dark satanic mills and were whipped
into submission by poverty and destitution, the craftsmen had
a tradition of independence and respectable status to fall back on.
When their status came under attack and faced the risk of
being withdrawn altogether, the reaction was an outraged
sense of justice (compare Edmund Cahn's article 'Justice'
in the 'International Encyclopedia of Social Sciences', 1968 edn).
In Germany they saw themselves as, of right and heredity,
members of the 'Mittelstand', a notion in no way synonymous
with 'arbeitende Klasse'. In France, they insisted on being
'gens de métier', practitioners of mechanical arts, people of
crafts and commerce - remembering that, as the jurist Loyseau
put it once,[37]

> trades which are crafts and commerce (mestiers et marchan-
> dises) combined...are honorable and those who exercise
> them are not numbered among the vile persons....On the
> contrary there are trades which rest more in the effort of
> the body than in the traffic of commerce or in the subtlety
> of the mind, and those are the most vile.

Still in 1848, at a handicraftmen meeting in Berlin a journalist
who used the term 'proletariat' 'was shouted down and made to
retract the expression. Indeed, what these workers feared
most of all was that they might be forced down into the 'proletariat'.[38] In England, they[39]

> kept a powerful vision of the past when their well-being
> had been preserved by custom and by paternalist legisla-
> tion. The Act of 5 Elizabeth had a reality in the notion of
> what *ought* to be, and to it, artisans, journeymen and
> small masters alike appealed. The repeal of the apprentice-
> ship clauses of that statute in 1814 may be viewed as mark-
> ing an end to the final crisis of paternalist protection.

The craftsmen's case against capitalism was, therefore, not
the capitalist expropriation of surplus. If they demanded better
prices for their products, or better wages for labour performed
for the hiring or putting-out entrepreneur, they did it on the
understanding that a certain level of income and expenditure
is necessary to maintain the status they wished to preserve.

But also when expressed in economic terms, at issue was always
the question of self-control, traditionally guarded by corporative rules and customs, versus control by the employer. The
craftsmen resisted capitalism because capitalism was the form
the expropriation of control took.

The conflict came to the boiling point with the gradual collapse of the 'employer's household' as the place of life and work
of the craftsman. The traditional master could well be no less
demanding and severe in executing orders than the owner of
a capitalist factory. And yet the 'task-continuity' had a psychological impact of blurring the boundary between work as such
and the way of life, between work discipline and loyalty to
the customary pattern of right and decent life. Neither the time
of work, nor the place of work seemed to be separate from the
totality of life activities. All this changed inside the factory
walls with its scores of apprentices, none of whom could see
his fate, task, or skills continuous with these of his employer.
The time of labour and the time inside the factory were now set
clearly apart from the rest of the apprentice's life. It was 'taken
away' from him and 'appropriated' by his employer. It was now
openly and blatantly outside his control. Nothing in the
corporative tradition of craft had prepared the journeymen
and apprentices to accept this situation. They would not accept
such control without battle; and those who wanted or needed
to impose it had to deploy all the powers they could muster.

THE BID FOR TOTAL CONTROL

The problem which the owner of an early factory confronted
has been since theorised as the clash between monetary stimulus and an unresponsive, because non-acquisitive, pre-
industrial worker. This interpretation, canonised finally in
Max Weber's 'Protestant Ethic' and since then taken for granted,
had absorbed uncritically the entrepreneur's perspective; from
the vantage point of the profit-oriented project, it must have
seemed indeed bizarre that the worker was not in all cases
prepared to sell himself into total submission if the price was
right; that he remained indifferent to what the entrepreneur
himself would consider a truly attractive offer. Later theorists
explained the phenomenon which so baffled the early entrepreneur by the immaturity of the homo oeconomicus. Immaturity
manifested itself in the visible absence, among the workers,
of the inner urge to maximise gains, which was seen, by definition, as an indispensable trait of rational behaviour. Much like
contemporary observers, later theorists saw the problem as,
above all, one of education; more precisely, as one of instilling
new morality, the 'work ethic' understood mostly in market
terms, i.e. as the willingness to work in such a way as leads
to the highest possible effects, measured mostly by monetary
gains.

Two remarks are in order in this connection.

First, the 'work ethic' is itself a value-ridden term. Its common interpretation reduces the inner value of work to its market value. The way it operationalises the idea of dedication to work dissolves what Veblen described as 'workmanship' in the pursuit of profit. The identity of the two is theoretically assured by the auxiliary notion of 'performance principle', which allegedly guarantees (at least, ought to guarantee) a high degree of correspondence between 'good work' and 'good income'. The concept of 'work ethic', if judged by its theoretical expositions and empirical applications, is therefore a misnomer. What it denotes, in fact, is the version of homo oeconomicus reserved for the life-long hired labourers when looked at from the perspective of their employers.

Second, the true sequence of events seems to have been exactly the opposite of what the early entrepreneurs implied in their complaints against shiftless and laggard workers, and later economists and sociologists accepted as a tested record of history. It was the advent of the factory system which spelled the crisis of the relationship between the craftsman and his work which the 'work ethic' postulated. The moral campaign recorded as the battle for the work ethic, or the training in the performance principle, was in fact an attempt to resuscitate basically pre-industrial work attitudes in conditions which no longer made them meaningful. The moral crusade aimed at the re-creation inside the factory, under the owner's controlled discipline, of the commitment to task performance which came to the craftsman naturally when he himself was in control of his time and work rhythm. What gave the crusade its vigour was the state of things apparently endemic to the fledgling factory system - a state bewailed several decades later by John Stuart Mill:[40]

> We look in vain among the working classes in general for the just pride which will choose to give good work for good wages; for the most part, the sole endeavour is to receive as much and return as little in the shape of service as possible.

One can easily notice that what Mill castigated in the quoted sentence was a kind of behaviour otherwise described as a perfect manifestation of market rationality (greatest gain for least cost). Appeals to work ethic were, so to speak, attempts to stem the tide, to exempt the workers from the rule of market rationality, rather than, as common interpretations would like us to believe, efforts to train the crude, pre-industrial labour force in the art of life guided by commercial reason. Under the guise of work ethic a 'discipline ethic' was promoted; the willingness of workers to renounce behaviour based on the calculation of interest, on behalf of a behaviour dictated by the stipulations of external control over an essentially meaningless productive process.

As Claus Offe suggested, the performance principle, which
the campaign for a work ethic employed as its major argument,
could seem a plausible explanation of the productive relations
only within the context of a small craftsman workshop (i.e.
exactly the context which the developing capitalist industry
was set to destroy). Three aspects of this context were of
particular importance.[41] First, the direct exposure of every
complete productive cycle to the evaluating scrutiny of the
market. Products, not persons or their possessions, were compared and assessed; by derivation, only such aspects of the
producers' behaviour as were directly relevant to the creation
of product (i.e. the skilfulness of their performance) seemed
to have been allotted their monetary equivalent. Second, the
division of labour inside the workshop, which was ultimately
embodied in the finished and assessed product, was task-
continuous: all levels of the internal hierarchy of command
and subordination, from the apprentice through the journeyman
and up to the master himself, were engaged in an essentially
identical task, which required, in principle, skills of the same
type. The levels differed from each other only in respect of
the amount of skill each one had had time to absorb; and,
consequently, in the expected quality of performance. It was
assumed that the master knew and could do everything his
journeymen or apprentices did, only better. Attributes of all
levels of the hierarchy were, therefore, plotted on the same
scale, and the way in which they were compared and differen-
tially rewarded was, so to speak, determined by the very logic
of the productive task. Third, with the notoriously slow pace
of technological change, skills once acquired could last for a
life-time of work, and hence length of service (reflected in the
achieved level of workshop hierarchy), seemed a fair measure
of the relative quality of contribution to be rewarded. When
projected upon the differential distribution of status and
income, this correlation of skills with seniority made the inequality of status seem fair and natural.

None of these three aspects of workshop production had been
preserved in the factory. And yet the performance principle
was adopted by the factory ideology in spite of the fact that the
context which once rendered it credible was gone forever. It
was called upon to legitimise a hierarchy grounded not in varying quantities of task-continuous skills, but in discontinuity
and asymmetricality of domination and subjection.

Thus the problem which the early entrepreneurs faced was
not the stubbornly idle 'pre-industrial man', oblivious to the
call of economic reason; and the way out of the problem sought
by the early entrepreneur was not to instil pious dedication to
work into the hearts of people unused to a continuous effort.
The problem, rather, was the need to force people, used to
put meaning into their work through controlling it, to expend
their force and skill in the implementation of tasks which were

controlled by others and hence meaningless. And the way out
of the problem that the early entrepreneurs sought was a blind
drill aimed at habitualising the workers to unthinking obedience
while performing a task the sense of which escaped them, As
Werner Sombart commented, the new factory system needed part-
humans: soulless little wheels of a complex mechanism. The
battle was waged against the other, now useless 'human parts'
of the factory hands. Or, to put it in a different way, the cause
and the purpose of the battle was the bid of the early entrepreneurs for the total control over the bodies of their workers
and the elimination of their souls from the productive process.
Such a control was relatively easy to achieve if the prospective
objects were women and children of the poor; they had had no
opportunity to learn the wonders of independence, so they had
nothing to forget once inside the factory walls. The docility,
not merely the cheapness of this kind of labour, was mostly
responsible for making women and children the entrepreneur's
first choice. The real problem arose when skilled men, brought
up in a culture of artisanship, had to be forced into the rigid
frame of factory routine.

   The problem was put in a nutshell by the anonymous hosier
of 1806, quoted by Sidney Pollard in his excellent sketch of
early battles for factory discipline:[42]

> I found the utmost distaste on the part of the men, to any
> regular hours or regular habits....The men themselves
> were considerably dissatisfied, because they could not go
> in and out as they pleased, and have what holidays they
> pleased, and go on just as they had been used to do; and
> were subject, during after-hours, to the ill-natured obser-
> vations of other workmen, to such an extent as completely
> to disgust them with the whole system, and I was obliged
> to break it up.

This statement, though brief, is remarkable for its comprehensive overview of the complex relation, and a clear insight into
its inner springs. The year was 1806: the conflict had not
been yet 'economised', and hence the monetary parameters of
labour contract had not been yet read into workmen's disaffection and resistance. The anonymous hosier had no doubt that
the workers rebelled against the factory discipline, not against
the wages; and that they rebelled against it not because they
failed to learn the art of self-interested conduct, but because
the impersonal schedule of factory work went against the grain
of their habit of controlling their productive activities according to their own will. He was clear as to his task; he knew he
had to 'break up' old habits.

   Much has been written since of how the old habits had been
broken. Factory discipline was forced down the throats of
recalcitrant workers with the help of finicky and intrusive
rules which between them tended to regulate every moment of a

worker's factory time. The Hammonds collected a long list of
such rules, testifying to the sinister inventiveness of the
capitalist pioneers. At Tyldesley mill, for example, the door
was locked for the duration of the working day; a shilling fine
was inflicted on a spinner found dirty, or alternatively found
washing; heard whistling; found with the window open (in a
temperature of 84 degrees).[43] The most remarkable feature of
such rules was their evident irrelevance to the efficiency of
labour; often the rules were impossible to observe because of
their contradictoriness, and in many cases their negative
impact on productive labour could not escape the notice of
the shrewd industrialist. One cannot, therefore, refrain from
concluding that the true objective of the rules was not so much
the promotion of rational organisation of the productive process, as forcing the workers into total and unquestioned
submission. What the rules expressed was not the battle for
the work ethic, but for the full domination over workers' bodies
(with their souls, preferably, kept far away from the battlefield). The very irrationality of the rules, inexplicable from
the point of view of the first aim, was, on the contrary, the
very condition of their effectivity measured by the second,
the true, objective.
   The battle for total control should not be interpreted as
arising from the sheer greed of power. Total domination was
not just an ambitious, arrogant dream of a new class; it was,
so to speak, a functional prerequisite of the new system of
production which this class represented – a system in which
not just the distribution of surplus, but the production of
surplus as well was subjected to the exercise of power and
could not be accomplished without it. One of the unavoidable
effects of the new system was that the workers cast in the
position of objects, not the subjects, of power, had to be
nevertheless entrusted for the duration of their working time
with precious machinery they had no obvious interest in preserving or keeping in good repair. Another equally unavoidable outcome was that the same workers had to be induced to
expend their energy in activities which bore no obvious connection to their own welfare and were exempt from the com-
munally regulated way of life. Both outcomes had the same
effect: the activities of the workers could not be left any more
to their own inner logic. They had to be regulated by external
agents, and subject to a routine deliberately designed in such
a way as to stifle and annihilate the 'natural' rhythm of the
producers' life, at least for the duration of the working day.
Following workers' own habits was foul, indecent, or immoral
not because it offended high ethical standards of the employers;
not even because it threatened the level of anticipated profits.
It was condemned simply as an expression of workers' autonomy.
It would be, one can guess, similarly condemned and persecuted
in whatever behaviour this autonomy might have been manifested.

The battle for total control was waged on two fronts. The first was a most meticulous and pernickety regulation of the workers' conduct in the work-place, often represented as the struggle for control over labour time. The second was a much broader moral crusade, purported to deploy a variety of social powers – the church, the school, the family – in the promotion of obedience to whatever order might be imposed for the working behaviour of the producers.

In his classic study of the elevation of time to the status of a foremost value in the capitalist moral code,[44] E.P. Thompson documented the struggle for the ownership of time spent by the workers in their bosses' employment. Buying a certain amount of time meant in the last account acquiring the right to full control over everything the persons, whose time had been bought, did; this was now the employer's time, and anything the workers did of their own will was tantamount to theft. As in all cases of property, what mattered was not so much the specific form in which the time sold/bought was used, but whose design and will determined this use. Thus in the end the question was of the extent to which the employer may and can control the conduct of the bodies of his employees.

This was, at least in part, a new situation, which arose with the advent of the factory. It is true that long before the factory farm labourers without land worked long hours, often longer than the proverbially endless workday in an early mill. It is also true that while so working they did not, on the whole, do jobs of their own choice. Still, as Thompson comments,

> there are obvious difficulties in the nature of the occupation. Ploughing is not an all-the-year-round task. Hours and tasks must fluctuate with the weather. The horses (if not the men) must be rested. There is the difficulty of supervision.

On top of the 'natural' limits arising from the type of work done in the field, a further tightening of the screw was difficult, even if desired, as long as agricultural employment was relatively abundant – a 'farm-servant could assert his annual right to move on if he disliked his employment'. Both limits were removed when the labourers had been transported from the farmland to the factories. The rhythm of factory work is largely insensitive to the capriciousness of nature. More importantly, the conditions under which the first factories were installed left the labourers little choice but to submit to the employer's will without murmur:

> Enclosure and the growing labour surplus at the end of the eighteenth century tightened the screw for those who were in regular employment; they were faced with the alternatives of partial employment and the poor law, or submission to a more exacting labour discipline.

The formidable task of total control which confronted the
early capitalists - the task they knew they had to perform
without help of the natural cycle, re-forged through centuries
of toil into a deeply internalised cultural rhythm - determined
the perspective in which they regarded their workers and
their behaviour. Any departure from the rules set for their
conduct - and, in particular, anything they did not do on the
behest of their employer or the supervisors he hired, was
seen as a manifestation of idleness, insolence, debauchery and
condemnable extravagance. What was previously accepted as
the normal rhythm of labour and life was now seen as ridden
with irregularity. It is not immediately clear, unless one takes
the employers' point of view uncritically, that the habits dubbed
'irregular', because operated by the producers themselves,
were necessarily less economically viable or, indeed, in the
long run efficient, than the meticulously defined routine with
which the employers strove to replace them. What made the
routine superior to old habits was not so much its debatable
economic effects, but its role in the entrenchment of employers'
domination over their labour force. The routine was, first and
foremost, an exercise in 'taming the savage'. After all, this is
exactly what the parishes, while transferring their measure
of 'dangerous classes' in to the care of the employer, expected
him to do. The factory, like the poor-house, was, before
anything else, an institution of public order and morality.

This continuity between poor-houses and factories explains
why the early entrepreneurs found it particularly easy to apply
their all-pervasive surveillance to those already drilled by the
extant poor laws: mostly women and children, but invariably
people with little or no skills, called merely to exert their
physical power and attention to keep machines going. In the
words of a French social historian, Michell Perrot, the typically
industrial 'system of micropowers' was not, in France, installed
'at a stroke. This type of surveillance and hierarchy was
developed first in the mechanised sectors occupied by mainly
female and child labour, that is by those already accustomed
to obey.'[45] This was true also of other countries industrialising
at the end of the eighteenth and the beginning of the nineteenth century - true certainly of Britain (in America, at a
later time, illiteracy and bafflement of recent immigrants played
a role similar to the trained docility of French and English
women and children of the poor).

The task was not that easy in the case of the male, adult,
skilled workers. However impoverished, theirs was poverty of
a different kind, not yet reforged into resigned dependency
of the good will of the rich and the powerful. Here the employers
had to do the job of drilling from scratch. They had no previous achievement to build upon. On the contrary, their efforts
to extend the patterns developed in their treatment of helpless
females and children were most likely to be seriously weakened
in their effects by the still fresh tradition of independence and

self-management which for the craftsmen of yesterday was,
if not reality, then a vivid memory.

One way in which the skilled workers could confound employers' intentions was simply to refuse the bondage of factory
employment. Unlike the retainers of parish charity, they could
not be forced into factories against their will. That this way
was indeed used, shows, for example, in John Fielden's testimony:[46]

> The hand-loom weavers are a very large body in Lancashire,
> extremely poor, very laborious, and the makers of some of
> the most beautiful of our manufactures; but their dislike of
> the factories is such, that, if they could obtain work in
> them and get better wages, they (except a very few com-
> paratively) will neither go into them, nor suffer their
> children to go.

Another way was, once in a factory employment, to stick stubbornly to, however meagre, symbolic areas of independence
against the employer's wrath and threats of penalty. The institution of *Saint-Lundi* or Holy Monday, raised to a symbolic significance by exasperated seekers of control over the labour force,
and commented upon over and over again by every social historian of industrialisation, was just one of the dramatic expres-
sions of this tendency: to retain some, however irrelevant,
field of discretion exempt from the employer's power. Craftsmen's liberties made the employers furious, and became an
object of a most vitriolic moral condemnation. But there was
relatively little the employers could do to chain their skilled
workers to the benches in the same way they did with their
female and under-age employees. This was the case for two
reasons. First, however large the surplus of labour force was,
skilled workers were always in a relatively short supply (partly
because of phenomena noted by John Fielden), and to lose their
services could be costly. Second, skilled workers occupied
strategic positions in the totality of the factory production;
hence their refusal to work, or just ill-will expressed in non-
co-operative attitudes, could effectively prevent the employer
from gathering the fruits of the docility of unskilled labour. As
Adam Smith had already noted,[47]

> half a dozen wool combers, perhaps are necessary to keep
> a thousand spinners and weavers at work. By combining
> not to take apprentices they can not only empress the
> employment, but reduce the whole manufacture into a sort
> of slavery to themselves, and raise the price of their labour
> much above what is due to the nature of their work.

At the early stage of industrialisation, the entrepreneurs
made in consequence little progress towards total control over
skilled labour. They were only too painfully aware that their

hands were too short for the task. Hence the practices of by-passing the problem with the eye on reaching the solution through a longer, but surer way.

A most prominent expedient was to leave the supervision to workers themselves; hiring an elderly, experienced skilled craftsman for a job to be performed under his surveillance by hands he would hire himself. This practice remained widespread both in France and in Britain for a better part of the nineteenth century; it meant an armistice in the war for control which was to last as long as it took the employers to accumulate the assets likely to change the balance decisively in their favour.

The armistice did not mean, however, that war activities stopped. The employers were busy in stocking arms and adding to the arsenal of weapons later to be used in the final confrontation.

One such weapon was the ongoing process of 'economisation' of the problem of control - something which will be analysed in more detail in the next chapter. Another was the keen development of technology able to 'de-skill' the skilled occupation, and thereby to make the process less dependent on craftsmen's discretion and thus to undermine the craftsmen's bargaining power. Thirdly, there was the moral crusade, waged simultaneously on many fronts, and aimed at deploying additional powers able to accomplish jointly what the factory-confined measures could not attain.

The moral crusade launched by the political and cultural powers of late eighteenth century society has been normally represented as an addendum to industrial training; as, in the last instance, a logical extension of the capitalist bid for greater productivity. This interpretation presents a number of notorious difficulties. First, it suggests a highly developed 'behavioural science' type of knowledge among at least the people directly engaged in profit-making activities, and a clear vision of the connection between productivity and health and life satisfaction. None of these is immediately evident in the argument sponsoring the case of moral crusade. Second, the interpretation implies that the measures to re-shape the 'total personality' of the workers came in the wake of the unsuccessful attempts to remould their work attitudes by inner-factory measures alone; again, there is ample evidence that even if the sequence were not exactly reversed, the two lines of action ran parallel, none enjoying a clear causal and logical precedence. Third, the interpretation has all the bearing of an ex-post-facto rationale when stretched to embrace elements of moral crusade aimed at the aspects of life far removed from the problems which the employer encountered in his factory practices. It runs counter to the contemporary evidence of the employers' insistence on the strict separation of their contractual duties towards hired labourers from any social obligation extending beyond the factory time, and their stout refusal to accept responsibility for non-factory aspects of a worker's life.

The employers, allegedly more than anybody else interested in enhancing the effectivity of labour they hired, had to be whipped into the ranks of the crusaders by the concentrated effort of the state and the forces of 'enlightened opinion'. Fourth, the interpretation fails to explain the composition of the crusaders' army. There was little correlation between the preoccupation with industrial profits and the intensity with which the moral improvement was preached. Unless a priori assumed, the motive of industrial efficiency is hard to be found in the actions of the principal actors of the moral crusade.

We have to repeat, therefore, that in all probability the relation between the growth of capitalist industry and the all-out offensive against moral turpitude of the 'lower classes' was, if anything, reverse to the one suggested by the popular interpretation. I have mentioned already that industrial employment was seen as just one convenient way of dealing with a much wider problem of taming the 'dangerous classes'. Moral crusade both preceded and followed the shuttling of the homeless and the indigent from poor-houses to the mills. If it made, in the long run, the employers' job easier, it was certainly not its primary objective. More important things were at stake than just the profits of industrialists. What gave the moral crusade its momentum was first and foremost the preoccupation with rebuilding social order under conditions where old powers and traditional instruments of social control increasingly demonstrated their inadequacy.

New problems are normally responded to with a call to restore old institutions; the very fact that the problems were absent, or unseen, when the old institutions were in command, is naturally taken as a proof of the causal connection between the appearance of the first and the demise of the latter. The moral crusade of the early nineteenth century reached unhesitatingly for the still fresh memories of patronage and paternalism, which, in the recent David Roberts' characterisation, 'emphasised those mutual bonds and differential patterns that defined England's organic and hierarchical society' and the 'duties of property and the role of the church'.[48] This time paternalism appeared as ideology rather than reality. The practical retreat of aristocracy and landowners in general, as well as the new rich, from the principle that 'property has its duties as well as its rights',[49] was widely bewailed and blamed for the growing restiveness of the poor. The preaching of the paternalistic approach to the poor gained in force considerably after the violent economic, political and social crisis which followed the Napoleonic wars. Frustrated expectations, depressed production and expensive food, lack of employment for propertyless labour and lack of markets for crafts and traditional trades, set English society, still off the routine course in the wake of a lengthy war, into turmoil. The last five years of the second decade of the century were the most violent in remembered history. Spa Fields meetings, the Blanketeers'

march, the Peterloo episode, the much inflated Cato Street
conspiracy, boded the awakening of new dark forces, which
the established elite, looking apprehensively to the other shore
of the Channel, did not feel confident to contain and domesticate. To the visible symptoms of popular unrest, the established
elite responded with panic. There was ample evidence of terror
and hysteria in the alarmist prophecies of the imminent Armaged-
don; the established classes lived and acted in the anticipation
of a popular revolution bound to erupt any day. The dominant
opinion perhaps grossly exaggerated the proximity of revolutionary outburst. Real or not, the fears spurred the frantic
search of remedy.

To the dominant classes, haunted by the ghost of Robespierre,
the deferential society with the poor safely locked in parish
workhouses and the few recalcitrant vagabonds in prisons,
looked like a haven of peace and order. It was this perspective
that made the case for paternalism convincing. Its advocates,
as it were, only rarely invoked now the ancient bonds and
eternal attachments as the source of perpetual duty of the
wealthy and the powerful. Paternalism was to be revived not as
an intrinsically superior and morally commendable form of life,
but because it could thwart the rebellion of the poor through
winning back their consent and deference. The preachers of
paternalistic relations on the land hoped, with Sir Henry
Banbury, that if land and cottages were leased to the labourers
at reasonable rates, if the wages were fair, and if – above all
– the employers talked to their labourers, talked with them,
came to know them, advised them, encouraged them – labourers
would not raise their arms against the landlords, and moreover
would accept the right of the latter to rule. Preachers of
paternalistic relations in industry, like Helps, had much the
same advice to offer: do not reduce your intercourse with
factory hands to mere cash payments, have a keen interest
in their plight, show it, try to influence their thought – and
they will respect you and obey. Setting the mighty patrons of
the past as an example to the up-and-coming rulers of the new
society, the Rev. Richard Parkinson complained in 1841 that

> there is far less *personal* communication between the master
> cotton-spinner and his workmen, between the calico-printer
> and his blue-handed boys, between the master tailor and
> his apprentices, than there is between the Duke of Wellington
> and the humblest labourer on his estate, or than there *was*
> between the old George the Third and the meanest errand-
> boy about his palace.

Given this ideal pattern, Parkinson had the following advice to
offer: treat a man like a friend, and you soon make him one;
'In no way are men so easily led – often, it is true, so blindly
led – as through the affection.[150]

It cannot be doubted that if master and man were in the habit of communicating more freely with each other, we should cease to hear so frequently as we do of those horrible outbursts of personal violence and outrage, with trade unions, and other combinations, are now enabled to nurse to maturity in fatal secrecy and silence.

As Gaskell's Carson explained on the pages of 'Mary Barton', workers should be 'bound to their employers by their ties of respect and affection, not by mere money'.

The number of industrialists who tried to achieve just this purpose was by no means negligible. People like Ashton, Greg, Ashworth, Whitehead 'were proud of their two-storey stone houses and their good wages' as much as of their 'schools, churches, chapels, libraries, playgrounds, reading rooms, news rooms, lecture halls, and baths and washhouses'.[51] According to Sidney Pollard, such comprehensive efforts to 'reform the whole man' were 'particularly marked in factory towns and villages in which the total environment was under the control of a single employer'. No wonder, since in such places the employer could not count on the assistance of public agencies; any slackening of social order in the town was bound to reflect directly on the inner-factory relations. Vice versa, factory hierarchy obtruded from the rest of local authorities as the contour of social order in general. The link was, therefore, direct and obvious; between economic, political and moral power there was no room for division of labour. Hence,[52]

factory villages like New Lanark, Deanston, Busby, Ballindaloch, New Kilpatrick, Blantyre, and Joseph Stephenson's at Antrim, had special provisions, and in some cases full-time staff, to check the morals of their workers. Contemporaries tended to praise these actions most highly.... Almost everywhere, churches, chapels and Sunday schools were supported by employers, both to encourage moral education in its more usual sense, and to inculcate obedience.

In the enlightened opinion of the era, a wider issue of moral standards in general and the particular concern with the obedience of the poor to the rule of their betters were hardly distinguishable. In fact, arguments in both directions were equally frequent and interchangeable. 'Blackwood's Magazine' wrote that 'the influence by the master over the man, is of itself a point gained in the direction of moral improvement'; on the other hand, it blamed moral depravity as one of main causes of insubordination. Rebellion was ascribed to the distress which is an attribute of life of the poor, which was in its turn explained by 'moral and religious destitution and ignorance' among other factors.[53] 'Edinburgh Review' (which represented an alternative conception of the solution to the present troubles) somewhat

caustically described the fervour with which some industrialists,
and members of the discussing public in particular, joined the
moral crusade:[54]

> It is not in (the charity) spirit that the new schemes of
> benevolence are conceived. They are propounded as instal-
> ments of a great social reform. They are celebrated as the
> beginning of a new moral order, or an old order revived,
> in which the possessors of property are to resume their
> place as the paternal guardians of those less fortunate;
> and which, when established, is to cause peace and union
> throughout society, and to extinguish, not indeed poverty
> – that hardly seems to be thought desirable – but the more
> abject forms of vice, destitution, and physical wretched-
> ness.

Rebelliousness was vice, insubordination was the sign of
idleness, foul language and refusal to obey the deadly factory
routine were equally important symptoms of immorality.
Obversely, the struggle for factory discipline was part and
parcel of the war against folkways now branded as moral
depravity. Shouting, whistling, loud talk, long sleep on
Sunday, sexual promiscuity, drinking and tenuousness of
family bonds all belonged, with insolence and disobedience
towards the masters, to one immoral syndrome which the joint
forces of the orderly society had to destroy and eradicate.
Whatever amounted to a separate way of life of the working
poor, whatever derived from their own inclinations supported
by tradition and communal influence over which the dominant
classes of society had no control – was seen not as a different,
but as an inferior culture; an evidence of immaturity, retardation, failure or inability to develop true human nature. The
working poor remained in the same relation to their betters
as the savage tribes were in relation to the 'civilised nations',
or children in relation to responsible adults. This perspective
put on the shoulders of the rich and powerful a duty similar
to this of the 'white man's burden': it called simultaneously for
the attitude of a stern and exacting master and a teacher carrying the torch of superior moral wisdom. It absolved the masters/
teachers from all scruples in their determined fight against
indigenous culture, perceived as the product of ignorance and
moral decrepitude. This perspective was shared by all shades
of political opinion; by the advocates of coercion and the
preachers of education, by the high-handed and the high-
minded, by those eager to condemn and inclined to despise and
those guided above all by pity and compassion. No one questioned the master/teacher role; their disagreements were concerned merely with the effectiveness of the birch and the
relative virtues of flogging against kindness and persuasion.
P. Gaskell, this kind-hearted, compassionate friend of the working poor, had no doubts about the nature of the problem:[55]

Judging them by the same rules which have been applied to
mark the advancement of man from a savage state, they
have made but a few steps forward; and though their primitive nature is disguised and modified by the force of external circumstances, they differ but little in inherent qualities
from the uncultivated child of nature, and show their distinction rather in the mode than the reality of their debased
condition.

In tune with the tendency to the 'moralisation' of social problems, Gaskell demanded that the manufacturers should have
separated the sexes in their factories, do their best to sup-
press displays of 'grossness and immorality', and ask for
testimonies of sobriety and morality before hiring their craftsmen; at the same time he wished to cast the employers in the
role of the teachers - he put among their main duties the task
to instruct their men that their own welfare is 'intimately
connected with the suppression and concealment of their separate desires and capabilities'.[56] He praised the growing ranks of
manufacturers who had already joined the moral crusade. He
blamed the reluctance of others to do likewise on the low origin
of most pioneers of industry, who had no time to efface the
blemish of low morality from which they arose:[57]

Master manufacturers...at the commencement of this
important epoch, were in many instances men sprung from
the ranks of the labourers, or from a grade just removed
above these - uneducated, of coarse habits, sensual in their
enjoyments, partaking of the rude revelry of their dependants....Destitute of every thing intellectual, and condemn-
ing every thing savouring of refinement, whether in manner
or thought, they were in some measure driven to the indulgence of their animal sensations.

It was in the struggle for the suppression of the 'animal' like
sensual sensations, these 'separate desires' which entailed a
constant threat to the social order, that it was proposed that
the new powers of the family be deployed. Family was the best-
known and most influential of Gaskell's recipies. His argument
tied together political concerns and moral tasks. It was dis-
armingly straightforward in presenting the family as the locus
of power which could be instrumental in supporting political
order by becoming effective as a moralising force:[58]

Let the mill artisans be assisted to shake off habits which
destroy them physically and morally; let them cultivate
home; let them become good husbands and good wives; and
they will, in a single generation, produce offspring who
will, in their turn, inherit their good qualities. Let them
discountenance agitation, combination, and political quacks.
Let them become a sober and orderly race.

Gaskell's contemporaries discovered 'sincere and pure'
'natural affections' among 'uneducated classes'. The Carlisle
and Sadler Committee wrote in its report of the 'instinctive
feeling and natural affection cherished among uneducated
children and parents'.[59] These 'natural proclivities' were thought
to have been stifled or fettered by the disruption which the
massive migration and conditions of employment brought to the
once warm and idyllic family life of the 'toiling classes'. The
selfsame 'natural proclivities' were now proposed to be restored
to their full potential which - so it was hoped - would be
employed in the service of public order. For this purpose,
however, the restoration of family life was deemed necessary.
Let the parents take responsibility for the children whom their
factory masters failed to advance on the road to moral and
orderly behaviour. Let women spend at least part of their
waking life at home, serving their husbands and tending their
offspring. Let each artisan have his home and his family, in
order that this home and this family could become a chapel and
a police station in the service of public order.

The overall strategy in the struggle to tame and domesticate
the 'dangerous classes', which finally took shape during the
first half of the nineteenth century, was perhaps most cogently
expressed in the words of R.W. Pilkington:[60]

No permanent and real improvement, I feel confident, can
be expected in the condition of the poor, but through the
improvement of their moral character; their increased comforts must spring from themselves, not from enactments to
supply their wants. Instruction may be given, but it is not
in schools alone that the great moral battle must be fought;
good instruction must be afforded, but *bad* instruction,
practically administered, through their interests and their
passions, must also above all things be withdrawn.

The family was to become one of the principal sources of good
instruction and one of the front units in the war against bad
influences. But it could not be trusted to accomplish the task
on its own, particularly in its current wretched condition. It
has to be assisted; and in a society inflamed with the holy
spirit of moral crusade, a society bent on eradication of savagery, villainy and crude manners, schooling was the obvious
choice.

Like hospitals, prisons, and poor-houses, schools were first
and foremost instruments of confinement. They kept the children of the poor off the streets and away from mischief. They
extended surveillance of their conduct over days and hours
when the factory foremen rested. Their contribution to public
order was therefore immediate and obvious. A somewhat less
obvious, but far more substantial, contribution consisted in the
long-term training of the young in the habits of obedience and
respect for the rules set by their superiors. As the Assistant

Royal Commissioner J.W. Cowell argued in 1834, 'who were the *best educated*, were likewise the *most orderly*'.[61]

> The promoters of the schools most often sought support on this ground that they were a form of social insurance. This was the easiest and the cheapest way to civilize the poor, to make them less dangerous to society, to render them more useful workers and, incidentally, to save their souls

A.P. Wadsworth summed up this second function of the schools in his splendid study of Robert Raikes's campaign for Sunday schools.[62] Some advocates of schooling for the poor presented the dissemination of useful knowledge as a rational substitute for inefficient and, indeed, harmful private or public charity which in the end panders to the base instincts and innate idleness of the inferior classes. H. Brougham was a most prominent representative of this train of thought:[63]

> The same money which is now not uselessly, but perniciously bestowed, might, by a little care...be made the means of at once educating all the children in the worst district of London, and of planting there the light of science among the most useful and industrious class of the country'.

There is already in Brougham's tract a note which was later to become foremost in the minds of the educators, though rarely, if ever, explicitly articulated. This was the idea of educational achievement as an antidote to class or communal loyalty. Whoever tasted the sweet fruit of knowledge, would remain preoccupied with personal improvement and the social rewards such an improvement might offer. He would have no time for communal interests and struggles. Schools shifted the loci of authority and wisdom from the community of fate to the authors of books and the teachers, their interpreters. They thereby made the member of the community into an individual. They directed the attention of so-produced individuals towards the ways and means of personal enlightenment, and re-articulated communal problems as the many tasks of individual enhancement. This latent function of the schooling for the poor was recently explored by Piven and Cloward, who suggest that:[64]

> literacy training is also necessarily training in ideological individualism. Preliterate peoples distill their shared experience into wisdom through a process of communication within the group; there is no other way to "know". But literacy implies that the individual is the sole agent of learning, via the printed word....The belief that the source of wisdom is external to the community, and the belief that the individual is the agent responsible for acquiring this wisdom, may thus tend - no matter what the content of literate wisdom - to

encourage a search for solutions to problems by individual self-improvement through the deferential process called education, rather than through collective struggle.

Of all powers deployed in the moral crusade aimed at the taming of the 'dangerous classes', schools for the poor seem to represent most fully the two aspects of the overall strategy; to use the terminology of prison discourse as an analogy, the schools promise to perform simultaneously the reforming and the retributive function. In the short run, they were expected to police a vital and most volatile and explosive part of the poor population. In the long run, they were hoped to divert the poor from subversive ways by directing their minds to the task of individual improvement; by, in other words, inducing them to play the game for the sake of its prizes.

The latter task seems to provide the substance of the process which will be analysed in the next chapter: the 'economisation' of the social conflict. We will try to show the role this process played in the formation of the working class and the form this class, in its maturity, assumed.

3 The self-assembly of class

What has been later collected under the generic name of 'the working class' was towards the end of the eighteenth century and long into the nineteenth a motley collection of working or unemployed people, destitute, poor, or not-so-poor, dependent on charity or their own masters, with numerous, unconnected traditions, tied to localities or trades, each keen to preserve, or kept perforce in, its own boundaries. There was little to unite them, plenty to divide. Each group was affected by the advancing industrial age in a different way. Some hardly noticed a change in the bleak life of stultifying drudgery. Some felt their world suddenly falling into pieces and the few secure orientation points around which their life cycle evolved disappearing. Some experienced an uncomfortable and frightening tightening of their weekly budget and growing difficulty in keeping up to the standards they considered to be normal. Some found their material standards improving thanks to the increased demand for their skills or products.

And yet a century or so later the existence of a working class has become one of those axioms of common sense which serve as a framework within which the experience of the world is organised and perceived, and for this reason cannot be challenged by this experience. On the level of interpretation and evaluation, the views differ as to the importance and social role ascribed to the class of workers. But as far as the prevalence of unifying, common attributes over local and occupational differences is concerned (which justifies the view of the working population as a class), there is a broad consensus stretching from the Registrar General through politicians and social scientists to the popular folklore. The materiality of class unity is further demonstrated by the presence of political parties claiming to represent the interests of the working class as a whole, as well as of tight or loose federations of trade corporations, claiming the same. The frame precepts of common sense together with the practices of the said organisations pre-form and process the flow of information about reality, thereby supplying continuous reinforcement of the dominant view and the reassuring proofs of its accuracy.

The task of this chapter is to explore how this fateful change came about.

The task is not new. It has been in the past and is still continually undertaken anew by historians and sociologists alike, anxious to discover in the events of past centuries the key to

the decoding of present reality. In practice, though, the handling of the task often defies the original intellectual stimulus. It
is exceedingly difficult to forget later experience while explor-
ing the world of the past. Historians and sociologists enter
this world with the queries born of the world in which they
live. Since we are trained to see social reality as historically
evolving, and the past as an earlier stage of growth of the
present, we tend to assume a 'developmental link' between the
past and the reality as we currently interpret it. Viewing the
past as a seed, or an embryo, or a chrysalis of the present
'mature' social organism seems to be as naturally and non-
controversially legitimate as perceiving a child as an adult in-
the-process-of-becoming. Accordingly, treating the exploration
of the past as the search for the pristine, inchoate, embryonic,
etc., forms of what we consider as fully developed (even if
still evolving) phenomena of the present, seems as natural as
organising our curiosity and our knowledge of child psychology as one of the adult 'coming of age'. For the research into
the origins of class this general tendency of cognition has
this consequence, that we are inclined to assign importance to
past events depending on the relative significance which has
been allocated to them at some later stages by the then authority
structures. Hence we can barely help but consider the currently known forms of class reality as the attributes of the
true, fully-fledged, mature, or at least relatively nearer
maturity, class formation, and to view phenomena of the past
as so many steps leading towards such attributes. This tendency
has been sanctioned as a methodological principle by Marx in
his frequently quoted, but rarely questioned, adage of the
'anatomy of man as the key to the anatomy of the ape'.
    Ontological determinism is the crudest manifestation of this
principle. This is an outcome of the projection of the logic of
our retrospective interests upon historical reality. Ontological
determinism assumes in effect that the later, 'mature' forms
had been, in one sense or another, contained in the earlier
stages, much as the body of a mature butterfly is concealed
inside the case of a chrysalis. This form of determinism prompts
the researcher to seek the 'objective necessities' truly responsible for the emergence of the phenomenon in question, and to
allocate to the motives, or objectives or indeed the actions of
the human actors of the process a merely epiphenomenal significance. Such necessities are most often found (or located) in
theoretical models, preferably detached from specific times
and places and contacting with historical events only through
examples and illustration.
    Understandably, ontological determinism in both its cruder
and more sophisticated forms is not seen as a serious proposition in the best of historical research. One of its latest
editions has been branded by E.P. Thompson as 'instant history', which prompts historians to dismiss the very idea of
historical determinism out of hand, rather than to explore its

possible cognitive potential. Thompson's earlier magnum opus,
'The Making of the English Working Class', was explicitly and
intentionally a manifesto against ontological determinism.
Emphatically, Thompson rejected the idea of class as a structure, or a category, promising instead to treat it as a historical phenomenon 'which in fact happens (and can be shown to
have happened)'. And yet, with ontological determinism dis-
credited, the impact of the re-projection of later wisdom on
the interpretation of the past is by no means dead. To forget
'how it all ended' would take an almost superhuman effort, and
the rejection of determinism in principle is exceedingly difficult
to be applied in practice. One could call this other, inadvertent,
against-the-will form of determinism 'hermeneutical', in that it
manifests itself above all in the tendency to take the researcher's
conceptual grid for the meanings and the perceptions of the
actors themselves. From Schleiermacher on, such an imputation
of meaning has been repeatedly legitimised in hermeneutical
theory. Though the presence of the interpreter's conceptual
grid in the interpretation cannot be avoided completely (without it no understanding is conceivable), its exact role is open
to argument and can be, with some effort, controlled. This
presence can, with a little inattention, lead to an outright confusion between the observer's and the author's perceptions -
a fault of which some recent writers accuse Thompson himself.
According to R.S. Neale, for example, Thompson 'seems to
claim to know these historical actors better than they knew
themselves and to do so with the aid of an *a priori* analytical
framework',[1] Francis Hearn suggests that the political meaning
of the communal consensus retained by English workers in the
nineteenth century was read into it by Thompson rather than
found there.[2] Whatever the justification of such criticisms aimed
at the foremost representative of 'determinism-free' historiography, there seems to be little question that the proclivity
to read the meaning into the actor's behaviour, rather than
from it, is widespread and unlikely to vanish soon. But the
role of the conceptual grid of the interpreter, indispensable
as it is, can be still redirected where Schleiermacher wished
to orient it in the first place. Through putting the conduct of
the actor in its contemporary context (which, in retrospect,
can be and is bound to be extended beyond the limits of the
historical actor's awareness), the interpreter can postulate
the 'true historical meaning' of action, which could, and perhaps must have, eluded the actors themselves. The vocabulary
the actors used to articulate their motives and to account for
their act must be in such interpretations distinguished from
the vocabulary only the interpreter can use to verbalise his
model of contextual totality which grounds the 'historical
meaning' of explored actions. The two languages must be, however, kept apart and clearly distinct throughout the research
and the presentation of its findings. The trouble starts when the
two are confused.

Thus, if the question of the 'meaning of the actors' sets, in principle, a limited task which with due care and enough time can be completed to a lasting satisfaction of students of history (barring the unlikely discovery of new documents which cast doubt on the totality of previously held beliefs), the issue of 'historical meaning' of events, their springs and the options they opened, is bound to be returned to repeatedly. It will be explored again and again with the widening or shifting of vistas which the changing historical experience inevitably brings forth. The conceptual grid forged in the smithy of this experience would lay bare ever new 'contextual totalities', forcing the communication between the present and its past into new discursive frameworks. The forms in which yesterday's present understood its past become for today's present an alien text itself to be interpreted in order to be understood. The new interpretation will prove its usefulness if it better serves the new conditions of understanding; though its usefulness is unlikely to outlive the conditions which determined it.

THE POWER-ASSISTED UNIFICATION

It should have become clear by now that one of the main contentions of this study is that the emergence of the new, all-penetrating, 'disciplining' power was a major factor in the forging together of otherwise heterogeneous categories of pre-modern population; eventually, it came to be instrumental (directly, or via the responses it evoked) in the process of class formation.

To a rather unspecified mass of the poor, the oppressed, the outraged, at which his 'Political Register' was aimed, Cobbett appealed in 1816 to respond with 'the correct idea of your own worth in your minds' to names by which they were banded together by the political language of the times: 'the Populace, the Rabble, the Mob, the Swinish Multitude'. These and similar terms of abuse, connoting a mixture of fear and contempt, expressed the tendency of the ruling opinion to telescope the variety of destitution and disaffection into a single problem of public disorder and disorderly classes. More sophisticated branches of the opinion sought terms able to entail diagnostic descriptions together with pragmatic prescriptions. Hence the numerous variations on the 'uncivilised condition' and 'ignorance' themes, which shared the advantage of connoting simultaneously the inferiority of their referents and the superior knowledge and ability of those who referenced them in such a way. In other words, such terms thematised the relation between the two sides as one between objects and subjects of action, or between the active and the passive roles in politics.

This more benign and condescending variant of the superiority theme was, several decades later, subjected to ridicule by John Stuart Mill:[3]

The lot of the poor, in all things which affect them collectively, should be regulated *for* them, not *by* them....It is
the duty of the higher classes to think for them, and to
take responsibility of their lot....[in order that] they may
resign themselves...to a trustful *insouciance,* and repose
under the shadow of their protectors....The rich should
be *in loco parentis* to the poor, guiding and restraining
them like children.

What united the crude and the sophisticated versions was, of
course, the theme of superiority and, ultimately, of power. In
both versions the structure of authority had been assumed
rightful, and defended. This structure of authority was precisely the factor blending 'the other side', the object of power
exercise, into a compound of 'lower classes'.

Power was not, of course, a new phenomenon which made
its appearance only in the dramatic era under consideration.
What was perhaps new was the objective of power, which determined its new 'unifying' or 'blending' effects. Power in a pre-
modern society was, if anything, discriminating and individual-
ising - towards categories if not always persons. It understood
liberty as a specific privilege or a concrete exemption from a
given rule. It discriminated between rights and duties of persons and collectivities, and related these rights and duties
selectively to other persons and collectivities. As I suggested
before, this, as well as other features of the 'old-style' power
can be accounted for by reference to its limited objectives;
after all, its only indispensable integrative function was to
design and to safeguard the channels through which the surplus product was pumped and siphoned off. The one thing it
had to accomplish was to determine the position of each person
or category alongside the channel and the share of the floating
surplus to which they were entitled. This kind of power was
not fit to generate a 'mass'. As Guy Fourquin summarised his
perceptive study of pre-modern social conflicts,[4]

It is because we do not discern any 'social dissolution', even
at the end of the Middle Ages, that we have largely avoided
using the term *mass.*...The day of the masses will come only
with the destruction of the societies of order. Before then,
the masses did not really exist, for individuals still had
well-defined stations and had not yet been 'equalised' by
a destitution more moral than material.

The 'social dissolution' to which Fourquin refers came later,
in the wake of the population explosion exacerbated by the
changing structure of agriculture and land utilisation. The
maintenance of order had become a much more complex task;
and so had the kind of power needed for the task. In the network of social rights and duties woven of the threads of
personalised patronage and loyalty, there were not enough

meshes to accommodate the now superfluous people. Hence the
'mass', 'the mob', 'the crowd', 'the rabble' - all these collective
notions trying to capture the new and terrifying phenomenon of
the undefined, indiscriminate, uniform-through-lack-of-attri-
butes. Hence also the urgent need of a new type of power,
able to reach the parts the old power could not reach and had
no need of reaching; a power capable of regulating not merely
the circulation of goods, but the daily actions of people; to
administer not just the products, but their producers and consumers. An omnipresent and all-penetrating power, which did
not discriminate between persons as loci of unique combinations
of rights and duties. Such a power had to unite the disjointed
and to homogenise the heterogeneous. This power provided the
first vantage point from which the motley collection of widely
distinct forms of destitution was seen as a uniform threat to
social order.

It is arguable to what extent the moral crusade launched by
the political and social authorities against the uncivilised and
uneducated 'mass' was the response to this threat (as was
suggested in the first chapter), and to what extent the sudden
eruption of the moral and proselytising zeal and the growing
numbers of well-wishers and charitable reformers arose from
the sui generis cultural revolution taking place among the
middle classes, which in no small a part drew its momentum
from the bourgeois resentment of the aristocratic domination.
It seems that both factors played their part, and the argument
about their relative importance is bound to remain inconclusive.
If anything, they contributed to each other's strength. As
Frank Parkin recently reminded us, the task of the self-
definition of a class is never complete unless ramparts and tur-
rets are erected on both the 'upper' and 'lower' borders.

Whatever the reason and the motive, the beginning of the
nineteenth century was a period of undeclared, but nevertheless
widespread and intense, cultural revolution among the urban
middle strata, and of a virtual Kulturkampf launched by these
strata simultaneously against the moral laxity of aristocracy
and the depravity of the poor. One of the many manifestations
of the cultural revolution was - at least in England - the vigorous evangelical movement. Religious revival meant not so much
a return to the institutional fold of the church, as an eruption
of strictly ethical concerns. Dorothy Marshall described the
evangelical movement, 'with its rigorous examination of conscience, and its insistence that grace is a secular garment, so
that the idle pleasure, the thoughtless word, brings with it
consequences not only in this world but in the next and that
therefore conduct, even in trifles, must be examined and
regulated'.[5] Yet the movement derived its impetus not necessarily from a latter-day revival of the puritan urge of the pious
to earn his salvation. The ethical revolution of the early
nineteenth century had from the beginning explicit political
connotations; a personal moral code and social peace and order

were perceived as inextricably linked and attainable only together. To quote Marshall again, 'Both the evangelicals and the polite world believed that the laxity, drunkenness, and idleness of the lower orders represented a threat to the nation....In 1787 the Proclamation against Vice and Immorality which included sabbath-breaking, blasphemy, drunkenness, obscene literature and immoral behaviour, was issued'. By the end of the Napoleonic wars, 'virtue was advancing on a broad, invincible front, though the impetus behind the advance was not solely religious. Infidelity and revolution were closely associated in men's minds and the summary discontent and half-concealed violence of the lower orders seemed to threaten social stability.'[6]

The immediate post-Napoleonic period was the time of the great scare. The state saw its authority rapidly being eroded under the barrage of unfulfillable claims and complaints of the 'lower orders'; the masters saw their thrust for control resisted and challenged; aristocracy feared an alliance between the growing wealth of the merchants and industrialists and the 'rabble', which could turn against its hereditary privileges; all experienced acute uncertainty in the face of the all the more evident bankruptcy of the old, limited power and the unprecedented scale of social dislocations. All sensed a Jacobin-type revolution round the corner and promptly defined every food riot or wage demand as its rehearsal. Drunkenness and the imminence of bloodshed and revolution were seen as belonging together because both were attributed to the 'lower orders'. The moral revolution seemed therefore the only alternative to a political and social rebellion.

Political criteria took precedence over social classifications. The threat of rebellion was imputed indiscriminately to all who might have been suspected of having a reason for discontent because of insecure existence and deteriorating standards. Hence the view from the political vantage point blurred not only the distinction between moral formlessness and political anarchy, but also the social boundaries between the food riots of the urban poor and the apprentices defending their traditional status. Meticulous, all-pervasive control over the totality of life, guarded and supported on one side by moral preaching, on the other by the twin threat of prison and poor-house, was the policy applied indiscriminately to all; it flattened the differences and brought together concerns and objectives otherwise distant from each other, if not altogether unconnected. Luddite protest against the stultifying routine of machinery and the riots against war speculators, demands of work and resistance against the masters' bid for total control, promotion of extended suffrage and apprentices' association mixing the memory of craftsmen's guilds with the anticipation of trade unions, were all cast on the same plane of unlawful and subversive activity against public order. Acts against combinations and riots forced all these diverse conflicts and varieties of

social protest into one category. Well before any unity between
them was forged in practice, they created its legally founded
illusion.

Defence of political authority was not an end in itself. The
state and the government stood for social order as such, and
this was not confined to the obedience to the acts of king and
parliament. Political repression was not only the means of keeping the rioters off the streets or preventing the seething discontent from gestating an organised political alternative. It
also secured the conditions for the crystallisation and entrenchment of the new structure of social authority able to meet the
requirements which the old, limited, 'sovereign' power had
proved unable to service. John Foster captured the essence
of the turbulent era in his assertion that:[7]

> the important thing is not so much the shape of social struc-
> ture itself as that of the authority system that sustained
> it....The overriding priority was to bind the emergent mass
> labour force to the new employer class - and to do so dur-
> ing a period when the old self-imposed disciplines of peasant-
> craft society were (at one and the same time) both disinte-
> grating and still dangerously potent.

The 'binding' did not mean just the need to switch the
workers' loyalty and deference from one class of social superiors to another; from the lord of the manor to the industrialist.
The 'binding' task was made all the more complex by the new
content of submission now required - a truly unprecedented
acceptance of complete control over productive activity of the
worker. The old loyalty, in addition, was woven into a complex
relationship in which one side pledged deference in exchange
for the other side's commitment to guardianship. In the new
configuration of dependence, the superiors still required
deference, while their subordinates vainly demanded the continuation of traditional guardianship. Each side appealed to
selectively memorised aspects of the old structure of authority.
According to the highly instructive recent study by Peter
N. Stearns, the French industrialists, much as their British
counterparts, assumed that 'the employer owed the worker
nothing but a wage....By paying the worker what he deserved
the industrialist had fulfilled his duties.'[8] On the other hand,
the employers now required the right to regulate their workers'
behaviour to an extent never experienced before.

Again, John Foster provides a most lucid synthesis of the
problem: 'The new system's most basic social tension was that
produced by the worker's immediate loss of control over his
labour.'[9] The importance Foster assigns to the issue of control
as the major source of social tension and conflict is novel and
revealing against the background of the majority of recent
research in social history which has by and large accepted
uncritically the 'economised' version of the class-formation pro-

cess. The earlier authors, read today rarely if at all, paid
much attention to the question of control, which they saw as a
factor playing a decisive role in determining the frontiers of
class division. Thus, in Witt Bowden's opinion,[10]

> more directly a result of the introduction of machinery and
> of large-scale organisation was the subjection of the workers
> to a deadening mechanical and administrative routine. Some
> of the earlier processes of production afforded the workers
> genuine opportunities for the expression of their personali-
> ties in their work, and some of them even permitted the
> embodiment of artistic conceptions affording pleasure to
> the craftsmen. The various processes were not so highly
> specialised, not so closely articulated and interdependent,
> and not subjected so minutely to the supervision of bosses
> and managers. The effects on the workers of the mechanisa-
> tion and super-organisation of production were early recog-
> nised. The great pioneer in the manufacture of machinery,
> James Watt, argued as early as 1785 that the real makers
> of goods are the inventors and the designers of tools and
> machinery. Others 'are to be considered in no other light
> than as mere acting mechanical powers;...it is scarcely
> necessary that they should use their reason'. The anony-
> mous author of *An Authentic Account of the Riots of
> Birmingham (1791)* explains the participation of workers
> in the riots by saying that the nature of their employments
> is such that 'they are taught to act, and not to think'.
> Various critics of the early textile factories based their
> objections on the fact that the workers were forced from
> their homes, where the work could be carried on inter-
> mittently and with some degree of initiative, into crowded
> quarters where they were subjected to routine and super-
> vision. This seems to have been one of the main objections
> of the craftsmen to machinery.

Later on in his study Bowden agreed that the loss of control
by the workers over their own productive activity was not
necessarily connected with, and certainly not determined by,
the introduction of machinery[11] - though he left unexplored
the obvious conclusion that the structure of authority, rather
than the technology of production, was at the bottom of social
re-alignment which expressed itself in the formation of workers
into a class. This latter view seems to have been represented
by the Hammonds in their pioneering series of studies in social
history. The Hammonds ascribed the major conflict of the era
to the fact that 'the English worker under the new industrial
system found himself receiving government, justice, discipline,
the ordering of most of his comfortless life, from magistrates
and masters' - but they link this suffocating experience of
total dependence not so much to the 'objective logic' of new
industrial machinery as to the substance of power relations:[12]

In the period discussed in this volume the upper classes
allowed no values to the workpeople but those which the
slave-owner appreciates in the slave. The working man was
to be industrious and attentive, not to think for himself,
to owe loyalty and attachment to his master alone, to recognise that his proper place in the economy of the state was
the place of the slave in the economy of the sugar plantation. Take many of the virtues we admire in a man, and they
become vices in a slave.

Casting the workers into the mould left over by slave economy
can hardly be ascribed to the technological features of machine
production. Rather, the introduction of machinery was made
possible by the reduction of the labour force to the passive
object of minute control. This reduction had been accomplished
under the pressure of the totalising viewpoint of dominant
classes bent on neutralising the threat presented by 'the rabble' independently of the role which the newly created masses,
or parts of them, played in the inchoate process of industrial
production.

The separation of the two processes (taming the 'rabble' and
recruiting factory hands) so often connected in later interpretations found its expression also in another feature of the early
industrial era somewhat overshadowed (and consequently forgotten) by the developments of the late nineteenth century.
The self-improvement and achievement ideology, which we are
prompt to identify as a permanent feature of the capitalist effort
to secure the consensus and obedience of their workers, was
in fact almost totally absent during the most vehement and
violent period of the struggle for the subordination and control
over the labouring poor. The struggle was launched in the name
of a permanent submission, the imposition of stable and immutable patterns of authority. If improvement of the lot of the poor
figured in the argument which accompanied the offensive, it
rarely, if at all, went beyond the old idea of the 'able-bodied'
poor who would be better off if forced to work regularly and
use their wages wisely instead of frittering them away in
drunken bouts. It was not expected, however, that in the end,
through industry and obedience, the labouring poor, or at
least a significant part of them, would lift themselves out of the
position of a subordinate class and humble existence. It had
been shown in recent historical research that, in general,
throughout the earlier decades of the nineteenth century there
was little recognition that the new machine tools augured the
advent of an essentially new type of economy capable of elevat-
ing the living standards of every member of society to unheard-
of levels. There was, on the contrary, a general lack of confidence in the permanence of the factory system; on the whole,
the opinion of the times was slow in noticing the forest behind
the trees. The argument that the labouring poor should dedicate
its effort to honest work in the name of the benefits which the

growth of industry would eventually bring to them all, was, therefore, hard to conceive. The most advanced minds of the era, who articulated the mood of the times for their contemporaries, thought about the foreseeable future in terms of a 'steady state' of economy soon to arrive; they expected the limits of economic expansion to be rather quickly reached, the 'wage fund' to remain stable; in other words (to use a much later terminology), the size of 'the cake' to remain practically unchanged, and, hence, the conflicts related to its division, to be permanent. Therefore the last thing the Kulturkampf wished to achieve was to arouse in the labouring poor ambitions and desires reaching beyond their limited, subordinated position in life, and above the subsistence level of existence.

There was, therefore, a continuous, frequently expressed concern with the potential dangers which the moral crusade contained; the campaign of moral improvement ought to be vigilant about the threat of excessive ambitions it could inadvertently foment. The concern was often so great that it led to efforts to thwart the spread of primary education in spite of the crucial role which had been allocated to it (as we have seen in the preceding chapter) in the overall strategy of the Kulturkampf. A typical objection was the one expressed by David Giddies during the parliamentary debate about the Whitbread bill to establish parish schools (1807): education of the labouring poor 'would teach them to despise their lot in life, instead of making them good servants in agriculture, and other laborious employments, to which their rank in society had destined them'. The advocates of primary education for the poor, who considered the advantages for 'moral improvement' outweighing the possible risks, were nevertheless quick to emphasise the limits which the educational effort should accept from the outset. And thus Patrick Colquhoun, in his influential 'Treatise on Indigence', went out of his way to draw a clear boundary which education of the poor should beware of overstepping:[13]

> Not that species of instruction which is to elevate them above the rank they are destined to hold in society, but merely a sufficient portion to give their minds a right bias, a strong sense of religious and moral honesty; a horror of vice, and a love of virtue, sobriety and industry; a disposition to be satisfied with their lot; and a proper sense of loyalty and subordination.

Note the reference to destiny which appears in both texts. This was certainly not a concept of education as a step towards social mobility and individual success. It was instead an idea of education as an inducement to accept willingly what is the inescapable fate of the poor. Hence, as its adherents with few exceptions insisted, educational effort must never be divorced from its moral content and become a pursuit of knowledge for its own sake; education is good only in so far as it serves social peace and order and stimulates satisfaction instead of social criticism. Perhaps the fullest presentation of such an educational philosophy was offered by 'Fraser's Magazine' in 1834:

> The knowledge of the art of reading only exposes [the labouring poor] to the designs of the vilest of men – the writers of cheap, obscene, lewd publications and low political ballads, in which their betters are held up to ridicule and contempt....Through the influence of these works, all the sharp and best-reading boys are early diverted from regular habits, and abandon themselves to idleness and debauchery, which leads to crime.

The remedy against the pernicious effects of 'education for its own sake' 'Fraser's' saw in the infusion of teaching with heavy and explicit moral message:[14]

> Education for the lower classes should comprise daily instruction in what is good for man to do, and what for him to leave undone; to inform them that they are moral agents, and that they may themselves know right from wrong, if they will exercise their reflection, and consult a certain innate feeling, which will be their guide through life under all circumstances of difficulty and doubt; that they have duties to perform, through which only can they obtain happiness, and which, if neglected, will inevitably lead to misery. The nature of virtue and vice, and their effects, should be expounded and illustrated every day by numerous examples from real life. Their acquirement in reading would then be a blessing instead of a curse to them.

To bring together again the major threads of our argument: powerful factors of social unification of diverse categories of people variously affected by the bankruptcy of the old rank and communal order and the growing inadequacy of the old, 'sovereign type', power – were the twin practices of coercion and moral crusade applied indiscriminately to all dislocated and disaffected groups. The tendency, as well as the declared objective of this practice, was to deploy centralised and diffuse means of control over the totality of behaviour of such groups; the effectiveness of such means of control was to be measured by the permanence of subordination grounded in the willing acceptance of the subjected, passive role. The practice derived its impetus and momentum not from the capitalists' desire to secure a smooth functioning of machinery and constant increase in efficiency of labour, but from the concern with social order among all the dominant forces of society. Only later was the already deployed and tested means of control, the new 'discipline power', employed in the service of industry; indeed, it made the success of industrialisation possible.

The forging of various destitute, or threatened with destitution, categories of people into a 'working class' characterised
by a unity of fate, interests and potential policy, was therefore
first and foremost the accomplishment of the concentrated bid
for control made by the established dominant forces in the
wake of the dissipation of the old regime. Paradoxically, what
later came to be considered as the working-class movement,
or working-class policy, was born of the resistance against
enforced unification. In particular, both the institutional forms
of the trade union movement, and the idea of workers' political
representation, were moulded in the course of the struggle of
skilled craftsmen against being lumped together with 'paupers'
and the 'indigent' and having extended over them the same
principle of unconditional submission which was first tested
and polished in parish poor-houses.

MEMORY AGAINST POWER

By the middle of the nineteenth century, even in England,
which was at that time the undisputed leader of the industrialising spurt, more than half of the population a sociologist
would classify as 'the working class' worked and lived outside
the factory system. Half a century earlier in the crucial years
for the formation of the institutional forms which were later
to play a decisive role in the practical blending of variegated
categories of the poor and the dependent into a class, the proportion of the labouring poor confined within the factory walls
was far too small for the experience of factory life to be held
responsible for the outlook and the actions of the class-in-the-
making. As we saw before, an overwhelming majority of the
factory population consisted at that time of children and women,
none particularly prominent in manifesting their resistance to
the advancing capitalist relations - and none in a position to
resist. The forces of order did not find the task of policing
them particularly problematic; local constables co-operating
with factory owners in capturing and returning to his 'rightful
master' an occasional strayed or fugitive child coped well with
the issue. Factories and mills were seen as cheaper and socially
more useful ways of dealing with the problem of poverty and
homelessness than the traditional parish poor-houses - not as
the agents of a new social order. Still less were they the areas
of danger where the ruling aristocracy and the rising middle
classes expected the ghost of the revolution to materialise. The
'labouring poor' whom the dominant classes expected to rebel
and against whom they built elaborate defences in the form of
successive anti-combination and anti-riot acts were not the
helpless children and women of the dark satanic mills.
    One is inclined rather to accept Witt Bowden's conclusion
that:[15]

the rise of a separate and distinct class of permanent wage-earning craftsmen without tools of their own and without control of the output of their labour had been proceeding independently of the introduction of machinery; and it was among this class that embryonic trade unions are first discernible....The rise of a dependent wage-earning class among the skilled handicraftsmen before the age of machinery was preparing the way in limited fields of labour for the formation of organisations similar in character to the modern trade unions.

The experience and the organisational forms of resistance and self-defence which later served as the practical framework for the unification of class were born outside the factory walls. They can be hardly explained by the impact of the blend of social coercion and economic exploitation which the factory hierarchy of power so blatantly demonstrated to those occupying its bottom rungs. Instead, for the configuration which provided the natural setting for such an experience and corresponding forms of action, one had to look into the processes eroding the autonomy and self-management of the pre-industrial urban craftsmen.

The first observers of the emerging and solidifying network of trade union organisations had little doubt that they constituted a direct continuation of the guild tradition, and particularly of the old craft unions. This view seems to have dominated British historiography completely until Marxist-influenced research began to underline the links and causal connections better geared to the theoretical model of class structure. Until then, the historical study emphasised the continuity, rather than a radical break, between the guilds and the trade unions; the latter had been depicted as the result of the gradual organisational separation of the journeymen sections of the guilds once their chances of promotion became remote and in the end unrealistic. Thus perhaps the most important theorist of trade unionism in the early years of the second half of the nineteenth century, George Howell, wrote, as of established historical fact, that:[16]

trade unionism is an outgrowth of, if not exactly an offshoot from, the old guild system of the Middle Ages.... Trade unionism not only owes its origin to the old English guilds, but the earlier Trade unions were in reality the legitimate successors of the Craft Guilds which flourished in this country down to the time of the suppression of the monasteries and other fraternities by Henry the Eighth, in the thirty-seventh year of his reign.

Another prominent trade union writer, J.M. Ludlow, declared unequivocally, that 'the trade society of our day is but the lop-sided representative of the old guild, its dwarfed but

lawful heir'.[17] It was these opinions, typical of the self-consciousness of the early labour organisations, which were
adopted and developed in historical research. In this a most
seminal contribution came from Brentano - whose carefully
documented exploration of the link between guilds and unions
exerted a decisive influence on the 'official' rendering of
trade union tradition by Sidney and Beatrice Webb.[18] A most
elaborate presentation of the continuity theory was offered
in 1904 by G. Unwin:[19]

> In tracing backwards the spiritual ancestry of the organised
> skilled workmen of the present day, the first link is undoub-
> tedly to be found in the small master of the seventeenth
> century. It is in his efforts after organisation, partly in
> their success, but quite as much in their failure, that the
> immediate antecedents of the modern trade union are to
> be sought.

More than later historical studies, Howell's or Ludlow's opinions,
however inadequately documented, throw an important light
on our problem. Whether the link between guilds and unions
was real or imaginary is, of course, a crucial question for
every historian concerned with verifying the true course of
historical events. For the class-formative processes this was,
however, a minor issue. What mattered was the historical
memory of the group, which directly influenced its expectations,
its standards for evaluating the present situation, and, in
consequence, its practices. Howell and Ludlow are the documents of such a memory.

There is ample historical evidence that memory of craftsmen's autonomy and self-government was fresh and palpable
at the time the organisations were born, later perceived as
the beginnings of the working-class movement. The attention
of historians has been, understandably, focused on the crafts
and trades most tangibly affected by expanding capitalist
markets and the competition of cheap factory production. These
trades, one would suppose, on the ground of the present
views of the nature of class separation and conflict, had most
reason to rethink and rearrange their former, now obsolete,
identities. Even in such trades, thoroughly researched by
the historians, powerful and by no means fading residues of
the old guild organisation have been found. The phenomenon
was impressively documented for France in a recent study by
William H. Sewell Jr, who showed the traditional journeymen's
associations gradually acquiring new concerns, vistas and
objectives without drastic interruption of institutional continuity and even without a noticeable change of vocabulary. What
is left, however, somewhat off the centre of historians' attention, is the fact that a great number of well-established and
influential trades and crafts were not adversely affected by
the early stages of industrialisation. Until well into the

nineteenth century, and in some cases up to the twentieth,
the expansion of capitalist markets brought prosperity to many
crafts catering for the growing numbers of well-off consumers
or performing important auxiliary functions for the factory
industry.

Thus some crafts and skilled trades, like shoemakers, sad-
dlers, cabinet-makers, braziers, pewterers, printers, tailors
and a good many others, experienced new, unheard-of opportunities, and consequently considerable improvement in business activity and the strengthening of the status of the craft
workshop. The expansion allowed the master craftsmen not
only to keep their workshops in operation without running the
risk of being squeezed out of business by the factory competition (as was the case of other, for example textile, trades),
but also to cultivate and, indeed, celebrate with added vigour,
the traditional guild ritual, complete with the unique type of
human relation which this ritual supported.

The printing trade, for example, kept the relationship
inherited from guilds intact throughout the eighteenth century.
Printing shops generally employed no more than one or two
journeymen each, and the regulations of the Stationers' Company put no important hurdles on the journeyman's road to
mastership. A thrifty and skilful journeyman could easily start
his own printing shop.[20] In 1818, of the twelve largest printing houses in London, only four had more than ten journeymen.[21] The first half of the nineteenth century saw master
printers multiplying like mushrooms after rain, as a contemporary account described it. The more ambitious journeymen
normally began by buying a printing press and a set of type,
and carrying out small orders on their own account after working hours. After a certain time they usually accumulated enough
money to open their own shops. In the brush-making trade 21
out of 23 workshops in London employed no more than one or
two journeymen each as late as 1835. In the workshop production followed the old arrangement, with the master sitting at
the same table as his journeymen.[22] A very similar set of relationships survived in the manufacture of cutlery, where essential tools were easy to come by,[23] in pottery,[24] and in many other
trades. No wonder that the Royal Commission of 1824 was
deeply impressed by the feeling of solidarity and community of
interests between master hatters and their journeymen which
showed unambiguously in the depositions submitted to the
commission.[25] The essentially intact small workshop pattern
helped also to preserve the feeling of trade distinctiveness and
the pride and dignity of craft status. During the period when
so many other patterns of human relationships were ripped into
tatters, the journeymen compositors issued a demand that their
traditional right to wear a sword and a top hat should continue
to be respected, with a reminder that an Act of Parliament had
accorded the status of 'gentleman' to members of their craft.
They also protested vehemently when a statement published

by the booksellers classified them in the same category as
other printing workers in the press room.[26]

What follows from these few examples, which can be extended
at will, is that throughout the period of gestation of trade
unions and other practices which cemented the labouring
population into a working class, the tradition of pre-industrial
craft was present not just as idealised memory of the past,
but as a palpable, active, all-too-real force. This tradition
included the task-continuity which united, rather than divided,
the master and his employees; the complex relations within the
workshop which stretched far beyond the mere execution of
the productive functions; the assumption of a transitory nature
of submission as an early station in the life cycle of the craftsman, to be succeeded by independence and self-management;
a good deal of self-control and self-regulation in the execution
of productive tasks; a complex network of guild-supported
guarantees of assistance and succour in case of ill fate and old
age; a long experience of 'closure by exclusion' (Frank Parkin),
perceived as an enjoyment of comfortable, even dignified,
status, a cut or two above 'ordinary labourers', and high
above the shapeless mass of the unskilled poor. Above all,
this tradition entailed a good deal of formal, and often real,
control by the craftsman over the use of his labour. All these
elements of tradition came under attack one by one in a growing number of formerly guild-organised trades. There was no
room for any of them in the new mechanised factories. And thus
the crafts still unscathed by the advance of the factory system
set the pattern of autonomy and control now visibly under
threat; while the expanding factory system, the embodiment
of the new disciplining power and total and impersonal control,
gave shape and flesh to the threat to be staved off. The basic
forms of the class organisations of labour were gestated in
the clash between the two.

I call the craftsman's tradition 'historical memory', placing
emphasis thereby not on the survival of pockets of the artisan
mode of life and work, but on the characteristic preponderance
of ideal normative patterns over potentially contrary evidence
of reality; and on the reluctance of learned cognitive patterns
to recognise their own counterfactuality. The artisan mode
of life was part and parcel of the total regime of 'sovereign
power' which left the productive process by and large to the
discretion of the producer, and which on the whole restrained
its intervention to the channelling of the circulation of surplus
through the rank hierarchy. The disintegration of the old
order and inescapable advent of the new, disciplining, power,
could not but sap the foundation on which the security of the
artisan mode of life rested. However powerful a role was played
in the demise of the traditional craftsmanship by the competitive
squeeze, the seed of destruction had been already sown with
the transformation of the power structure. Long before it was
delivered a coup de grâce by the expanding mechanised

production, the artisan mode of life was condemned to slow but irreversible decay by the corroding forces of the new pattern of social power. The presence of crafts where the old mode survived relatively unimpaired longer than elsewhere allowed the process to be seen as an aberration rather than a trend, and thereby added to the vigour and resoluteness of the resistance. The defence of old rules and customs derived its impetus from the determination of craftsmen not to be pulled down to the level of dependent factory workers and not to be dissolved in the depersonalised mass of labourers deprived of status and of control over their own work and life.

Half a century ago Selig Perlman advanced a theory of labour movement which attempted to look beyond the overt rhetoric of conflict into the inner motives of workers' resistance. Perlman articulated his model of industrial conflict in terms of 'scarcity groups', suggested by the current understanding of the mechanism of market competition:[27]

> 'Scarcity groups' regularly endeavour to 'own' as groups the limited opportunities at their disposal. Thus no issue relating to the conditions upon which they will permit an individual to connect with an opportunity can escape becoming strongly tinged by this fundamental aspiration to 'own' all the opportunities extant. It would be erroneous to try to account for an industrial struggle solely by the specific demands which are its proximate causes: wages, hours, freedom from discriminating discharge, etc., while leaving out this group 'hunger' for controlling the job opportunities to the point of 'ownership'...behind each strike there always lurks the struggle for the control of the jobs.

Perlman's interpretation is itself more than just 'tinged' with the market-inspired vision of the individual motivated overwhelmingly by the desire to hold, and to maximise, his possessions; he obviously believed that the specificity of workers' behaviour in industrial conflict could be dissolved in the generality of 'scarcity group' struggling to defend and expand the opportunities at their disposal. The uniqueness of the problem encountered by the workers, as located at the receiving side of the power structure, all but disappears, and labour organisations become - together with their employers - partners in a game in which both sides pursue the same prizes. This tendency to gloss over the particularity of the task which gave rise to, and maintains the energy of, the labour movement (but not of many other 'interest groups' which also compete for an increased share of the surplus), is a major flaw in Perlman's theory. This weakness should not deter us, however, from appreciating the advantage this theory holds over many an interpretation of labour history, which has taken at face value the explicit 'topicalisation' of labour struggles and without further questioning accepted them as the true account of the motives and the objectives of collective action. Perlman invites us to take our search for motives beyond the surface of declared aims and grievances. Moreover, what would become apparent from his argument, if not for the vocabulary of market competition in which the argument is couched, was that the ultimate cause of the struggle was the issue of control over jobs. It is this contention which our own argument intends to support.

'Control over jobs' is, to be sure, a notion already 'processed' by the discourse of power. It results from the condensation of a much wider and more principal issue of individual autonomy and self-management into a specific topic of rights and duties in a 'hired work' situation, thereby rendering the issue amenable to treatment in terms of a power-determined labour contract. What the idea of 'control over jobs' stands for is the unresolved issue of control over body and spirit of the job-holder.

The conflict is ineradicably rooted in the fact that the labour cannot be bought separately from the labourer; the employer cannot 'expropriate' a labour force without acquiring the right to control its holders' conduct. In this crucial respect, 'selling of labour' is distinct from selling any other commodity; in this crucial respect, that is, labour is not like other commodities. Mutual dependence of the sides to contract begins, not ends, with the agreement to sell. In this sense, one could say, slavery was much less ambiguous an institution, as it took proper account of the intrinsic logic of the management of the process of production. A labour contract creates an inherently equivocal, underdetermined relationship; it cannot be implemented without affecting aspects of the worker's life which, on the face of it, were not the subject of negotiation and agreement. Hence the 'buying of labour' inevitably leads to a permanent power struggle in which the 'glossed over' issues of autonomy and control are resolved. The conflict between employers and their employees is, therefore, a permanent and irremovable feature of 'contractual' labour relations. Its inevitability results from the very ambiguity of the power situation which the labour contract cannot help creating.

The degree of overall control over any situation depends directly on the number of vital parameters of the other side's behaviour which can be determined. The strategy of any group aiming at the extension of its control over the situation consists in eliminating as much uncertainty from the behaviour of the other side as possible - which amounts ultimately to depriving this other side of freedom of manoeuvre. Control is greater the less 'unpredictable' the conduct of the other side becomes, the more one can depict it as repeatable, routine, subject to invariable rules, etc. This effect can be achieved by various means. It can be achieved by coercion: the penalties for deviant conduct are set at such a high level that the prohibitive costs of non-compliance render disobedience improbable. It can be achieved by cutting off the information about alter-

native states; this makes the conception of the contingence of
the current power structure, and hence the action aimed at
its modification, highly improbable. It can be achieved also by
practical limitation of the other side's choices – by reduction
of its functions to routine activities which do not allow for
variations and leave no room for initiative. The outcome of
the whole process would not depend then on the other side's
decision; the other side would cease to be a 'source of uncertainty' – one could disregard it as a source of action and,
consequently, as a factor in calculating the results. Theoretical
grounds of this strategy (control as proximity to the sources
of uncertainty) have been developed as a general cybernetical
problem by W. Ross Ashby;[28] they have been applied to the
theory of organisation by Michel Crozier in his classic, 'The
Bureaucratic Phenomenon'.

From its inception, one can discern in the labour conflict
(both in the strategy of the capitalist employers and in the
organised response of the workers) all the aspects of the above
strategy. The almost total control the employers enjoyed over
women and children employed in the first factories had been
attained by the combination of all theoretically conceivable
strategic devices to a population already reduced to the
status of a passive object of action. This was not, however,
the case of a small, but crucially important group of skilled
craftsmen, whose labour was strategically located in the
decisive points of the productive process. I have quoted before
Adam Smith's observation on the power 'half a dozen of wool
combers' may exert on their employers (and their fellow workers)
due to their irreplaceability and the importance of their contribution for the final outcome of production. This privilege of
the strategically vital position was used as the prime resource
in the craftsmen's fight against the control of employers.

Trade unions had been formed among such craftsmen, steeped
in the memory of the autonomy of an artisan workshop; their
objective was to maintain control over access to skilled trades,
which was necessary in order to keep the monopolistic, strategically crucial position inside the productive process which in
its turn was the only available means of preserving the traditional craftsman's control over his work and, more generally,
over his own actions as a person. Trade unions had been
created in order to fight for the survival, or the restoration,
of the old regime of guilds, or some modified and updated
version of the guilds. This general tendency had been epitomised in the vociferous and universal demand to bring back
and observe the apprenticeship clauses of 5 Elizabeth. It was
hoped that by retaining control over the entry to their trade,
skilled craftsmen would remain an independent factor with
which the employers would have to reckon in their calculations.
In terms of Ashby's theory, they would remain a 'source of
uncertainty', and hence an independent agent in the game of
power.

The obvious adversary in this struggle was the employer,
naturally interested in undermining the foundations of the
craftsmen's power by taking over the gate-keeping functions
and thus depriving the craftsmen of their traditional control
over skilled labour. He was not, however, the only adversary.
The fight for the gate-keeping prerogatives boiled down, in
practice if not in theory, to the collective refusal 'to work with
those whom they did not regard as "fair" workmen'.[29] According to John Rule, the 'closed shop' was a very early invention
certainly deeply rooted in the guild tradition; it was seen as
the defence of the customary laws of the guild against the law-
breaking actions of the masters who usurped the right to
increase the number of apprentices at will. More often than not,
however, the wrath of journeymen fell upon the backs of their
fellow employees. The long campaign of weavers over the
apprenticeship issue reached its culmination in the first decade
of the nineteenth century; aimed at 'limiting the spread of
the factory system by preventing the employment of unskilled
labour', it revealed the strength of the weavers' clubs which,
among other things, brought prosecutions against 'unfair workmen' in over fifty cases altogether.[30]
   Paradoxically, it was the middle-class intellectuals who picked
out for condemnation such divisive practices of early trade
unions - divisive, that is, in relation to the stipulated unity of
labour. In 1838 the 'Edinburgh Review', in its extensive
research report on the activities of trade unions, wrote that:

> in order to secure the monopoly of the skilled part of the
> trade, it is usually enacted by the ruling committee, that
> no master shall employ more than a small proportion of
> apprentices to the skilled workman....The skilled labourers,
> that is, a twentieth or thirtieth part of the mass, alone are
> consulted.

Trade Unions, the 'Edinburgh Review' concluded, are 'monopolies of skilled against unskilled labour'.[31] The author of the
article was sufficiently perceptive to sense deeper and wider
issues behind the overt preoccupation of unions with wages
and hours of work. If the trade union concern with the number
of employees could be explained away in purely economic terms,
the other objects of trade-union struggle clearly owed the
attention paid to them to other than economic purposes. Among
such objects were demands that 'the employer must submit to
their directions, in regard to the overseer or manager whom he
is to employ to superintend the combined workmen', or that
the master should have no right to choose his workmen alone,
without consent of the craftsmen's union. Such demands were
difficult to explain in the usual terms of 'maximisation of profit'. They made sense only as far as one accepted that the moving force behind the early trade union activity was the desire
to stem the masters' offensive against the established autonomy

and self-control of the craftsmen.

The struggle waged by the early trade unions had not been victorious. Neither had it ended in a total failure. In fact, it still goes on; an outcome only to be expected, knowing the inherent and inescapable ambiguity of the issue of control over labour and the labourer. The struggle did, however, undergo vital modifications as either one side or the other scored partial, though never conclusive, successes.

A most seminal modification was, to employ John Foster's expression, the transformation of the 'old craft elite' into the 'new labour aristocracy'.[32] To take the engineering industry as an example, the skilled craftsmen had been accorded the privileged, semi-autonomous role which they sought, as the pacemakers and the taskmasters in relation to the rest of the factory employees; but this role was simultaneously riveted into the new power structure which supported the indisputable management rights of the owner. 'While the self-imposed work routine of the craft worker served to insulate him from employer control', the new routine, regulated from outside by the rhythmical rotations of the engine, 'equally firmly identified the skilled worker with management'. The degree to which the latter was true depended on the extent of the mechanisation of work. The reduction of the uncertainty inherent in the craftsmen's control over vital skills, if inachievable in a straight battle, could be and eventually was, attained by a longer route: by technological means, which imposed a high degree of routinisation also on the traditionally skilled jobs, to the extent that the skills themselves have become the properties of the machines rather than their operators.

Many years after the first clashes, and many transformations of the working population and the trade union structure later, the issue of control is still alive. Moreover, it seems to remain the crucial explanation of the trade union activity. It has been repeatedly shown by economic research that the actual distribution of income between industries and occupations depends on trade union activity to a degree much smaller than is needed to account for the utmost importance which the trade unions accord to wage bargaining. Quite often specific moves of trade unions are impossible to interpret in terms of market rationality and 'maximisation of profits'. One remembers the bewilderment of the last Labour government at the insistence of trade unions on 'free collective bargaining'; the spokesmen for the baffled government argued, and rightly in the economic sense, that with free collective bargaining everybody would be in the end as well off or as badly off as in the beginning, with weaker money and sapped economic confidence as the only difference; if the spokesmen were at a loss in trying to comprehend this apparently irrational behaviour of the unions, it was because of their belief, induced by the 'common-sense' view of the 'interest groups', that the struggle is in the end for more money. In particular, the verdict of irrationality was grounded on a total neglect of the issue of autonomy and control.

If bargaining for wages and hours of work came to play an increasing role in the activities of trade unions (simultaneously with the gradual disappearance of the formerly dominant topics of the management prerogatives), it was mainly because of the fact that with other, more fundamental issues having been resolved to the satisfaction and benefit of the managers, wages were left as one of the few issues around which the autonomy of the workers could be maintained and defended. In a sense, the wider issues of the power structure were 'bought off' in exchange for economic benefits, or rather removed from the agenda, 'de-topicalised' by shifting the conflict on to a purely economic platform.

From a recent, most perceptive study of the shop-floor power structure we learn that the 'managerial prerogative', a code word for the right of the managers to control and command, has turned after years into common sense, and that like all commonsensical presumptions it has ceased to be an overt topic of discourse. The authors of the study conclude that 'at present there is not, in the culture of most workers, anything corresponding to the principle of managerial prerogative which could justify any demand for increased control'. The asymmetry of power relations in the modern factory has been absorbed into the very vocabulary used to conceptualise and 'think' inner-factory relations, and as such it precedes their experience and prevents its own topicalisation. Profitability is spoken about as 'efficiency', and hence any behaviour which may lead to the diminution of profit is automatically seen as the advocacy of inefficiency, and thus another corroboration of the already assumed inability of the workers to control their own conduct in accordance with their true interests. As a Pennine work engineer put it, the craftsmen 'know their stuff, but they do not know what is to their benefit, particularly from the long-term point of view. As a manager *does know* what is good for them in the long term, they should accept managerial viewpoints and decisions as being in their long-term interests'. More often than not, if the power structure is brought into the topic of discussion, it is defended in terms of 'self-evident common sense' which every sane man or woman must accept. The authors of the study challenge the widespread assumption that the workers' acquiescence, at least in the sample of factories they investigated, 'rested solely on a calculation of the odds stacked against them. Indeed, the very deployment of this kind of power against individuals depends on the absence of mass revolt.' 'In a fundamental sense', the authors conclude,[33]

management establishes the basic strategic elements of the situation through its control, *ab initio*, of the technical and formal social organisation of the workplace....Workers' principles, on the other hand, appear to be more usually expressed in responses to managerial moves or defensive reactions to other changes, rather than in initiatives taken 'out of the blue'.

The quoted study confirms, in a systematic and well-docu-mented way, that the issues which once led to the crystallisa-tion of class conflict, and its institutionalisation in the form of organisation embodying a separate worker identity, are largely absent from the modern agenda of conflict between workers and their managers. That the craftsmen do not control their own labour has become a commonsensical, uncontested principle of the factory power structure. But it was against it becoming a principle that the craftsmen of the early nineteenth century revolted, re-emerging from the revolt with a new identity of 'permanent workers'. As John Foster has shown admirably, the temporary fusion between craftsmen's resistance and the preachings of the middle-class radicals was due essentially to the radicals' appeal to the independence of small producers.[34] Foster's own conclusion is that 'although the movement was mainly political in composition...it seems too early to talk about "working-class consciousness"'. What the conclusion assumes is the retrospective knowledge of the later acceptance of the permanence of an asymmetrical power structure in the factory, of the permanence of the workers' subordinate position, and hence of the distribution of surplus as the main, if not the only, issue of conflict and struggle against the owners and the managers of the work-place. It was on the ground of this series of acceptances that what has become identified as 'work-ing-class consciousness' gradually emerged, once the initial attempt to preserve the pre-industrial pattern of control was thwarted by the joint effort of 'discipline power' and state coercion.

The story of the formation of the working class and its later institutionalisation exemplifies the paradoxical role played by historical memory in the dialectics of continuity and change. Memory of pre-industrial craftsman's autonomy and self-management served as the ground for the resistance against the encroachment of the new power structure, which the crafts-men encountered directly in the form of the capitalist factory. The conflict between craftsmen and their capitalist employers came into being in the course of this resistance. The craftsmen appealed to the traditional authorities - the king and parliament - to restore and to defend the old laws and the tradition-hal-lowed customs, only to find out that state policy is aimed at compressing their status into that of the indiscriminate mass of the 'labouring poor'.[35]

The government, to which they had looked not without a certain confidence for the maintenance of stable conditions... was now almost invariably on the side of these changes which left them at the mercy of increasingly powerful employers. They naturally in consequence resorted to the processes of self-help by means of organisation.

The sense of the outraged justice resulted in political radicalism, intended to force the powers that be to do what they refused to agree to when peacefully petitioned. Still, the political action was backward-looking and derived its impetus from the wish to stem the advance of the factory and extinction of the crafts- man's workshop. In the course of this action, permanent forms of new working-class organisations emerged, inspired by the only form of collective action known to the craftsmen and preserved in their cultural tradition - that of the guild and journeymen's association; the remembered forms were now subjected, however, to a slow but steady process of adjust- ment (of their vocabulary, daily concerns, and express objec- tives) to the permanence of the new power structure (a process superbly documented for France by William H. Sewell Jr). The battle for control for which the troops took up arms was lost, but the troops remained. Their very existence retained some residues of the original objective - it dented the essential asymmetry of the new structure of power and preserved the conditions for contesting the absolute limits of employers' control. But, by and large, the sweeping ambitions of the original war aims have been forgotten; a good part of the second half of the nineteenth century (after the 1848 'Spring of the Nations' episode and after the petering out of the Chartist movement in Britain) can be seen, on the whole, as the period of forgetting, when the inchoate working-class organisations left over from the initial all-out struggle slowly dissociated themselves from their own historical memory.

THE 'ECONOMISATION' OF CLASS CONFLICT

The parallel processes of the 'forgetting of origins' and the incorporation of the labour organisation into the capitalist system (later dubbed 'the emergence of working-class con- sciousness') were accomplished primarily through the economisa- tion of the conflict. By this I understand the substitution of the wage-and-hours bargaining for the initial conflict over con- trol of the process of production and of the body and soul of the producers.
   Like the condensation of widely different categories of population and cultural traditions into a single class of 'labour- ing poor', so the economisation of the employer-employee relationship was given its initial push by the pressures arising from the changing power relations. The aspect of change of particular importance in this context was the accelerated dis- sipation of patronage and paternalism - the age-old pattern of trading obedience for security. As I tried to show before, this pattern collapsed not so much under the pressure of the new, market-inspired avarice, as because of its inadequacy

to the task of domesticating and keeping at bay the growing
surplus of population for which the old economic structure had
no room. The demise of paternalism was neither an easy nor
a straightforward process. It lingered in the collective memory
on both sides of the new conflict as a norm long after it ceased
to be a viable solution to their problems. The new patterns of
power relations gestated in the shadow of struggles and arguments still clinging to old topics and now unrealistic objectives.
It was against this background of confusion between the normative order suggested by historical memory and the realities of
the day that the enlightened spokesmen for the emerging order
launched their uphill struggle for the re-articulation of the
power structure in a new way, free from the illusion that the
old foundations of domination and obedience could be retrieved.
The main thrust of their effort was to redefine social relations
as, essentially, economic ones.

This point was made with rare clarity in one of the many
articles of the 'Westminster Review' dedicated to the analysis
of the 'causes of the present trouble'.[36] Because of the com-
prehensiveness with which the case for the new articulation
had been made, the article deserves to be quoted at length.
The article declares that: 'we are now encountering the difficulties of a transition state, in which former rules and ties
are loosened, and the new ones fitted to our changed conditions are as yet unformed, or imperfectly recognised.' Previous
eras associated subjection with protection - either absolutely,
as in the case of slavery, or partially, as in the case of a
system defined as 'feudal vassalage'. The new era, however,
brings a totally new arrangement, 'that of bargain or mutual
agreement', in which 'simple service is balanced against simple
payment' - with, so to speak, no strings attached on either
side. The sides to the conflict failed, however, to notice the
novelty of the situation, and they still expect an extension of
their mutual obligations in the direction which would be at home
in the earlier system but which does not fit the logic of the new
one.

> In the case of both capitalists and labourers...they do not
> see clearly, or feel invariably, in which of the two pre-
> viously mentioned relative positions they intend to stand.
> Each party borrows some of the *claims* of the preceding
> relation, but forgets the correlative *obligations*. The artisan
> conceives that he is entitled to claim from his master the
> forbearance, the kindness, the assistance in difficulty and
> distress, which belong to the feudal relation; but he for-
> gets to pay the corresponding duties of consideration,
> confidence, and respect.

Conversely, the employers would be foolish to expect from their
labourers love and gratitude in addition to the discipline they
buy for the wages they pay. As the 'Edinburgh Review'

admonished the employers the same year,[37] ours 'is not an age
in which a man can feel loyal and dutiful because he has been
born on his estate....Obedience in return for wages is a different matter....But good-will and gratitude form no part of
the conditions of such a contract.' Though the two journals
occupied different sectors of the contemporary political spectrum, they expressed the same practical concerns. The first
concern was with the way of securing discipline of a thus far
rebellious, sometimes riotous, labour force under conditions
when the old entitlements to obedience and deference had
lost much of their former hold. The second concern was with
the limits of domination which ought to be recognised in advance,
in order to prevent the social explosion which their wilful or
inadvertent transgressing was, as recent evidence had shown,
threatening. As to the latter, the 'Westminster Review', offered
unhesitant, though somewhat resigned, advice: 'The only plan
which appears to us at once sound in its principle, and promising as to its prospects, is to spread instruction among the
masses by every means in our power, and then leave them
to "work out their own salvation"' - the familiar idea of a moral
crusade as a remedy, at the same time, against the imminent
rebellion and against 'destitution caused by indolence and
improvidence', which was its constant source.

The crucial aim of the suggested 'instruction among the
masses' was to teach the labourers to accept the principle of
'simple payment' as full equivalent for the 'simple service'
they render; in other words, to teach them the new art of
exchanging submission for wage rather than for security; and,
subsequently, to take care of their security themselves using
the resources the wages offered. A social relation between
classes was to be re-articulated as an economic exchange of a
'commodity' (labour) for money (wage). By the same token,
the two classes confronting each other in the social relationship
were to be redefined as economic categories.

In his recent study of the origins of labour economics,
Paul J. McNulty emphasised the relatively late arrival of this
idea. The concept of free contract and the belief in its desirability made tremendous advances in all areas of economic life -
but not, until quite late, in the field of labour relations.[38]

> Throughout the sixteenth, seventeenth, and even, to a
> large extent, the eighteenth centuries, when the medieval
> regulatory principle of just price had been generally aban-
> doned in favour of the free interaction of market supply
> and demand, the desirability of wage regulation nonetheless
> remained a widely accepted postulate of social analysis.

One would add that throughout all this period wages were not
seen as a purely economic problem. They were naturally conceived of as an element in wider social relations, which included
considerations clearly not belonging to the sphere of the

economy - like security, social order, or status rights. The
reduction of wages to an economic issue pure and simple was,
in its turn, part and parcel of a wider process of 'de-socialisa-
tion' of labour relations. This, as is stressed repeatedly through
our argument, was not a matter of new economic theories or
even of the changing economic climate, but the result of a profound social transformation, of which the deployment of new
'disciplining' power in the service of social order was a most
prominent factor.

The new economic view of labour which gradually established
itself in social theory reflected the emerging power structure
in which tools of labour and the labour process itself had been
separated from those who laboured and who operated the tools;
and where the initiative of action and the right to plan and
supervise it had been concentrated on the side of the tools,
with the living labour left entirely on the passive, receiving
side of the relation. McNulty searched the writings of social
theorists of the time for indications of the cognitive perspective
within which the reduction of labour relations to economic power
took place. And thus he quotes Adam Smith's lecture of 1763,
in which the great Scottish moral philosopher sadly concluded
that 'it is remarkable that in every commercial nation the low
people are exceedingly stupid'. This view of the labouring
poor was later developed in his magnum opus: the labourer,
as Smith found him,

> has no accession to exert his understanding, or to exercise
> his invention....He naturally loses, therefore, the habit of
> such exertion, and generally becomes as stupid and ignor-
> ant as it is possible for a human creature to become. The
> torpor of his mind renders him not only incapable of relish-
> ing or bearing a part in any rational conversation, but of
> conceiving any generous, noble or tender sentiments, and
> consequently of forming any just judgement.

Smith undoubtedly bewailed this condition; he hoped that the
growing division of labour would eventually improve the unpre-
possessing character of the labourers, but he saw the improvement chiefly as the question of making the poor more eager to
exert themselves, less 'slothful and lazy'. Smith's verdict
telescoped the universally held view of the era. On the one
hand, this view denied the labouring poor any capacity for
initiative and self-management; in particular, it refused to
trust them with the control of the productive process - something they were still in full charge of a couple of centuries
earlier. On the other, it pointed to economic pressures (division of labour meant in practical terms narrowing down of
individual tasks and designing and regulating them from outside
of the individual workplace) as the only factor of any conceivable improvement in the quality of the labouring population -
whatever content was put in the notion of 'improvement'.

McNulty points out the clinching role of David Ricardo in
this gradual process of re-articulation of the 'lower classes'
as the subordinate side of the process of production:[39]

> Ricardo solidified the identification of labour as a factor of
> production with labour as a social class....The class con-
> cept as employed was deficient from an analytical stand-
> point in that there seems to have been a confusion between
> groups of people interacting socially and manifesting com-
> mon modes of thought and behaviour (sociological classes)
> and economic agents whose contributions to the processes
> of production are of a common type (factor classification in
> economic theory.)

Perhaps the collapsing of the two concepts which social scientists would rather keep apart can be seen as analytically defi-
cient, but the meaning of Ricardo's model is not a theoretical
error. The substance of Ricardo's theory, when seen against
the background of contemporary processes, within both the
power structure and its diagnostic reflections, is revealed as
consisting, above all, not in the identification of 'sociological'
and 'economic' aspects of labouring classes, but in dissolving
the first in the second. Ricardo's idea of labour simultaneously
'de-socialises' and 'economises' the concept of class.

Ricardo's model of the 'factors of production' does not present
capital and labour as symmetrical partners in the game of
production and distribution. In so far as it represents the
reality of the society Ricardo wished to comprehend, it sub-
sumes, as a commonsensical assumption rather than a postulate,
the domination-subordination relationship between capital and
labour. In other words, it interprets the taken-for-granted
power structure of the society as, in its essence, an economic
relationship.

That this is the case is shown by the difference between the
relationships of, respectively, the analytical category of 'capital'
to the social category of capitalists, and the analytical category
of 'labour' to the social category of labourers. Capital does not
'exhaust' the 'totality' which is the capitalist; it is only a part
of this totality, and, what is more, a detachable part. It is,
as it were, separable in such a way that it can be used or
abused or left idle without this use or abuse or unemployment
being necessarily transferred on to the rest of the whole. Above
all, capital is separable from the person of the capitalist - his
body and soul; what is done to capital is not done to the body of
the capitalist. The rhythm of the work to which capital is subject when put to use in no way determines the life rhythm of
the capitalist as a person. All this is, obviously, untrue of the
other 'factor of production' - labour. This is not 'detachable'
from the body and spirit of the labourer. It cannot be used or
abused or left idle without the labourer undergoing the same
experience. If labour means anything, it means the bodily

exertions of the labourer, engagement of his person in a specific kind of activity. A 'limited company' of labour is an absur-
dity. The 'rhythm of labour' can be nothing else but the life
rhythm of the labourer.

Once the asymmetry of the two 'factors of production' in
Ricardo's model is taken into account, it becomes immediately
evident that the asymmetry of the power structure had been
incorporated into the model in spite of its apparent egalitarian
assumptions. In all probability, the 'economisation' of class
relation cannot be accomplished without the expedient of presenting the asymmetrical as equivalent. This is exactly what
Ricardo's model, this culmination of the protracted process of
theorising the emergent 'discipline power', had accomplished.
What the intellectual articulations of the new-type power in
general, and Ricardo's model in particular, glossed over, was
that production, organised as the encounter between capital
and labour, does not engage capitalists and workers in the
same way. The first group remains, as an aggregate of persons, free and undetermined; the second becomes determined
by the encounter not just in their material gains, but in the
totality of their life activities. The economic model takes for
granted what the early tradition-bound struggles of journeymen against the advancing factory order opposed: namely,
the transformation of control over production into control over
producers. Only when such an association is established, can
the exchange between capital and labour, as depicted in the
model, take place.

The economic model of class, therefore, implicitly (by glossing over its power structure, de-topicalising the power structure, shifting the focus to the rules of the game played in
a setting no more under discussion) legitimised the industrial
society, if we define it as a society which deploys old and new
agencies of power for a new task of controlling the productive
activities of its members. In other words, it legitimised the new
power structure in the sphere of production, in the same way
as the old sacred or secular model of rank society legitimised
the power structure in the sphere of distribution. What the
economic model of class spectacularly failed to achieve was
exactly what the rank model had accomplished with impressive
efficiency: it failed to legitimise power-operated principles of
distribution.

Because of this organic weakness, Ricardo's model contained
a virtual time-bomb. It was simply a question of time for the
discontented and antagonised victims of the industrial order
to note that the model, which (if only by default) maintained
the necessity of an asymmetrical position of 'factors') in the process of production, did not offer any equally 'objective' guidance
as to the means by which the relative value of contribution of
each factor should be judged and the joint output distributed.
And once this had been noted, Ricardo's model, unambiguously
and irrevocably 'pro-industrial' in the previously explained

sense, could be used as a powerful anti-capitalist weapon. The small, but vociferous and influential group of 'Ricardian socialists', from whom Karl Marx was later to borrow the basic tenets of his economic model of class, were quick to spot and to develop this inherent potential of Ricardo's concept of class. But the rift between production and distribution, faithfully reflecting the conquest of production by the new power achieved at a price of shifting the power struggle to the field of distribution, was not solely a matter of socialist interpretation. It has become a canon of economic thinking in general. The t's were crossed and the i's were dotted by John Stuart Mill, who put it among the principles of political economy that 'there is nothing optional about the natural laws of production - which depend upon antecedent accumulation, the ultimate properties of the human mind, and the nature of matter, while the distribution of wealth is conducted at the discretion of society'.[40]

What the 'discretion of society' consisted in was an open question. The one thing beyond dispute was that - as all open questions - this one could be solved only through controversy and struggle. The economic model of class, therefore, legitimised class conflict; but it shifted this conflict into the sphere of distribution. Having done that, the model took a rather neutral position as to the specific solutions to the conflict. The economic model of class, by itself, does not determine the way in which the surplus product should be divided between the 'factors of production'. The line of split could move from one theoretically conceivable pole to another without coming into disagreement with the basic assumptions of the model - since these basic assumptions are concerned with the power structure of production, not distribution. In a sense, the model postulates separate sets of factors determining respectively the sphere of production and the sphere of distribution, and their relative independence of each other.

Legitimation of any concrete principle of distribution or its application required in consequence auxiliary theories. And these were not slow to appear. Around the middle of the nineteenth century a great number of such auxiliary theories competed with each other, covering between themselves the whole range of the potential continuum starting from the absolutisation of the current historical (and thus contingent) division of surplus, biased heavily in favour of the capitalist owners of industry, and ending with radical arguments denying the right of the capitalist to any part of the final product (as the capital allegedly constituting their entitlement is no more than the accumulated and 'solidified' labour of the past). The theories of the 'iron law of wages' or 'wage fund' occupied one extreme; various arguments justifying labour's right to the whole product occupied the other.

In his classic study of the 'right to the whole product of labour', Anton Menger wondered at 'a surprising circumstance that the English political economists (by whom Menger under-

stood only those gravitating to the conservative pole) and
Thompson (one of the most prominent 'Ricardian socialists')
draw from identical propositions such opposite conclusions'.
Menger satisfied his curiosity by deciding that: 'Thompson
and his followers are only original in so far as they consider
rent and interest to be *unjust* deductions, which violate the
right of the labourer to the whole product of labour. So that
here...the difference between the two views is rather juridical
than economic.'[41] In this distinction between the juridical and
the economic Menger followed the established canon of political
economy of his time - 'the economic' being accordingly limited
to the inevitable and the necessary, to wit, to the sphere of
production. Inadvertently, Menger lets out the consequence
of the exclusion of distribution from such a sphere: from
identical propositions (regarding production), opposite conclusions (about distribution) can be drawn. This consequence
should not have caused Menger's bewilderment. If anything,
it seems inescapable. The economic model of class can achieve
the legitimation of the asymmetry of power inside the productive process only at the expense of proclaiming the power
struggle in the sphere of distribution unsettled and bound to
continue.
   Nobody theorised this consequence in a fashion more convincing than the 'Ricardian socialists'. Thomas Hodgskin,
in a highly influential tract published in 1825, argued extensively that capital, in addition to being merely a condensation
of past labour, cannot contribute to the final product of itself;
its contribution 'must depend altogether on the peculiar skill of
the artisan and mechanic, who has been trained to practise
different arts'. Hence, if judged in terms of the relative value
of the contribution, 'the whole produce of labour ought to
belong to the labourer'. Hodgskin's conclusion is straightforward:[42]

> Masters cannot therefore rationally expect a termination to
> the present contest. On the contrary, it must continue.
> Even if it should be stopped, it will again and again occur.
> It is not possible that any large body of men who are
> acquainted with their rights will tacitly acquiesce in insult
> and injury. The profits of the masters, as capitalists, must
> be diminished, whether the labourers succeed in obtaining
> higher wages, or the combination continues, or it is from
> time to time renewed. In the former case, the masters, as
> skilled labourers, will share in the increased rewards of
> industry; in either of the two latter, not only will their
> profit be destroyed, but their wages will be diminished or
> altogether annihilated.

There are several elements in Hodgskin's pamphlet which are
of particular significance for our problem. First, it is conceived
in response to the unrest among journeymen (the reference

to it constitutes the subtitle of the book); Hodgskin attempts
to interpret the hidden causes of the persistent trouble (hidden, perhaps, for the journeymen themselves), and finds the
answer to his query in the improper division of the product of
labour. The reason which journeymen themselves offered for
their resistance – the usurpation by masters of an unlimited
control over their labour and its conditions – does not disappear
altogether from Hodgskin's argument, but its significance is
reduced to the material cause of the excessive profits which the
capitalists allot themselves.[43] Thus, in Hodgskin's interpretation,
the true cause of journeymen's dissaffection is not the subordinate position into which they had been forced, but its
impact on their wages. Hence their grievances might be met
by increasing their share in the final product – which, by
itself, need not necessarily undermine the superior position of
masters in the process of production. The latter can become
acceptable to men, providing the former is the case. Second,
the proclamation of the 'right to the whole product' means in
practice that no set limits exist to the demands which at one
point or another might be voiced by the journeymen. The practical limits are determined by the force the journeymen may
muster in support of their claims, and the concessions they
can compel their masters to concede in consequence. Third,
since a gap is likely to persist between practical and theoretical
limits of the struggle, the conflict is likely to remain endemic.
With the power structure as such removed from the agenda,
the consequences of its continuing operation will manifest themselves in a permanent battle about relative shares in the surplus produced within this structure. Fourth, the labourers
whose 'right to the whole product' Hodgskin defends are,
explicitly, journeymen as defined by the tradition of crafts.
Their rights are argued in terms of superior skills, the knowledge of arts 'they have been trained to practice', artisanship,
which transforms immobile objects into living tools of production.
The message is clear. It is not the domination, as such, which
affects all labour alike (in deed or potentially), which Hodgskin
'economises' and proposes to compensate with monetary equivalents, but a specific dispute over control over labour between
the masters of production and skilled craftsmen who used to be
their own masters or expect to become ones in due time.

The lengthy argument produced by William Thompson at
approximately the same time (1824) was organised, by and
large, along the similar lines. It assumed the inviolability of
the principle of possession; in fact, it took it as the criterion
by which to measure the degree to which the inherent rights
of labourers had been satisfied in the society which avidly
guards the property rights of its members, 'For what reason is
it that the free disposal of the *products* of labour must be
respected, for which we should not also respect the free
disposal of *labour itself*?'.

> We deprecate the forcible seizure of an article of wealth,
> not for any evil, any ill effect, to be produced on the
> article itself, on the inanimate object, but for the evil to
> be produced on the intelligent agent, on the mind of the
> producer. The article itself is not necessarily injured,
> is equally capable of use whether transferred voluntarily
> or involuntarily; but the alarm, the sense of insecurity,
> the discouragement of future production, the disinclina-
> tion to labour which is defrauded of its rewards, are
> produced equally by compelling labour, or seizing, or
> giving an unsatisfactory equivalent for its products.[44]

Insecurity, disaffection, resentment, which gave rise to the
craftsman's resistance to the factory system, are here explained
by the compulsion to which labour had been subjected. But
at the same time – throughout the book – the experience of
compulsion, of deprivation of freedom, of the 'involuntariness'
which the conditions of labour entails – are interpreted as the
mental impact of the inability on the part of the labourers to
secure full and rightful remuneration for their product.
Labourers suffer and revolt because they anticipate that the
product of their exertion will be seized by their masters. And
they see it as a seizure, as expropriation, because they do not
receive for their labour the price they would fix if allowed the
position of free agents of exchange. Again, much as in Hodgskin's
tract, what is at bottom a conflict about power and control is
re-projected upon the plane of bargaining about the price of
labour. Again, much as in Hodgskin, the case of labour would
be vindicated were it given the right price – or, rather, were
the masters prevented from imposing on the other side a division of surplus which fits only their interests.
    Hodgskin and Thompson have been quoted here as examples
of the most radical conceptualisation of the conflict between
the workers and their masters. But their writings provide
also a proof of the extent to which the market-inspired vision
of human relations helped to de-conceptualise the problem of
power and control over persons by substituting the problems
of goods and money instead. This shift of discourse from the
relation between groups of people to the relation between
economic categories played a decisive role in the assimilation
of the conflict, which potentially threatened the pattern of
control itself, within the framework of the power structure
which this pattern generated. Once the economic interpretation
of conflict had been embraced and adopted by craftsmen's
unions for purposes of self-definition and determination of
strategy, the question of asymmetry of power ceased to be an
object of the ensuing struggle. The constant pressure exerted
upon autonomy and self-expression of the (now dependent)
producers continued to generate resentment, disaffection and
resistance. But the resulting militancy was now redirected
into the channel of wage bargaining. The side-effect of the

re-channelling was putting on the wage conflict a crippling
burden of the vicarious defence of workers' autonomy and the
need for self-assertion. Because of this additional burden it
had to carry, wage bargaining tended continually to spill over
from the purely economic framework of labour, as commodity,
seeking to maximise its price on the market. Rather than confine itself to this model-economic function, wage bargaining,
as the sole vehicle of workers' self-assertion, could not but
become and remain the manifestation of workers, as persons,
seeking to maximise the realm of their autonomy and their
share of social power. However narrowly economic in their
declared objectives and ostensible concerns, labour organisations carried into economy the unsolved and continually seething problems generated in the sphere of power structure.

In their recent important study, Offe and Wiesenthal objected
to the habit of political scientists of equalising the unequal
and comparing the incomparable. One manifestation of this
habit came particularly under attack: that of subsuming
capitalist companies and labour unions under the common category of monopolies, set to deflect the trading terms in their
favour and thus to maximise their market chances; or presenting business associations and trade unions as two variants of
essentially the same phenomenon of interest groups, lobbying
the state agencies to obtain a better share in allocated resources or more favourable rules of allocation. Offe and Wiesenthal
point out that, contrary to this widespread conceptualisation,
the organisations of workers are not like their alleged business
equivalents; their sociological meaning is altogether different.
'Since the worker is at the same time the subject and the object
of the exchange of labour power, a vastly broader range of
interests is involved in this case than in that of capitalists,
who can satisfy a large part of their interests somewhat apart
from their functioning as capitalists.'[45] Offe and Wiesenthal
go on to argue that the capitalists' associations are, by and
large, instrumental-utilitarian, pursuing the enhancement of
the interests of members as individuals through collectively
operated measures; while the workers unions 'always find themselves forced to rely upon nonutilitarian forms of collective
action, which are based on the redefinition of collective identities - *even if* the organisation does not have any intention of
serving anything but the members' individual intents, for
example, higher wages'. Rather, however, than explain the
excessive vigour of the defence of economic interests by the
'nonutilitarian' tasks (like the establishing and maintaining
of collective identity) which, under the conditions of industrial
power structure, can be accomplished only through economic
competition, Offe and Wiesenthal reverse the relation between
the explanans and the explanandum. They explain the peculiar-
ity of workers' organisations by the unique features of labour
(for example, non-liquidity), and the absence of power assets
outside the organisation itself ('the potential to sanction, as

well as to make concrete decisions to bring this potential to
bear on a particular situation, reside outside the organisation,
namely, with the individual capitalist in the case of business
organisations, whereas the potential has to be built up in a
communicative process *within* the association of workers, whose
individual potential to sanction is minimal because of their
atomisation'). In other words, Offe and Wiesenthal's argument
boils down to the familiar inferiority of bargaining power of an
individual worker when confronted with an equally 'individual'
capitalist. A true unity of the workers' organisation and its
capacity for a truly unified action must be therefore communica-
tively perpetuated, if the bargaining assets are to be balanced,
or the endemic imbalance at least partly redressed, in the
workers' favour.

This argument, however, tacitly assumes that the ultimate
cause of conflict is indeed the distribution of surplus product,
and that whatever is peculiar in the sociological character of
workers' organisation stems from the logic of redistribution.
I have tried to suggest an opposite order of explanation. 'The
communicative process within the association' is not a strategic
device made necessary by the objective of wage bargaining.
It is, rather, the wage bargaining which, under the conditions
of entrenched 'disciplining power', provides the sole available
outlet through which the self-identity and relative autonomy
of the labouring population can be defended and maintained,
and limits of its subordination can be drawn and guarded. The
establishment of group identity is, therefore, the end in itself
- while its manifestation in the struggle for redistribution of
surplus is best understood as its means. Hence the vehemence
and determination with which workers' organisations fight at
times for an apparently negligible 1 or 2 per cent which separate their claims from the employers' offer, and the readiness
to sacrifice much more in lost wages than the eventual victory
of strike may bring, irrational as they are in terms of profit
maximisation, appear entirely sensible as displaced manifestations of endemic power conflict. The same applies to the
workers' preference for closed shops, to their insistence on
the observance of consultative procedure, to their resistance
to many managerial decisions solely on the ground of their
unilaterality, to numerous 'demarcation' conflicts and many
other peculiarities of workers' collective behaviour which only
too often are condemned for their 'irrationality', measured
simply by monetary gains or losses.

This does not mean, of course, that the significance of the
means is fully reducible to the ends. Still less does it mean that
the selection of means, or the outlets for the energy generated
by the conflict, is unimportant - or that it has no consequences
of its own. On the contrary, the fact that the power conflict
has been channelled into the struggle for the distribution of
surplus, that the autonomy and self-identity of the objects of
the power hierarchy had been allowed to express themselves

and 'materialise' only in economic gains, has had profound
influence on the whole course of development of the industrial
society. It accomplished what the direct assault on the body
and spirit of producers in the early years of industrial revolution tried in vain at the enormous risk of a popular rebellion:
it instilled in the minds and the actions of the workers not so
much the 'spirit of capitalism', as the proclivity to access one's
own value and dignity in terms of monetary rewards; and to
make up for the lost control over one's own productive contribution by an increased share in consumption. This effect has
determined the further history of industrial society. It seems
to lie as well at the roots of its present troubles.

4 The tendency of industrial society: an interim summary

In its sociological sense, the industrial revolution consisted in the subjection of the bodies and the thought (in so far as the latter was operative in the action of the bodies) of the producers to the control of other people than the producers themselves. During the industrial revolution this way of organising the process of production, which formerly played a secondary, even marginal, role in the totality of social production, had become the norm.

The pattern of control which the industrial revolution made the social norm was not a development of social patterns which had emerged and gestated in pre-industrial productive units. One cannot trace it back to the craftsman workshop for at least three reasons: in such a workshop, the position of subordination was ostensibly temporary, defined from the outset as a stage leading to, and an instrument of, emancipation and eventually mastership; for the duration of subordination, the co-ordination which the output required was accomplished, by and large, through task-control, rather than body-and-person control, and on the whole did not include the subjection of apprentices and journeymen to a uniform rhythm of physical exertion; the relationship between superiors and their subordinates spread well beyond the requirements and the intrinsic logic of the production process - approaching the totality of a social bond incorporated fully into a shared community membership and culture. With somewhat more justification one can seek an embryo of the industrial pattern of control in the economy of the manor and the category of farm-hands, numerically growing on the eve of industrial revolution. Also in this case, however, similarity was limited by two crucial circumstances: however rhythmical and routinised the productive activity of farm-hands tended to be, the rhythm was only secondarily imposed by man-made design, having been first and foremost determined by natural cycle and conditions to which both labourers and their overseers had to submit - which set unencroachable limits to the discretion of the controllers; and though the shared community membership and culture were absent, the relations between the masters and their hands extended beyond the framework of production proper. Most importantly, it included the characteristic exchange of deference for protection and the expectation of security.

The typically industrial pattern of control over procedures gestated outside the framework of pre-industrial forms of production. It emerged and developed in the dealings of the state power with the first 'mass' of history (if one does not count the episode of the Roman proletariat) - the poor and vagrant population which the locally organised, small-scale, productive units could not contain and accommodate. Before the industrial revolution, the phenomenon of the poor, as the result of its unprecedented size, had been re-articulated as a question of public order, rather than an issue of communal charity and individual salvation as before. The treatment of the poor became increasingly the problem of developing new, more comprehensive and efficient, means of punishment and drill; above all, of direct supervision of the totality of behaviour. This was best attained under conditions of confinement and direct surveillance; the latter revealed their fullest potential when applied to the uniformisation and routinisation of the life-activities of the inmates. The routinisation was not subject to the logic of productive tasks. In poor-houses, the output - if expected at all - was a secondary consideration, almost a by-product of organisations designed with other objectives in mind. If assessed and consciously attended to, the patterns of routinisation were guided by the aim of transforming the unruly and unpredictable (and hence dangerous) into the orderly and repetitive (and hence controllable). If standards were set for the end which this treatment was to achieve, they had been articulated in terms of moral improvement, not the enhanced productivity of labour. Routinisation and surveillance developed as means of, simultaneously, punishment and moral education, with physical labour serving both.

The first factories emerged thanks to the combination of favourable market opportunities and the availability of a large, destitute and uprooted excess of the population complete with the techniques of controlling their bodies, and the power to apply the techniques. In the sociological sense, the first factories are best seen as continuations of parish poor-houses or 'hôpitaux' rather than of pre-industrial workshops. The first factories had been populated with the inmates of workhouses and often served as alternatives to prisons. They were keen absorbers of machine technology because they had been already engaged in forcing their labourers' conduct into a closely watched, repetitive rhythm which made their bodies machine-like well before the introduction of machines; machine technology was well geared to the pattern of control developed in the service of the public order and subsequently adopted by the factories.

Routinised and mechanised production also proved highly profitable, which gave the owners of factories a distinct competitive advantage over the small-scale, custom-bound activity of the craftsmen. Sheer economies of scale left the craftsman with little chance once his customary market had been invaded by the factory output. Some traditional crafts prospered for a while thanks to the rising opulence of their

customers. But the number of trades which faced the threat of
extinction was growing, as the evidently successful method of
profit-making developed in the first factories invited emulation.
For the apprentices and journeymen of the threatened workshops, this meant descending to the level of the 'labouring
poor', and subjection to the discipline power applied heretofore
to the women and children transferred forcibly into the factory-
owners' care from parish poor-houses.

If the labouring poor, ground in the mills of Poor Law and
anti-vagrancy regulations before they passed the factory gate,
had no tradition of independence and self-management to
recall as an alternative to their present fate, the craftsmen
were in an entirely different position. They had a fresh and
rich memory of the guilds, kept alive before their eyes within
the few crafts not only unscathed, but strengthened by the
initial stages of industrial revolution. They were not to surrender without struggle. The weapons of the struggle had
been supplied by collective memory – and this was so in a
double sense: the preservation (or, rather, restoration) of
the guild order with multi-faceted relationships of reciprocal
services between a master and his men, self-regulation of the
work process, limited numbers of apprentices to every master,
was the obvious objective of the struggle against new trends
which had yet to demonstrate their legitimacy against the sense
of outraged justice; short of attaining their backward-oriented
aims, craftsmen derived from their memorised past the knowledge and the experience of organisation and collective management of their joint interests – the skills which could be used
in self-defence or pursuit of their claims, even if the initial
objectives of the struggle proved unrealistic and had to be
adjusted to stubborn realities.

Hence if the discipline power could be imposed on the labouring poor by sheer force and lack of articulated alternatives,
one could not extend it to the journeymen of yesterday, the
skilled workers of today, without first securing their compliance by other means than naked coercion. In the long term,
one could dispose entirely with their strategic role in the
factory production through transferring their skills to new,
more sophisticated, machinery. But this was too vague and
distant a possibility to figure prominently in contemporary
calculations as a realistic solution to the current problem. In
the meantime, therefore, the subjection of skilled workers to
the pattern of labour controlled and made rhythmic developed
in the factories had to be achieved by deploying other methods.
Two methods proved to be crucial in this battle for control:
the moral crusade and the re-articulation of labour relations in
economic terms.

The moral crusade did not mean just the pressure of religious
and secular preaching or the propaganda of bourgeois virtues
of sobriety, routinisation of emotional life and calculated self-
interest, though there was no dearth of these. It meant also a

decisive crackdown on all and any residue of indigenous folk
culture and a determined effort to exterminate all its manifestations, including the most innocuous ones, devoid of any direct
relevance to the ostensible objectives of the battle. Above all,
the moral crusade meant the deployment of old and new social
agencies in the service of retraining the free-spirited and
refractory craftsmen in a fashion more appropriate to the
discipline of the factory. Among those deployed, the family
and the rapidly expanding system of education were perhaps
the most prominent. Both acted as grass-roots, diffuse and
ubiquitous agencies of discipline power. Their primary impact
consisted in the 'individualisation' of workers, achieved simultaneously through the weakening of communal authority and
reorientation towards personal success. Their other function
was an early training in other-directed behaviour.

The re-articulation of labour relations in economic terms
(called here, for the sake of brevity, 'economisation of the
class conflict'), would have been, perhaps, impossible without
the moral crusade. But on the whole it is to be seen as a
separate but correlated process. Like the moral crusade,
economisation of class conflict was not simply a matter of shifts
in theorisation or of the development of a new economic model
as the framework for political discourse. Changes in dominant
theories and, in particular, the gradual acceptance of these
theories by the labour side of the conflict, were, obviously,
a necessary component of the process, but they cannot be
assigned the prime responsibility for its occurrence. At the
bottom of the economisation process lay the steady loss of control over production by the craftsmen; the gradual, but unstoppable transformation of the journeyman into a skilled factory
worker, for whom the surrender of control over his own productive activity had become a condition of livelihood. Redeployment
of social power decided the outcome of the battle for control
over production of surplus. As it happened, having secured
the structure of domination in the productive sphere, it
simultaneously left undefended the battleground of distribution. The principles of the distribution of surplus had been
made vulnerable to attack by the same process which rendered
the principles of the control over production impregnable. Once
the issue of control over production had been settled, the war
of control over distribution was doomed to become endemic and
permanently inconclusive.

Within the pre-industrial order, the redistribution of surplus
was conducted outside the framework of its production. The
sovereign power guarded, and maintained in a working order,
the channels of surplus circulation which led from the immediate
producers to the groups wielding political and military power,
but playing no direct role in the production of surplus; but
this power did not claim, nor contest the control over the
activities which resulted in the production of surplus. Control
over the totality of the productive process, including the

possession of the finished product, was unquestionably in the
hands of the producers. The division of surplus between producers and other users of surplus began where the production
of surplus ended. The principles of this division were explicitly
unconnected with relative contributions to the production of the
divided surplus. The distribution was an aspect of the social,
not economic structure. It derived its stability and continuity
from the strength of political, religious and cultural forces,
normally engaged in the business of the perpetuation of social
structure.

In the industrial order, and more generally with the advent
of the 'discipline power' and the dissipation of the 'sovereign'
power, the situation is reversed. It is now the production
itself which turns into the theatre of power; it is now the
bodies and life functions of the producers, as agents of
surplus creation, which become the objects of power control.
But with the weakening and gradual dissipation of the sovereign
power, distribution of surplus is no longer safeguarded by the
overwhelming forces of culture and social structure; hence it
becomes an open question and invites contradictory claims
pursued from positions of strength.

The pre-industrial order, which legitimised participation
in the finished product by categories which did not partake in
its creation (through taxes, levies, rents, tithe, begging
or charity) kept the direct possession of the product by its
producers unproblematic. The right to the whole product (i.e.
the right to preside over its primary distribution) was therefore the legacy of the pre-industrial order sedimented in the
collective memory of the producers. But with the advent of the
industrial system it ceased to be self-evident who the producers
were who exercised these rights to the compound result of the
productive process. An increasing number of producers were
excluded from control over the products, having been first
excluded from control over production itself. Their historical
memory suggested that the product belonged to its makers.
Hence the sense of outraged justice with which they reacted
against the departure from the traditional order.

Historical evidence shows that the wrath was initially directed
at the ultimate cause of the outrage: forcing the producers
into conditions and a rhythm of labour which they did not
control - the substitution of the factory system for the craftsman workshop, of skilful machines for skilful artisans. As
the hopelessness of the battle for the restoration of the old
craftsmanship order was becoming increasingly evident in the
face of overwhelming odds, the struggle focused more and more
on the conditions of surrender: having lost the control over
production (and hence over their own productive labour, and
their own bodies as receptacles and instruments of this labour),
yesterday's journeymen, now skilled workers, claimed the right
to participate in decisions about the way in which the product
of their labour was to be divided.

There was a highly significant continuity between the battles over distribution of surplus in pre-modern settings and the later struggle for the right to wage bargaining inside the capitalist factory. The former punctuated the history of pre-capitalist society in spite of the grip in which the sovereign power held the circulation of surplus. Battles occurred whenever the state or the landlords attempted a departure from the established way of splitting the product. Peasants took to arms in defence of their 'Rechtsgewohnenheiten'; French 'Cahiers de doléances' were filled with peasants' and town-people's complaints about 'abuses' of traditional prerogatives manifested in the growing greed of landowners, traders or state officials; towns rebelled when the king levied new increased taxes or withdrew old privileges. In all such circumstances the rebellion was triggered off by the sense of outraged justice; the established way of dividing the surplus provided the standard with which justice had been measured. Pre-modern battles over distribution were relatively rare (though their number grew rapidly in the course of the final disintegration of the sovereign power) and episodic precisely because an unambiguous standard of justice was so provided. With the emergence of industrial order, while historic memory suggested that attack against the norm of distribution was unlawful and was to be resisted, the standards to be defended were no longer clear. Occasional battles, prompted by contingent reshuffles of stakes, turned into an endemic war. They have become an institutional attribute of the new system.

The continuity between the two systems, and the dramatic shift-within-the-continuity which took place in the first half of the nineteenth century, have been amply documented and much commented upon, though more often than not the commentators place emphasis on the break in the continuity rather than the continuity itself. An illuminating summary of historical evidence for England, which avoids simplification of the dialectical complexity of the process, has been offered by Patricia Hollis:[1]

Until the late 1820's, working-class writers had located poverty as the gap between the value of a working man's labour, and the value of his wage; and taxes, parasites, the theft of land, and competition were held to account for it. The enemy was primarily aristocratic government buttressed by land and by church. The result was a radical analysis of wrongs, a view of society that Chartists could and did share with the Anti-Corn Law League. Middle- and working-class radicals saw themselves confronting a common enemy in the aristocracy. But the articulation of political economy in the 1820's, justifying the new industrial capitalist system, encouraged working men to compare their wage with that of the capitalists. The discrepancy was held to be exploitation, the enemy was the capitalist

and the middle man, and the result was a socialist analysis
of working-class wrongs. Former middle-class allies in the
radical attack on aristocracy were now class enemies.

While Patricia Hollis's account has the unique virtue of capturing the dialectics of the process in all its interplay of continuity
and discontinuity, it seems to take symptoms for causes of
the radical shift in the content of the analysed struggle. The
'articulation of political economy' was such a symptom, particularly regarding the facility with which the drifting, inchoate
labour organisations took it into their sails. The combination
of two factors seems to hold responsibility for the smoothness
and ease with which the transformation had been accomplished.
One was the industrialists' need to obtain the skilled workers'
compliance with the employers' control over their labour - if
necessary by concessions in the splitting of surplus. Another
was the memory of the skilled workers themselves, who knew
from their journeymen's past the legitimacy and the means of
defending the distributive norms.

The typically working-class battle over the distribution of
surplus differed, however, from the past occasional outbursts
of outraged justice not only by its novel institutional location
(within, rather than beyond, the cycle of production). Its
crucial novelty consisted in the endemic ambiguity and the
irreparable lack of legitimation of distributive norms in the
new setting. For the clarification of this ambiguity the memory
of the pre-industrial order (which took for granted what had
now become the prime topic of the contest, namely the natural
link between the producer and his products) could offer no
guidance. In the absence of clear cultural tradition, the question of distributive standards had been articulated as the issue
of power confrontation, and ever-continuing power confrontation. Working-class organisations, or rather associations which
transformed labouring masses into the working class, differed
from their ancestors', the journeymen's, associations, in that
they specialised in the contest over the control of distribution
and not over the control of production. The centrality of the
distributive contest has been brought up sharply in Allan
Flanders's classic summary of trade union characteristics:[2]

> As in other industrial countries, trade unions in Great Bri-
> tain came into being, established themselves on firm founda-
> tions and extended their power and social influence mainly
> as agencies for collective bargaining. This is to say they
> succeeded as a form of organisation which enabled employees
> - at first only wage-earners but later also salary-earners -
> to regulate and thus improve their wages and working condi-
> tions. All the activities which the trade unions have under-
> taken and all the other purposes they have acquired must be
> regarded as a by-product and auxiliary to this, their major
> activity and purpose, since success in it has been the condi-

tion of their survival and the basis of their growth.

An indirect confirmation of the decisive role of wage bargaining in the self-assembly of the working class is the fact that
most students of the process, without necessarily rendering
the underlying theory explicit, identify the emergence of
'true working-class politics' and 'working-class consciousness'
with the conjunction of the acceptance of industrial system
and the challenge of the legitimacy of capitalist profits. What
is normally understood by the birth of the working class
(though this interpretation is not necessarily spelled out in
so many words) is the de-topicalisation of control over producers (by now firmly held and uncontested, at least not contested directly), and the institutionalisation of the struggle
for the share in consumption.

This institutionalisation is not a contingent feature of one
type of organisation. It seems, on the contrary, to be a crucial
attribute of industrial society as such. It derives from the very
essence of this particular social system, which consists in shifting the power-regulation of social order into the sphere of
production and simultaneous de-legitimation, and opening up
to the power struggle of the sphere of distribution and consumption.

Skilled workers were the first in the long, theoretically
inexhaustible series of categories which were to react on the
new situation by institutionalising the defence of their share
in social consumption and their claims to its increase. Once the
maximisation of gains and possessions had become the sole
substitute for personal autonomy and the only symbolic expression of group identity, an enormous social and psychological
significance was attached to the preoccupation with consumption. At the same time, patterns of consumption ceased to be
regulated by tradition. The combined result of these two factors was the history of industrial society as a succession of
battles over the redistribution of surplus product, punctuated
by the self-constitution of ever-new groups joining in the distributive battle and mobilising their powers in support of their
claim to a greater share.

The consequences of the seminal power shift were not
immediately realised. The most powerful minds of the early
industrial era thought of their society as evolving towards a
'stationary state' - a model theoretically substantiated by
David Ricardo and accepted by J.S. Mill as a canon of political
economy. In Ellen Frankel Paul's summary, Mill believed that
'the increase of wealth was not boundless', that 'profits would
fall because there would be a constantly diminishing field for
new investments', that 'eventually the progressive state must
end in the stationary state'. 'To counteract the effects of such
stagnation upon the poor, he urged that restraint on population
must be recommended to the labouring class and they must be
impressed with the desire to keep up their standard of living

by limiting their numbers'.[3] Well after the new industrial power
structure transformed the distribution into the major battleground of society, this society saw itself through the lens
inherited from its pre-industrial past: what it saw through this
lens was a change leading from one stability to another, an
improvement between two successive stationary states, a
society capable of increasing its wealth but still essentially
finite; a society with great, but nevertheless limited, potential.
The most perceptive thinkers of the period were preoccupied
with the means of 'keeping up' the existing standard of living,
rather than greatly enhancing it. Demographic policy coupled
with moral education were to serve this purpose. Decent life
conditions could be safeguarded if a limited, even if slightly
increased, product was distributed among a stationary number
of claimants. The idea of improvement rarely appeared in this
thinking. To Jeremy Bentham, the maximisation of happiness,
which a good society was expected and obliged to bring, consisted in subsistence, security, abundance, equality – but
hardly in constantly growing standards of material possession.
Adam Smith dreamed of a 'cheerful and hearty state to all the
different orders of the society' – but this was rather an image
of the fast-receding past, adorned by benign memory, than
a prevision of the acquisitory bustle buttressed by ever-faster
economic growth.
    The one consequence of the emancipation of distribution from
power regulation which was perceived with rapidly growing
clarity was the necessity of some supra-societal regulation of
needs which market-operated distribution is not capable of
satisfying. From Adam Smith on, the state was seen as the
agent of such regulation. Once the distribution ceased to be an
aspect of a hierarchical system embracing the totality of human
life and needs, some needs were bound to be left wanting, and
the state had to step in to do what the market could not. The
state could not possibly improve on the productive performance,
since production was subject to inexorable objective laws (i.e.
regulated by adequate and uncontested, diffuse social powers).
But it could, and should, watch closely the way in which the
produced surplus was divided and used up, and attend to the
interests neglected in the process. Smith, Bentham, Senior
and Mill were all (though with varying degrees of enthusiasm)
in favour of state interference with spontaneous, market-guided
distribution; all of them, at the same time, would most strongly
object to any attempt of the state to interfere with the management of production; the latter could not possibly serve any
useful purpose. The criteria were clearly set by Mill:[4]

Before making the work their own, governments ought
always to consider if there be a rational probability of its
being done on what is called the voluntary principle, and
if so, whether it is likely to be done in a better and more
effectual manner by government agency, than by the zeal

and liberality of individuals.

Government agencies are likely to be more effectual in setting
aside some of the social surplus to cater for collective needs
like education, health, or recreation, which the market, which
operates the production of surplus so well, is not fit to provide
properly.

The immediate consequence of the separation of distribution
from the overall structure of social power was the increase in
the active role of the state: not just in guarding the already
operating rules by force, but in articulating and re-articulating
these rules. Gradually and imperceptibly, the distribution of
surplus was becoming a responsibility of the state. This process had, in its turn, two more unanticipated consequences:
first, it led to a consistent increase in the size and the powers
of the state; second it caused the distributive claims to be
addressed in a constantly growing degree to the state, and
hence the issue of distribution to be politicised.

Throughout virtually the whole of the nineteenth century,
and - somewhat more arguably - through a considerable part
of the twentieth, it was hoped that the sui generis division
of labour between the state and privately operated industry
would be maintained infinitely as sufficient for the solution of
social problems as they might arise: the 'discipline power'
vested with capitalists and only obliquely supported by the
state would take care of the production of surplus, while the
state would attend to its optimal distribution, by the same
token taking the pressure off the powers engaged in the running
of production. This was, however, not to be. Once distribution
was designated the sole area of social contest, once the power
struggle was left alone on the battleground as its sole determinant, the claims which the state was supposed to handle were
bound, sooner or later, to exceed the volume of surplus which
the market-operated production was able to supply.

As the result, the line of demarcation between production
and distribution was bound to be crossed. Much like merchants
who, unable to obtain sufficient quantities of goods for which
they have good outlets, are tempted to step into production to
keep the supply high and steady, so the state, faced with
periodic depressions, successive waves of unemployment,
chronically under-employed industrial potential and cyclically
falling output, and yet obliged to discharge its responsibility
for the welfare of the affected, was not likely to stand aside
for long. Diffuse disciplinary power focused on control over
production and producers proved to be inadequate in coping
with the social forces which it had itself set loose. In this sense
the disciplinary power - the method of securing social order
typical of industrial society - was self-destructive. Once the
state had to interfere with the sphere hoped to remain its
exclusive domain, the issues of domination and subordination
which it seemed to settle and conclusively 'de-topicalise'

became politicised. Distribution of surplus, which the order
buttressed by discipline power left under-regulated as an
epiphenomenon of production which presented only minor
corrective problems, grew gradually into the focus of a social
conflict which could not be coped with without modifying,
curbing or displacing the power structure within production
itself. Among the problems put on the agenda by the maintenance of social order, meeting the claims pressing on the
agencies of distribution was raised to the supreme position
and came to determine the tasks of production. In other words,
consumption replaced production as the arena of power conflict
critical for social order and its dynamics.

This is why industrial society with its characteristic pattern
of power distribution and control could not for long maintain
the fiction of the 'stationary state'. As the outer horizon of
the current problems, it was eventually replaced by the vision
of infinite economic growth. What made this vision so tempting
was the hope that the relentlessly accumulating consumer pressures could be neutralised by the increase in the sheer volume
of goods which growing production would make available. Perhaps in no other place was this idea so artlessly spelled out
as in a statement quoted by W. Arthur Lewis in the book which
could be read as the epitome of the new spirit:[5]

> I sincerely doubt whether the struggle for redistribution
> can be held in check except in the context of a growing
> economy. Labour in particular will insist on a steady
> increase in its material well-being and unless total material
> output is increasing, the full force of this insistence will
> be felt in pressure for redistribution of incomes.

Thus the responsibility of the state for the 'socially correct'
distribution of surplus was slowly transformed, under constantly
growing pressure, into the state responsibility for the production of surplus. Stimulation of economic growth had become
the primary and decisive goal of state policy and the crucial
legitimation of state power.

To make the situation still more complex, however, the
constant growth of industrial production (in addition to many
difficult-to-procure factors) requires a constant growth of
consumer power – if the consumption, that is, is satisfied by
the mediation of the market. The growth of effective market
demand is not correlated with the simple growth of investment,
but with the increment in the steady rate of growth. Consumer
pressure, if it were to be satisfied entirely through the market,
would require an unthinkable expansion of production. According to standard opinion expressed by P. Samuelson, 'even the
richest of such nations, the United States, would have to be
hundreds of times more productive than it now is to give everybody as comfortable a standard of living as is now enjoyed by
our most fortunate few'.[6] The distributive claims tend, there-

fore, to grow faster than the market-effective consumer demand. The excess of distributive ambitions over consumer demand tends to manifest itself in a political struggle, not in economic activity in the market. But this excess is constantly enlarged by the exacerbation of consumer appetite, which for profit-oriented industry is the prime condition of survival (i.e. of realisation of output). Having effectively deprived the great majority of the population of the role of homo faber, the profit-operated industry must do its best to train them in the role of consumers; in practice, this amounts to the continuous chan-nelling of all and any social grievance and disaffection into the demands for a greater share in some or other consumer goods. While barred from turning into a market-effective demand, the so-channelled claims acquire directly a political character, without losing their economic relevance. The resulting paradox is the constant increase of social tension as a consequence of the effort to defuse it.

This is, in essence, the theme of the remaining two chapters.

5 Corporatism and its discontents

'Who now, except a complete imbecile, can still expect a *guaranteed* progress?' asked John Dunn recently.[1] Better than so many elaborate, densely argued analyses, this short, sharp indictment captures the spirit of the end of the century. This century has been remarkable for speeding up the travel of things, images, and ideas, and simultaneously losing its sense of destination. If the last century looked towards the completion of its works as a beginning of an era, this one lives through its last decades as an end to the 'world as we know it', with no new world in sight. It is hard to imagine a more thorough change of mood. Mistrust came to replace confidence, self-deprecation has supplanted the pride of achievement; above all, as carefully documented by J.F. Clark, all change came to be identified with deterioration and decline, while the power of intellect has been denied the credit for the progressive improvement of civilisation.[2]

A hundred years earlier (in 1874-7) a Frenchman, Léon Walras, produced 'the biggest utopian dream of them all',[3] a phenomenological insight into the mechanism of a 'perfectly competitive system'. Contrary to its later interpretation, this was not intended as a description of the reality of capitalist economics: nevertheless, as all successful explorations of a pure, necessary essence of a historically contingent phenomenon, it was an effort to capture the inherent potential, the overwhelming tendencies, the developmental horizons of the economic system which, in fits and starts, was coming of age throughout the nineteenth century. Reality from this perspective appeared as an imperfect, still distorted or immature, rendition of a perfectly equilibrated, self-perpetuating system kept on course by the combination of perfect mobility of resources, perfect flexibility of prices, and perfect accessibility of information. Reality could be measured against this ideal; departures from the ideal were contingent and, in principle, reparable; a real economy tended (and could be assisted in this tendency by properly designed policies) towards the ideal which at the same time constituted its true essence and its constantly present potential.

Walras's view of the capitalist economy (like, with some time-lag, Parsons's view of society of a similar epistemological provenance) was in no way idiosyncratic. It shared in the mood of the time, anticipating a perfect society just round the corner or not much further behind – a society whose healthy

roots are already well-established just below the squalid ground
and soon, with a little help from a caring gardener, will produce vigorous plants. It was the time when Max Weber toyed
with his majestic vision of scientific rationality as the unstoppable tendency and final destination of Western history: when
the best-selling book was Karl Pearson's 'The Grammar of
Science', boldly declaring the imminent end to the extant
mysteries of the world and announcing that in science humanity
had found the best, and the ultimate, weapon in its struggle
for survival. It was a confident generation, relishing the soli-
dity of facts and transparency of the world without enigmas
and transcendental duties, foretasting the certainty science
will bring, averse to eccentricity, ill-disposed to lyricism and
embarrassed by displays of emotions. This generation enjoyed
peace, comfort and wealth comparable to nothing in human
memory. It seemed, indeed, that the elements of nature and
history had been finally tamed. The philosopher's stone of
ever-growing happiness had been found in the human productive activity in its constant expansion.

In economics proper, Walras was in tune with the most powerful
and influential minds of the period: Menger in Austria, Jevons
and Marshall in Britain, Clark and Fisher in the US, Pareto
and Barone in Italy or Wicksell in Sweden. Each in his own
way, sought a 'general theory of equilibrium', and they all
believed that conditions of equilibrium, such as logic and
precise scientific analysis may dictate, are attainable through
the purification of competition as institutionalised in the capitalist market. Their optimism regarding the future came paradoxically from their inability to anticipate its actual course.
Phenomena which were to determine the economic scene of the
twentieth century looked, from the vantage point of the
Walrasian model, like impurities; like problems, perhaps calling
for some concerted action, but not affecting the essential logic
of the market, which always carries the potential of equilibrium
in its innermost core. Like so many ostensibly anticipatory
models, Walrasian vision sought the secrets of the felt satisfaction with the world, the conditions of which had been left
behind already during the life of its generation. The foundation of the balanced economy - perfect competition - was to be
attained when each economic agent is so small that neither
through his demand, nor through his offer can he noticeably
influence the prices of market commodities; when from the
perspective of each economic unit taken apart, prices appear
as 'the hard facts of reality', which - like other phenomena
determined by the laws of nature - one cannot change at will.

In a sense, the Walrasian model suffered from the dearth of
ambition. In a truly nineteenth-century style, it viewed nature
as a set of inviolable rules, which one has to learn to respect,
instead of disregarding; nature as a target of adjustment in
the first place, an object of mastery only in the second. The
specific nature of the market explored by Walras was constructed

of the autonomous decisions taken by individual buyers and
sellers; the possibility of such decisions being deliberately or
wilfully tampered with, or otherwise deprived of their inherent
autonomy, did not count among the assumptions of the model.
But this possibility was real in Walras's time and became actuality shortly after. Once this had happened, the prospects of
prices ever becoming 'natural facts' turned exceedingly remote.
Some economic agents could now view the market as a weakly
defended territory, ripe for conquest, and likely to obey the
laws of the invader. For some economic agents, therefore, other
people were themselves objects of potential manipulation, natural
objects rather than autonomous subjects of decision; they sought
to manipulate these objects' behaviour by shaping and re-shap-
ing the very structure of the market situation, which Walras
and his contemporaries viewed as determined by ruthless laws
of nature. This dramatic change of perspective was not, of
course, a result of deliberate decision or ill will. It was an
obvious corollary of disparities in power, the one factor conspicuously absent among various forms of market assets that
'perfect competition' would tolerate. With this factor in action,
economic agents were bound to lose quickly their alleged
'equality-through-smallness'. Perhaps the perfect market of
Léon Walras could permanently guarantee its own equilibrium.
But such a market was not to be the 'phenomenological essence'
of the twentieth-century economy.

Theoretical lag is not an ailment unique to economic science.
In general, the theory's past successes quickly turn into its
worst enemy. Thomas Kuhn, and the many writers who picked
up and elaborated his seminal idea, have amply documented
the psychological and institutional mechanisms responsible for
the widespread phenomenon of theoretical inertia and the
lasting incapacity for articulating novel experience. In the case
of the 'perfect market' model, some extra ideological factors
perhaps reinforced the usual tendency. Arguably the most
important factor among them was the facility with which the
traditional theory, in its canon established towards the end
of the nineteenth century, had disposed of class and class
conflict as social phenomena. In William Krehm's words, this
theory[4]

> shifted the whole discussion of value from the sphere of
> production, where it had begun to get rough and unman-
> nerly, to the market. Everything - not only the price but
> income distribution - was explained in terms of impersonal
> market forces. Instead of assessing the workers' input by
> how long they worked, their contribution was *defined* by
> what they were paid. Value was simply where supply met
> demand and the market was cleared....In place of classes
> and a social question, economists were left with traders on
> a variety of markets.

This theory, in other words, clinched the long process of
'economisation' of social conflict. It extrapolated the experience of the second half of the nineteenth century and, so to
speak, looked into the liminal forms which the tendency was
hoped to bring about, if unravelling undisturbed: the extension of the 'natural logic', which J.S. Mill established for the
sphere of production, on to the sphere of distribution - and
as the latter accommodated the totality of power conflict between
classes, also on to the task of the perpetuation and constant
updating of the power relations within the society. The theory
can be seen, in retrospect, as a manifestation of the hope
that essential conflicts of the society can be, in principle,
routinised as the free play of prices and wages, and that
once this happens, the pattern of control established within
the sphere of production will be made secure and, moreover,
will continually generate the quantity of commodities sufficient
to render it immune to attacks. Prices and wages would again
and again return to equilibrium, markets would be cleared
and ready to be replenished. In short, the market as the substitute for class conflict would take care of the political stability
and integration of the society as a whole.

The belief that a self-equilibrating market based on a near-
perfect competition bears, or may bear, the burden of social
integration and safeguard stability seems today so bewildering
that most writers doubt whether such a market ever existed
in the past. Moreover, the model does not seem to be a good
framework in which to analyse the working of economic mechanisms as they are; it does not seem possible to consider the
many plagues of economic life as so many contingent departures
from the ideal type.

Doubts as to the self-equilibrating capacity of the market
were never in short supply - indeed not since Adam Smith set
aside a number of vital social needs that the market, in his
view, was unlikely to satisfy by its own logic. The doubts
grew in force with the writings of John Stuart Mill, Alfred
Marshall and Wicksteed; a forceful indictment of the innate
malfunctions of the market emerged from under the pen of
Joseph Schumpeter as early as the beginning of the twentieth
century. Often, however, these doubts merely drew the outer
limits to the dominant optimism. Whatever state economic initiative they prompted or legitimised did not move far beyond the
idea and the practice of corrections. The state initiative was
considered as supplementary to the job performed by the
market; it was not meant to replace, or even confine, the
market competition whose tendency to perfection continued
to be trusted.

It is often assumed that the optimism epitomised by Walras's
phenomenological insight suffered a decisive blow only in the
result of the Great Depression of the 1930s. The shock caused
by an unprecedented and unanticipated collapse of an economy
apparently nearing the height of prosperity achieved overnight

what a century or more of carefully argued warnings and
cautions could not: it made the public discourse respective to
the idea that the natural tendency of the market is not a
perfect competition and solution to all social and political problems, but the very opposite: generation of problems which the
market-based economy is incapable of solving on its own.

The spectacular catastrophe of the Great Depression undoubtedly dramatised the bankruptcy of the dream and hopes of
yore. It can be argued, however, that it did no more than
crush the lid of complacency and inertia which concealed new
pressures and tensions accumulating for a long time, in fact
since the power conflict of the industrial society had been successfully 'economised' and relegated to the sphere of distribution. In the long run, it is these tensions which should take
responsibility for the acute crisis in which the 'perfect market'
idea found itself in the middle of the twentieth century, and
for the subsequent rethinking of economic realities and their
relation to social conflicts and political structures. Ultimately,
it was the ever-increasing pressure on the social surplus
(caused by the very success in translating all the power conflicts into the language of consumer demands) and the evident
inability of the established power patterns to relieve it, that
resulted in what Gardiner C. Means calls a revolution in economic thought, which brought in its wake a revolution in political
practice. Both revolutions came to be associated with the name
of John Maynard Keynes.[5]

> This revolution rejected the principle that under capitalism
> automatic forces would tend to maintain full employment and
> that any significant departure from a prosperous condition
> is only temporary. It rejected the principle that automatic
> forces would tend to bring to each individual an income in
> proportion to his contribution to production, and that
> unemployment is the product of an individual's own laziness
> or moral lack. It rejected the principle that automatic forces
> of supply and demand would tend to maintain a fair balance
> between farm and industrial prices.

ECONOMISATION OF POLITICS

According to Keynes and his followers, even if all the now
rejected ideas were once a fair approximation of reality, they
had to become anachronistic following the fundamental changes
in the structure of capitalist economy. These changes consist,
first and foremost, in the continuous concentration of capital
and the emergence of a new form of enterprise which need no
longer worry about adjustments to the demand it does not
control; it is now able, thanks to its share of the market, to
manipulate the needs of the consumer. In Philip A. Klein's
words:[6]

the normative implications of emergent prices in a system
in which corporate businesses produce whatever they choose
to produce and then persuade consumers (through advertising, appeals to snobbery or class, or whatever) that
this is also what they want, are most assuredly *not* what
they would be in a system in which prices reflected the
efforts of business firms to adapt to the 'sovereign' wishes
of consumers.

Administrative competition and administered prices become the
rule. Indifference of dictated prices to the play of supply and
demand together with their impotence in solving the self-
inflicted problems the economy tends to accumulate, is not,
however, a disease of the otherwise healthy competitive system.
It is, on the contrary, its natural tendency, an outcome of
'normal' development. The rationality which market competition
breeds and rewards matter-of-factly consists in gaining immunity from the vagaries of supply and demand. This is, in fact,
what happened and what continues to happen in the history of
capitalism. In the United States, in 1968, the 100 biggest firms
held a larger share of assets than 200 firms in 1950; while the
200 biggest firms the same year disposed of the volume of
assets as large as that of the 1000 biggest firms in 1950. In
Germany at about the same time 1 per cent of firms produced
40 per cent of the total industrial output. According to
A. Shonfield, 'large industrial concerns in the Federal Republic
are not only able to make most profits and to control the market,
but they also have a sort of guarantee...since the state is
forced to preserve these concerns in the interest of full employment'.[7] In Britain, the share of the 100 largest manufacturing
firms in the net output of manufacturing increased from a mere
15 per cent in 1909 to 45 per cent in 1970.[8]
'The growth of competition finally ends competition' - summarised the experience of economic history for Leopold Kohr,
and he then went on to explain the mechanism of this paradox:[9]

As long as market areas and business units were relatively
small, the scale of fluctuations they could produce was so
limited that no external stabiliser was required. For, as the
various then emerging self-generating theories pointed
out, each phase of the cycle - prosperity, recession, depression, recovery - created automatically the forces leading
to the next phase....Only three of the four phases of the
cycle were now still capable of producing unaided the forces leading to the next: recovery, prosperity, and recession. Depression had become a terminal stage.

Fred Emery had expressed the same observation in more
general terms, presenting the changes in the conditions of
economic activity as a case of system theory. The substance

of his argument is that both the actions by the system on its
environment and the goals and noxiants presented by the
environment for the system depend not only on the inter-
dependencies within the system, but also on the inter-depen-
dencies within the environment - remaining by and large
beyond the systemic control. Some kinds of environment exercise particularly effective determining power, which from the
point of view of the system appears as a blind, unpredictable
force. The 'turbulent' environment is such a kind. Once such
an environment has been set in operation:[10]

> the dynamic properties do not arise just from the interaction
> of particular systems but from processes that are set off in
> the environment itself. The environment ceases to be a
> stable ground on which organisations can play out their
> games and counter-games. With shifts in the ground the
> ground-rules change in unpredictable ways....When insti-
> tutions and organisations are large enough and powerful
> enough, their efforts at producing changes in the environ-
> ment can trigger off social processes of which they have
> no forewarning, in areas they never even thought to con-
> sider and with results they had certainly not calculated
> on....
> It is perhaps not completely idle to speculate on what
> happens if the uncertainty and complexity of a turbulent
> environment is compounded by the prevalence of maladaptive
> responses. Theoretically one would expect something like
> the...randomised environment to emerge where there is no
> longer any hope for a strategy for survival.

The message of both Kohr and Emery is that size has consequences. Beyond a certain critical point the precarious balance
between the system and its environment is thrown into disarray,
their relations become unruly and uncalculable, and rational
responses only exacerbate the chaos. Let us recall that size
was precisely the one variable missing from the world gently
guided by Adam Smith's 'invisible hand'.

In more specific terms, the concentration of capital, in itself
a process determined by the logic of capitalist economy, created
a situation where a contradiction exists, and grows, between
the requirements of the economically rational behaviour and
the conditions of reproduction of the capitalist social order.
In other words, the economy becomes a major source of imbalance of the system as a whole. Instead of supplying the
essential factors of systemic integration (being, in a sense,
its own police and its own ideology), it now generates what
from the systemic point of view can be seen only as disturbances. Left unchecked, the capitalist economy may well make
the perpetuation of the capitalist system impossible. This economy demonstrates on an increased scale its intrinsic propensity to develop generalised disorders, like drastic falls in

employment; and its continuity generates 'local' disorders,
like inability to maintain the production of goods and services
essential for the reproduction of capitalist economy at large.
These two afflictions, further exacerbated by the contracting
environment, made Heilbroner repeat after a growing number
of economists that 'there is no alternative to planning if capitalism is to be kept alive at all.'[11]

In the perspective of the Keynesian economic theory, most
adverse phenomena which trouble the capitalist economy can be
reduced to one major failure; the inability to generate sufficient
demand, i.e. demand large enough to clear the market of the
goods the factories are producing or are able to produce; consequently, to cure, or at least to alleviate, the ailments of the
capitalist economy means, above all, to generate such a demand
by other than the obviously inadequate market mechanisms.
This is how the concerns and intentions of Keynesian theoretical and practical reform are normally articulated. It could
be argued, however, that this articulation reverses the true
order of significance of the factors responsible for the tremendous interest Keynes's suggestions aroused and the impact they
had on the political thought of the time.

It could be argued that the problem which rendered the Keynesian revolution both necessary and inevitable was not so
much the dearth of demand, but, on the contrary, excess of
true demand over the fraction of it which could be made 'market-
effective' under the condition of power structure still dominant
in the field of production. As we noted before, the perpetuation
of this power structure was accomplished by means of 'opening
up' the conflict over distribution, and thereby setting loose
consumer demands and expectations which could not be satisfied without undermining the very power structure, the preservation of which made them necessary in the first place.
Within the framework of this power structure, the distribution
of surplus had to remain permanently overburdened with social
tension which it was unfit to resolve, as social demand could
not be fully translated into economic (i.e. market-effective)
demand. The gap between social and economic demand could
not be absorbed as an economic problem dealt with by the market with its ownership-determined distribution. This gap,
therefore, was bound to remain a political problem; and it was
this gap which became a major factor in the steadily rising
'planning' ambitions of the state.

To what extent the government intervention in economic
affairs which has developed since the 1930s answers the name
of 'planning' is, of course, a contentious matter. It depends on
the degree to which one would be prepared to stretch the
meaning of the term. There is little doubt, however, that the
economic activity of the state has acquired in the last half
century entirely new dimensions which can only be interpreted
as a change in kind.

The first of the many economic functions of the state is at

the same time the most traditional. It consists in providing
general conditions for the continuation of economic process:
a relatively protected market and a framework of 'law and
order', which make for an 'orderly' environment in which
the decision-making process, calculation of profit, etc. are
possible; and in initiating, through the re-allocation of resources, the construction and maintenance of the necessary infrastructure of economy, among which the road network is a classic example. In principle, this function does not significantly
alter the role of the state as envisaged already by Adam Smith;
nor is it necessarily in conflict with the liberal view of a minimal state, tolerated even in the heyday of laissez-faire economy.

Other economic functions of the state most certainly represent
a novelty hard to reconcile with the liberal theory. First, the
state acts as a kind of huge insurance company, underwritten
by the fiscal capacity of the whole population and its total
economic assets, in relation to the giants of economy. We have
already quoted Shonfield's finding about the state-assured
security of large German firms, which further strengthens
their powerful grip over the economy. The situation is not very
different in other countries with great concentration of capital.
In Britain, where by 1969 in each of the twenty industries
surveyed three major firms controlled between them from 50 to
90 per cent of the market, the 'government hastened to bail
out these giant concerns when the world recession and their
own economic policies put their liquidity or production at
risk'.[12] The reason is always the same: exactly because of
the enormous size of the firm in trouble its collapse would have
widely reverberating effects on the rest of the economy and
in the end could seriously undermine the political stability of
the system. When a firm controls a third of the market, its
collapse is not a merely economic problem. This means, however, that the economic health of privately owned units becomes
dependent directly on political measures, to the same extent
as the ability of the body politics to perform its function is
dependent on the performance of an economy it normally does not
control.

State insurance of giant concerns (which increasingly entails
the compensation for the falling rate of profit – the maintenance
by indirect, political means of what the firms are no more capable
of assuring by direct, economic action) is just one aspect of a
much more general function of the state: exercising of the
responsibility for the supply of elementary factors of the
capitalist production. In Offe and Rouge's formulation, 'the
most abstract and inclusive common denominator of state
activities and state intervention in advanced capitalist societies
is to *guard the commodity form of individual economic actors*'.[13]

In other words, the 'insurance' function of the state goes
beyond the explicit Keynesian prescription of running macro-
economic policies which facilitate economic growth. It aims at
nothing less than 'administrative recommodisation' of both

labour and capital; at creating and perpetuating conditions
under which capital and labour can go on behaving as commodities. This task includes the maintenance of the saleability
of labour: the prospective labour force must be supplied with
necessary skills through the state-financed system of education;
it must be provided with the basic facilities required by the
life process conducted in modern densely populated cities;
it must be enabled to secure accommodation in the areas where
capital is seeking labour; it must be also kept in reasonably
good health. The task also includes the state sponsorship of
economic initiatives aimed at increasing capital's competitive
power; assisting the firms, particularly the large ones, in
getting round the awkward corners of economic recession or a
successive technological upheaval; developing retarded regions
to prepare them for capital investment, etc.

The next item for the insurance policy is the social risks
arising from the inability of individual firms to protect security
of jobs, not to mention life security. The state responsibility
for so-called 'social rights' amounts to the socialisation of risks;
individual firms are, so to speak, absolved from worry about
the social consequences of their decisions. They do not have
to feel responsible for the plight of the aged, the ill, or the
unemployed. They never did, since the collapse of paternalism,
but until recently they have not needed to fear pressure to
take such a responsibility upon themselves. With labour well
organised and powerful, avoidance of responsibility is no
longer conceivable. And so the state comes to the rescue. The
firms may go on 'rationalising' their production and tending to
the high level of profits without being troubled by the fate of
the work-force thrown out of work as a result. The potentially
inflammatory problems are defused thanks to the protective
institutions run and financed by the state. The costs of social,
ecological and all other 'externalities' generated by individual
firms are spread by the state over the entire community. In this
indirect way business profits acquire a wider, and more secure
basis than labour directly employed by a firm, considered as
a self-contained economic unit.

It is the biggest firms which most naturally and most palpably
benefit from this 'socialisation of risks'. In Robert Lekachman's
terse summary, 'by and large government largesse further
enriches the wealthy and enlarges the power of the already
powerful'.[14] The costs of economic rationalisation grow exponen-
tially with the increase in the size of the unit: soon they
become so devastating that without government-administered
redistribution they would not be absorbed by the national
economy – much less still by the socio-political system. In a
sense, the state activity insures the big firms against the
unwelcome consequences of their bigness. It secures the conditions for further concentration of the capital by maintaining
the equilibrium of the system, which otherwise would be unable
to survive the political and social pressures.

As the big firms need an economically active state most, and as their action, because of its sheer scale, has a dimension which renders political administration an indispensable complement of the business cycle - it may seem that the many agencies of the twentieth-century state and their unprecedented penetration of the previously autonomous economic and socio-cultural sub-systems defend and serve the interests of big capital. On the other hand, however, big business is the reality of modern industrial society. There is no other economic organisation of the reproduction of society except the one based on immense concerns which dominate output, employment and distribution. By cushioning the most vulnerable groups and areas of social life against potentially devastating side-effects of large-scale business, and by turning out in mass quantities the properly 'commoditised' labour such as business needs, the economically active state defends and serves not a particular class, or a particular section of a class, but the capitalist society as a whole - in the form which historically emerged as the outcome of the capital-concentration process.

The ill-famed and much vilified adage of Charles Wilson - 'what is good for General Motors is good for the United States' - is not just an act of arrogance or the love of a paradox. It reflects the reality of the highly industrialised capitalist society as confirmed by the horizon of its fundamental political institutions and the political culture they support. 'Enlarging the power of the already powerful' is the only option these institutions can pursue, the only 'realistic' way in which they can perform their global societal function of perpetuating the conditions of societal reproduction. There is no contradiction, in this sense, between the preference given to big organisations and the assertion of Offe and Rouge that

> the state does not patronise certain interests, and is not allied with certain classes. Rather, what the state protects and sanctions is a set of *rules* and *social relationships* which are presupposed by the class rule of the capitalist class. The state does not defend the interests of one class, but the *common* interests of all members of a *capitalist class society*.

If, as said before, the chief concern of this state is to guard the commodity form of individual economic actors 'this, again, does not directly mean the general interests of a particular class, but guarding the general interests of all classes on the basis of a capitalist exchange relationship'.[15] By identifying the defence of the 'general interest of all classes' with the perpetuation of a system dominated by big organisations, and by securing this perpetuation through the means of political administration, in the space between the polity and the remaining sub-systems contradictions are generated which render the task in practice self-defeating. But this is a different matter, to which we will later return.

CORPORATISM, OR SIMULATED POLITICS

The last decade brought a spate of writings aimed at the re-
adjustment of the theory of state to the new knowledge of big
business dominance, and at a synthesis of scattered intuitions
regarding the related transformations of the political process.
The numerous publications following the programmatic state-
ments by Ray Pahl and Jack Winkler, Philippe Schmitter and
Gerhard Lehmbruch, quickly supplemented and elaborated by
Bob Jessop, Colin Crouch and Leo Panich (to name only the
most popular readings among many), contributed in their
various ways to a rather fundamental revision of the pluralist
model of the state; a model which conceived of the political
process as, essentially, a competition between group interests
within society, represented on the legislative level (through
the mutually complementary, but simultaneously dissonant,
processes of articulation and aggregation) by political parties,
and promoted on the executive level by various interest groups
organised for the exercise of pressure. To this model, recent
writers prefer the theoretical framework of the 'corporatist
state'.

The reader interested in the detailed argument, and controversy between the proponents of the corporatist theory, will
find the updated information in 'Trends Towards Corporatist
Intermediation', edited by Schmitter and Lehmbruch (Sage,
1979), and in the lucidly written, comprehensive 'Pluralism
and Corporatism' by Reginald J. Harrison (Allen & Unwin,
London 1980). We will confine our discussion to conveying the
gist of the corporatist idea, while omitting the fine distinction
between the many yet unsynthesised variants of the theory.
And the 'hard core' of the corporatist hypothesis is that the
modern state is best understood not in terms of the representation of diffusely articulated interests (as the traditional liberal
theory of the state would wish), but as a network of consultation, bargaining and compromise between functional 'simulators'
- leaderships of big and powerful organisations each standing
for one of the constituents separated within the functional
division of the system. What used to be 'interest groups' -
extra-constitutional, politically unrecognised crystallisations
of collective concerns with varying degrees of continuity and
organisation - have spawned permanent, institutionalised
spokesmen, regularly called for consultation and accorded the
right to validate, by consent, the decisions of the state. These
former interest groups, or rather the products of their condensation into the institutionalised leadership 'simulating' the
interests of theoretically represented groups, have now become
in more than one sense extensions of the state.

The other side of the same process is that the traditional

functions of parliament - enactment of laws, the control of
taxation and public expenditure, and scrutiny of government
coupled with redress of grievances, have all become much
more difficult to perform. In Bob Jessop's view, parliamentary
power 'in all the domains has declined substantially'.[16] The
permanent functional sub-division institutionalised in the corporatist framework acquires growing immunity against volatile
and contingent aggregations of diffuse interests embodied in
the vicissitudes of inter-party rivalry. Again, the ascendancy
of the corporatist network is to a great extent the function of
the size of the organisations entailed. Almost by definition,
the network includes only functional divisions comprehensive
and powerful enough to be commensurate with the global scale
of issues determined by the economic dominance of big business.

A considerable controversy persists as to what extent the
modern states in general, the British state in particular, are
approximating the model of the 'corporatist state'. A conclusive
decision on the matter is not made easy by the vagaries of
party political fortunes and apparent reversals of trends. As
the whole phenomenon is of a relatively recent origin, vacil-
lations - minor in a longer historical perspective - may well
confound the perception of trends when seen at a close
distance. An agreement is difficult to reach also because of
the fact that the corporate bias, as Middlemas points out, 'never
acquired the patina of legitimacy which hallowed the nineteenth-
century parliamentary constitution....It existed in the twilight,
the dark side of the double standard of political morality known
to consenting participants but publicly deprecated if not actually denied.'[17] Corporatism never was, and is unlikely ever to
become, a dominant political Utopia of a society after the pattern of the liberal vision of representation. It has, therefore,
no intrinsic power to impose itself upon the popular perception
of social realities and mould the self-awareness, or the self-
deception, of the political process. The socially constituted
view of reality is, for this reason, likely to resist a corporatist
treatment. And yet among scholars a wide consensus is emerging that even if one should beware of prematurely announcing
the arrival of the fully-fledged corporatist state, or at least
deciding that such an arrival is a foregone conclusion, one is
fully justified in speaking of a 'corporatist tendency' - a
tendency, in Middlemas's words, 'always to run to one side'.
There are powerful forces within modern society which lie
behind this tendency and make it likely to persist.

For the central topic of this book, some consequences of the
corporatist tendency are of particular importance.

First of all, the corporatist tendency is - in one of its many
senses - a further reinforcement of the economisation of social
conflict; more precisely, of the accommodation of social conflict within the confines of distribution. The corporatist tendency is an ultimate embodiment of politics organised as an
authoritative allocation of scarce resources against which

contradictory demands are made. The corporatist tendency
entails the deployment of the state in the service of economisation of conflict; the state with a corporatist bias is an instrument of translation of social antagonism into the vocabulary of
distributive policy, and simultaneously the institutional basis
of the legitimacy of such a translation. In a more outspoken
way than ever before, political issues are now articulated as
the arbitration between irreconcilable claims on the shared
basis of the law and order, i.e. the preservation of the extant
structure of power and control.

Perhaps the most immediate consequence is the partial defusion of class conflict in the form institutionalised towards the
close of the nineteenth century. The one organisation historically developed as the functional representation of labour tends
to become, together with other constituents of the corporatist
framework, an extension of the state, with the leadership
caught in a double bind between counter-pressures of the
membership, which it continues to represent functionally, and
the 'global interests', for the articulation of which it bears
a partial responsibility. To quote Middlemas again, 'corporate
bias is better put as a system which encourages the development of corporate structures to the point at which their power,
divergent aims, and class characteristics can be harmonised,
even if that harmony involves a partial loss of class distinction,
individuality and internal coherence'.[18] A similar point has
been recently made by Richard Scase with yet more bluntness:
the state 'is an "uneasy compromise" of class interests, in
which some of the aspirations of the dominated classes become,
at least partially, incorporated'.[19] Consultations carried inside
the corporatist network simulate a public debate between classes and other class-like organised interests. Simulation is
based on the effort to hypothesise the likely assessment of
alternative measures by classes and groups as they calculate
the balance of their respective benefits and losses. Hypotheses
of this sort have not much to go by except the memory of
similar calculations in the past; they tend, therefore, to stabi-
lise and perpetuate the historically shaped definitions of group
interests. Above all, they tend to trim such definitions to the
extent required by the framework of consultation and bargaining. Both the ineradicable conservative bias of simulation and
the trimming draw a limit to the effective accommodation of
interests in the output of consultation. Within this limit, however, the functional groups admitted to the network can go a
long way towards preventive action, staving off the possibility
of direct confrontation of interests. Though institutionalised
consultation of the corporatist type has been historically, at
least in part, an outcome of the rising 'confrontation power'
of the dominated classes and, particularly, of the conspicuous
practical manifestations of this power, the personal participants
of the corporatist network come to see the absence of open confrontation as both the measure of their efficiency and the

condition of the continuing effectiveness of their action. This kind of 'institutional bias' turns into an important factor in its own right for the elimination of antagonistic interests from the rhetoric of public debate.

This rhetoric, instead, draws on the vocabulary of 'scientific politics'. What is, in fact, a contention between simulated, but still assumed to be diverse, interests - is wrapped in the vocabulary of objective laws and optimal policies, and represented as following the pragmatics of truth-searching. The very notion of 'political representation' has undergone a subtle, but fateful change. It is now interpreted as the pursuit of beneficial results of particular policies as anticipated by the experts, while its old measure, the constitutionally expressed will of the given group or of the nation in its majority, is reduced, at best, to the 'popular mandate' for a particular team to stand at the helm of the ship navigated with the help of the blandly non-partisan, disinterested compass. When the strategy of the struggle for consensual ends (a continuous and possibly high economic growth being the key one among them, in terms of which any short-term objective must be justified) has been placed in the safe hands of the experts, the 'big issues' are kept away from the public debate. Political contention is confined to the simulation games within a corporatist network, properly truncated to fit the consensual frame. The by-product of the process is a growing 'privatisation of the public sphere', coupled, according to Jürgen Habermas, with the 'publicisation of the private domain'. The latter means that essential elements of survival and welfare slip away from the control of the individual, as they become increasingly dependent on the public supply of the means of collective consumption and social wages, the public fight against, and prevention of, disutilities, publicly initiated stimulation or retardation of investment, employment, etc. But the 'public sphere', inside which all these decisions or non-decisions, affecting the individual living by definition, belong is not constituted by a genuine public debate. The public debate, true to its name, i.e. a debate of issues dividing the interested parties, is merely simulated - and in its most decisive parts hidden from public view. An effort is made to prevent an active involvement of the public by the bid for an adequate representation of its interests by the leadership of the functional organisations. Hence the 'privatisation' of the public sphere: whatever remains of the public scrutiny of the activities of public personalities, is concerned with their personal qualities and private relations more than with the substantive issue of the representation of interests. Political struggle is presented and viewed as a series of private fights and squabbles, the public attention is focused on dramatic gestures and personal invectives, loyalties and 'defections', rather than the arguments advanced. First and foremost, however, rules of evaluation proper for small-scale, intimate relationships are extended over the personalities of the public stage;

they are judged in moral and characterological terms (sincerity,
personal honesty, consistency, steadfastness, overall likeability)
rather than in terms of the policies they stand for. All these
tendencies are pushed to the extreme by the popular media.
It is particularly the tabloid press which excels in drawing the
concept and the standard of 'publicness' back to the pre-
modern times, when it meant inviting of a selected audience to
witness private functions of the rulers. Trivialisation of public
debate, a makeshift ethicality and personalisation of the public
presentation of political struggle, seem to be closely correlated,
as a tendency, with the ostensible drive towards the 'objective',
scientifically based politics.

The personification and objectification of politics are, in fact,
as Alan Wolfe pointed out several years ago (in 'The Limits
of Legitimacy', Free Press, New York 1977), closely associated
with each other. Both phenomena are associated with the
bureaucratisation of conflict in its economised form, and a tendency to divorce the distributive allocation from public debate
and, above all, collective action. To be successful, the emancipation of conflict-solution from public involvement and control
would require what Wolfe called a 'depolitical socialisation' (or,
in Habermas's terminology, an extreme 'familial privatisation').
Its success - if at all conceivable - would be, however, a mixed
blessing. On the one hand, the mechanism of conflict-resolution
may in time lose much of its relevance to the actual tensions it
was meant to unload. On the other hand, a thorough bureaucratisation of distributive decisions would leave social conflicts
without a legitimate channel of expression, with a constant
challenge to the 'law and order' as an inevitable result.

As the carrying capacity of a bridge is equal to that of its
weakest pillar, so the ability of the corporatist network to
initiate change is that of its most reluctant and conservative
member. Two reasons are responsible for the inherent conservatism of the discussed systemic tendency. The first has
been already mentioned: the natural inclination to follow past
experience in simulating interests and will deprived of the
opportunity of discursive self-constitution. This inclination
naturally favours familiar solutions and tried methods; any
innovation drags the system into an unexplored territory, with
the tools for charting it missing. Another reason is the thoroughly informal, extra-constitutional character of the corporatist arrangement. Because of this character, clear-cut rules
of procedure such as an objectified definition of the point when a
decision is interpreted as attained and binding are exceedingly
difficult to articulate, much more so to apply with consistency.
In the absence of 'objective' criteria to invoke, an ill-definable
general consensus is the only rule of thumb which can guide
the on-going process of negotiation. The principle of consensus
means in practice the right of veto; this again favours the
partner least inclined to depart from the well-trodden track of
past precedents. The joint result is the situation well portrayed

by Middlemas: 'Backward-looking in its aims, gradual in method, revisionistic in theory, the new system accommodated itself to change by moving at the least speed commensurate with the interests of each governing institution.'[20]

Such an open-ended, under-determined, no-rules situation we have encountered before: it had been created, in the area of wage bargaining, inside capitalist factories as an inevitable correlate (and a counterweight) of the removal of the power hierarchy in production from the agenda of contest. The quasi-corporatist state elevates this situation to the national and political level; now the state - its force of coercion and its political legitimation - undersigns the power framework in which the surplus is produced, and the state becomes, accordingly, an arena for the open struggle for the distribution of surplus. It took the London 'Junta' of 1851, and then several long decades of trade union resilience and dogged determination, to institutionalise and 'normalise' the power game of distribution. On its new, 'nationalised', level, the game remains at the moment in a relatively early stage, when not just the division of prizes, but the rules and, indeed, the legitimacy of the game itself are at stake. Hence the erratic, seemingly inconclusive development of the corporatist bias. What in retrospect looks like an unstoppable historical tendency of capital-labour relations on the factory level, from the too short perspective of the brief history of the 'nationalisation' of conflict may well seem a once-in-a-lifetime episode, if not an aberration, much like trade unions looked to the writers of 'Blackwood's Magazine' in the 1830s. The history of the quasi-corporatist state has been to date, and is likely to remain for some time yet, punctuated by withdrawals of partnership by one side or another and, above all, by the attempts to deny permanently the partnership status to the weaker side. This factor additionally detracts from the, however meagre, potential of the corporatist 'simulated debate' to establish its authority and render its agreement binding.

This latter point is the Achilles heel of corporatism for another reason: the 'nationalisation' of distributive struggle means an enormous lengthening of distance between the represented interests and their active representation. Hence another troublesome problem bound to haunt a corporatist state however well established: that of a continuous dialogue and renewed agreement between the leaders acting on behalf of the functional divisions and the groups they theoretically represent. True representation, based on a discursive articulation of generalised group interests reached with an active participation of all concerned, would be jarringly at odds with the pragmatics of simulated debate and, indeed, with the consensual principles embodied in the corporatist tendency. Without such a discursive articulation of interests, however, there is a real danger of a widening gap between the organisational interpretations of interests and the will of the group which

theoretically legitimises the organisation's authority. There is
nothing in the corporatist agreement to guarantee a smooth
accommodation of the changing mass opinion; even if the stands
taken by the partners were not confined by the abovementioned
'double bind' and not subject to often contradictory loyalties,
they would still be forced, in the absence of true public discourse, to rely on potentially deceptive intuitions and 'gut
feelings'. As the fiction of representation remains a crucial
factor in the relative stand within the corporatist network,
efforts must be made to make the intuitions 'stick'. This can
be achieved either by a random test of mass opinion and the
current distribution of preferences and/or limits of endur-
ability, or - preferably - by an active management of opinion.
The latter measure requires, however, for its success, an
institutional guarantee of the continuous commonality of language between the representatives and the represented - and
this also, particularly in the long run, can come under stress.
If the stress becomes unmanageable, only a forceful re-
assertion of the legitimising rights by the ostensibly represented will restore the balance on a new level; in so far as no
opinion-management methods thus far available are potent
enough to withstand the inroads against the established notions
of interests, an occasional confrontation between leaders and
the rank-and-file seems to remain an indispensable complement
of the corporatist arrangement. In most cases, confrontations
play an essentially positive, integrating role; however violent
and unruly this form of bargaining-through-withdrawal-of-
assent may seem, it often leads merely to the uplifting of consensus to a higher, more secure because updated, level. There
is no institutional guarantee, however, that the endemic confrontations will continue to support the functioning of the
corporatist network. It should be noted that massive action
has never been mobilised so far in defence of the corporatist
mechanism as such (as the TUC leaders learned the hard way
through the abominable failure of their 'Day of Action' called
to support the network of consultation rather than the results
it was supposed to show), while a mass action challenging the
corporatist agreements may well push the events beyond the
boundary of what may still be re-negotiated and in the end
accommodated.

However important the malfunctions of the corporatist tendency so far listed may seem, they all look relatively insignificant in comparison with the powerful delayed-action bomb
deposited in the very heart of corporatism. The corporatist
network may be interpreted as the most extreme development
of the universal (in Frank Parkin's view) tendency of all
privileged groups to 'closure by exclusion'. The deepest roots
of the corporatist tendency lie in all probability in the re-
arrangement of heretofore major antagonistic forces of industrialised societies; in the fact, that (in Norbert Elias's words)
'the representatives of the industrial bourgeoisie and the

established industrial working class now form the primary elite
in the nations'.[21] The more intimate connection of the well-
entrenched forces of society with state power has further
reduced the influence of such forces as have failed to pass the
test set for the members of the corporatist network, and
diminished their chance of passing such a test in the future.
The wind of social protest blowing from the weak and disprivileged quarters could be captured in the sails of one or the
other of the great class forces publicly engaged in the battle
for political supremacy. With these forces coming to an arrangement, actively engaged in the search for a mutually convenient
consensus, and substituting a simulated debate for an open
political discourse, the winds of grievance may well seek a
passing sail in vain. A simulated debate is by definition an
exclusive affair; attendance is by invitation only. The chasm
between the guests and those remaining outside is accordingly
deeper than ever before. The powerless become at best an
object of political action – they are denied the status of the
subject with institutionalised means of expression. A prudent
state would not allow the deprivation to sink too deep, or the
size of the deprived category to grow too large; it would, as
a rule, attempt to alleviate the plight of the destitute under
the pressure of their only hypothesised rebellion; the simulated debate also ponders the anticipated responses of such
groups as the theoretical limits to the freedom of decision. As,
however, no participant of the corporatist network has the
destitute group as its permanent constituency, the likelihood
of an open, violent confrontation between the group in question
and the state authority is high. Unlike in the previously discussed leadership-membership case, such a confrontation is not
confined to a sporadic correction of state policies gone astray,
or an occasional sobering of the politicians who have lost the
feeling of the rank-and-file mood. It is, in principle, just a
more visible, because dramatised, manifestation of a permanent
conflict and a continuously seething antagonism, both lasting
at least until the group in question is given institutionalised
representation within the corporatist framework. The latter is,
on the whole, a function of the degree of self-articulation and
the manifested 'breaking power' of the deprived group. One
wonders, however, whether the corporatist tendency, however
radical, will ever lead to the incorporation of all potentially
rebellious groups and categories. Whether, in other words, such
a viability as the corporatist arrangement may possess does
not derive precisely from the limited extent of incorporation;
from the comfort and benefit the members of the network gain
thanks to the fortification of their relatively privileged position
against the importunities of the excluded. If corporatism is about
replenishing the authority of the power structure through the
expedient of distributive consensus, this consensus, in its
turn, rests in a not inconsiderable measure on what Andrew
Tylecote in his recent thought-provoking study 'The Causes of

Corporatism and its discontents

Present Inflation' (Macmillan, London, 1981) called the phenomenon of 'boosted escalator': the experience, by the established and unionised part of the labour force (for instance, white or male) of a relative progress in their share of available goods because of the influx of weakly unionised, under-represented and hence downtrodden outsiders. The soft stance, which renders the consensus plausible, is less likely to survive for long the disappearance of such an experience.

THE ULTIMATE LIMITS OF ECONOMISED POLITICS

So far we have discussed internal, structural contradictions of the corporatist tendency. They are related to our topic in so far as the corporatist arrangement is the institutional form in which the evolving relationship between economy and polity has manifested itself to date. It is, of course, debatable whether the state, summoned to help the ailing capitalist economy, must spawn the corporatist tendency; whether the marriage of convenience can, theoretically at least, take other forms as well. The many weaknesses of the corporatist arrangement, some of which have been listed above, do provide a stimulus for some to search feverishly for a safe way to divorce; explorations of this kind will most certainly be periodically undertaken, each time inspiring premature pronouncement of the 'end to the era' or a 'reversal of trend'. It is necessary, however, to consider that some most strongly felt failings of the corporatist network do not arise from internal reasons, from the precariousness of its structural provisions. They are related directly to the very contradictions which triggered off the corporatist tendency and which the institutions born of this tendency failed to eliminate or even rectify. These are substantive, not formal issues. They derive from the ends against which the performance of the corporatist network (as indicated by its policy output) is measured and evaluated. It may well be that the demonstrable lack of progress in approximating these ends has little to do with the corporatist bias of the state; that the ends themselves are self-contradictory and no institutional structure can be devised which will render them realistic.

Let us recall that the 'economic management' state gradually developed as a response to the failure of the capitalist economy to reproduce the conditions of its own existence and to cure the social ills which it had itself incurred. If such a state is viewed as a salvaging operation aimed at the survival of the capitalist society, its tasks must be defined, accordingly, as mobilisation of resources to meet the costs of keeping both capital and labour in their commodity form fit for a capitalist system, and to finance the transfer payments hoped to ward off the threat of major social and political disturbances. Both tasks are the logical continuation and development of the

general tendency of industrial society: to secure the permanence of the pattern of control which serves as the framework
for the production of surplus, at the expense of the 'economisation' of power conflict, and hence at a constantly increasing
cost of growing distributive claims. This tendency being in
the long run self-defeating, the corporatist tendency is hardly
to blame for the lack of success in their implementation.

The resources which the state has to mobilise in order to
perform its tasks are indeed enormous. Perhaps the most costly
of new political responsibilities in the economic field is the
reduction of risks threatening the increasingly vulnerable
economic units in the age of huge markets, volumes of output
and fixed capital investments. Liabilities are too immense to be
dealt with by individual firms; and yet the firms are big enough
to set off an earthquake when falling. James O'Connor spelled
out clearly the resulting contradiction:[22]

> there is the assumption of government rather than the
> individual risk associated with the operation of the eco-
> nomy. The state under-writes business losses sustained
> during economic crises and arising from the anarchy of
> capitalist production. Direct lending, indirect lending
> via intermediaries, and loan insurance and guarantees
> socialise business risks and create huge government lia-
> bilities that can be guaranteed only by further private
> capital accumulation of growth - and hence more loans,
> subsidies, and guarantees. State capitalism is no tempor-
> ary phenomenon that will be dismantled once capitalism
> finds its way back to 'normalcy', but rather is the inte-
> grating principle of the modern economic era.

The growth of a capitalist economy requires intense financing
by the state, but the latter cannot be done without a further
growth of the capitalist economy; the interdependence acquires
its own dynamic momentum and becomes self-aggravating. The
capitalist economy and the state rotate around a common axis
with economic growth as the fly-wheel. The distinctive prospect
of this wheel not running forever sets the limit to the new
political solution to the old problem of economic vulnerability.
It may well happen that the only effect of the new solution will be
to bring forward the moment when the energy and resources
are used up and the fly-wheel is grinding to a halt.

Other immense liabilities of the state, as we have already
seen, arise from the necessity to finance education, which in
addition to the production of skilled and hence saleable labour,
serves the capitalist system by inculcating consumer drives
and predispositions, and reproducing the social status of
middle-class children; from defraying the social costs of private
production, which may be of a most diverse kind ranging from
the fight against industry-born pollution up to the prevention
of urban decay or the provision of means for the delivery of

labour to its work-place. All these expenses are topped up
by the constantly growing costs (to employ Talcott Parsons's
glib phrases) of 'pattern maintenance' and 'tension-management'
functions (put in a simpler way, welfare and police), deemed
indispensable for the continuous and orderly environment of
economic activity.

The new role of the state as a most powerful financial broker,
called upon to solve the problems generated by the capitalist
market, has become a source of new problems. The most obvious
of them, called by James O'Connor 'the fiscal crisis of the state',
derives from the natural and widespread dislike of taxes, which
the state is obliged to impose in order to support its wide-
ranging responsibilities. Taxes ostensibly add to the costs of
the selfsame private firms whose interests the state which
collects them is supposed to guard. In fact, the burden of
taxes is spread wider. Big concerns have a way of passing on
the added costs to the consumer. To the extent to which they
dominate the market, they are free to adjust the prices to a
new level set by the increased taxation (the recent rise of pet-
rol pump prices simultaneously with an 'oil glut' being a classic
example). Given the substance of the social functions financed
from the taxes, big concerns pass on to the consumer the
costs of defusing the same social problems which they generate
and which present a threat to, above all, their own survival.
Via the 'administered prices', big firms are able to shrug off
the cost of unemployment which they perpetrate, of the provision of basic shelter which they fail to supply, and of all
other public goods, for which - as Galbraith has demonstrated
- a price mechanism is missing for supply and demand to seek
a mutual equilibrium. Taxes become a major source of continuing inflation of prices; and through the inflation, a 'concealed
tax exploitation' of consumers takes place. By helping to shift
the source of profit to the producer-consumer relations, the
state assists the capital in the defusing of its conflict with its own
employees; the latter are now exploited in their role of consumers rather than producers.

As consumers, however, they are in an endemically ambiguous
situation. On the one hand, they are interested in paying less
direct or indirect taxes, either in the form of wage-deductions
or in the form of higher prices entailing the element of company
taxation. On the other hand, however, they are the beneficiaries of the many tax-supported public services, which play a considerable role in maintaining their standard of living. And the
experience (which tends to be repeated as soon as it is forgotten) shows that whenever taxes are reduced, it is the rich
who have their taxes cut while the less fortunate have cuts
in their services. Once the power conflict has been shifted to
the area of consumption, the 'rational interests' of parties
involved (indeed the parties themselves) are difficult to define.
There is no longer a clear-cut strategy for their defence. Whenever they attempt to defend one aspect of their interest, the

consumers lose on the other front. They have the choice of
the channels through which their share of the national product
is pumped away to finance state expenditure; but hardly more
than that.

Hence the recurrent 'tax revolts', which, as O'Connor realised well before the working-class enthusiasm for the Tory
'cut the taxes' clarion call, and well before the popular cele-
bration of the slaughter of state services in California, are
'not presently organised along class lines'.[23] Apart from bringing together strange bedfellows, tax revolts indicate political
limits to the strategy of saving the capitalist system through
the redistributive activity of the state. They are a reminder
that the means are permanently in conflict with the end; that
the system to be cured militates against the medicine. They
show, in other words, that the traditional contradictions of
capitalism have not been eradicated or transcended, but
merely shifted into a new sphere. It is now the administrative
responsibility of the state to avert crises and other disturbances of growth. It is now the conflicts arising in the course
of the exercising of this functional responsibility which should
have provided foci for the crystallisation of major antagonistic
classes, but which in fact create the curious, unprecedented
landscape, 'no longer dominated by classes acting as person-
ages', a shifting mosaic of class-like relations without classes.[24]
Contradictions arising within the administrative system produce
less sharply divided groups and less clearly defined issues;
it may seem therefore that the intensity of inner-systemic
tension is now mitigated, and integration accordingly strengthened. In fact, the very equivocality of possible articulations
of problems, and of the identities of their potential standard-
bearers, render the chronic 'rationality crisis' (Habermas)
exceedingly difficult to handle. The transformation which it
was hoped would restore the environmental certainty of the
small enterprise and the nature-like market era has brought up
a situation of acute ambiguity. According to Jurgen Habermas's
analysis,[25]

> (i)n the administrative system, contradictions are expres-
> sed in irrational decisions and in the social consequences
> of administrative failure, that is, in disorganisation of areas
> of life. Bankruptcy and unemployment mark unambiguously
> recognizable thresholds of risk for the non-fulfilment of
> functions. The disorganisation of areas of life moves, in
> contrast, along a continuum. And it is difficult to say
> where the thresholds of tolerance lie and to what extent
> the perception of what is still tolerated - and of what is
> already experienced as intolerable - can be adapted to an
> increasingly disorganised environment.

The point at which the dislike of taxation, constantly bred
by the persistent market pressures, recedes before the dislike

of disorganisation, which threatens further existence of the
system complete with the market and its pressures, is not
clearly fixed. This leaves considerable freedom to the simulated
debate, allowing a dangerous accumulation of irrationality.
There is no inbuilt safeguard against the volume of accumulated
irrationality passing the threshold of unmanageability. Fluctuations of income have an immediate effect on living standards
and are therefore psychologically well-defined and visible.
Deterioration of various environmental aspects of the life
process (less frequently repaired roads, less frequent transport services, larger school-classes, long queues at the out-
patient clinics) progresses in small, often imperceptible and
seemingly insignificant steps; it is noticed only in retrospect,
but even then not too easily, as the very gradualness of
change favours psychological accommodation and blunts the
sensitivity to change. The resulting bias in favour of the
more immediate and more distinctly felt benefits makes it all
the more difficult for the state to deliver the volume of public
services necessary for the reproduction of the public consent
and loyalty.

In a consumer society, propertyless, hired labour cannot
be seen any more as rallying steadfastly on the side of 'social
rights' and the state cannot be seen as digging into private
pockets in order to provide them. In spite of the fact that
labour's standard of life is more than at any time dependent
on factors administered and financed by the state, the choice
between 'cheap government' and an active, taxing and redistri-
buting state is not presently an indicator of the great class
divide. Workers' interests and rational responses to them are
inherently ambiguous. Equally so are the interests and attitudes of other traditional classes.

Much has been written about the changed structure of the
middle class. A hundred years ago, the bulk of the middle
class consisted of self-employed individuals and their families,
some of them using their capital to employ other people, some
selling their own services; a member of the middle class, typically, was 'in business' and 'his own master', and for this reason
inclined to praise the virtues of individualism and resent the
sprawling state both for its innate collectivism and its costs.
The self-employed, the entrepreneurs, the businessmen are
still a considerable part of the middle-class; for many, including themselves, they may well remain the pace-setters of
middle-class political dynamism. They are not, however, 'the
bulk'. And they are not socially self-sufficient; they cannot
reasonably hope to reproduce their social standing in the next
generation in the form they enjoyed. For this reproduction they
are dependent on the thousands of prestigious and highly paid
jobs offered by the civil service and its numerous novel extensions. Employment by the state or by one of the institutions
it supports and indirectly administers, is now an integral part
of the middle-class mode of life. If it is not the source of

status and income for a given number of the middle class, it
will be, in all probability, for his close relatives, and above all
his sons and daughters. Both branches of the new middle class
come from the same social pool. They attend the same schools.
They belong to the same clubs. They read the same papers
and journals. They share cultural preferences and mode of
life. They are, sociologically speaking, one category; this does
not mean that they are identical; but one can safely assume
that the variations across the branches are not greater than
the difference between the individuals belonging personally
to the same branch.

Because of this new composition of the middle class one would
expect an ambiguity no less confusing than the one found in
the working class. The 'public sector' is, indeed, a heavy
financial burden. But it is also the source of status and income,
and the institutional basis for their transmission to the next
generation. The larger it is, the more cumbersome becomes the
fiscal pressure, but the wider are career opportunities, and
the more secure is middle-class status. The middle class cannot
be seen, therefore, as unequivocally set against further expansion of the state and its various ramifications. From this perspective as well, the attitude to the expanding state ceases to
be an indicator of class conflict. One would expect instead the
middle-class attitude to oscillate between the traditional suspicion of a voracious and omnipotent government and the pressure for 'more room at the top' in the numerous state-supported
hierarchies of power and prestige.

If one could abstract from the interest in the public sector as
an institutional basis of the stable and secure status, the
middle-class attitude to the state would still remain ambiguous.
This applies even to the traditional core of middle-class members with personal stakes in private enterprises, i.e. to the
modern equivalents of the nineteenth-century ideal-type
capitalists. They need the state for their survival as capitalists
– in many more ways are they dependent on the state than their
predecessors a century ago. The state is not only the safeguard
of law and order, but the agent able to provide (or failing to
provide) an orderly, manageable environment for economic
activity, to guard the regular supply of capital and labour,
and to stretch a safety net mitigating the impact of business
risks and miscalculations. On the other hand, the state can do
all this only on the condition of constraining the very autonomy
of the private enterprise which its economic initiatives are
expected to boost. One would anticipate this highly contradictory relationship to prompt an appropriately ambiguous attitude,
best expressed as one of love-hate. In practical terms, the
paradox begets rather jittery, inconsistent political pressures
which further exacerbate the rationality crisis of the administration torn between contradictory and incompatible demands.[26]

The outcome is portrayed in dramatic terms by Habermas:[26]

On the one hand, the state is supposed to act as a collective capitalist. On the other hand, competing individual capitalists cannot form or carry through a collective will as long as freedom of investment is not eliminated. Thus arise the mutually contradictory imperatives of expanding the planning capacity of the state with the aim of a collective-capitalist planning and, yet, blocking precisely the expansion, which would threaten the continued existence of capitalism. Thus the state apparatus vacillates between expected intervention and forced renunciation of intervention, between becoming independent of its clients in a way that threatens the system and subordinating itself to their particular interests. Rationality deficits are the unavoidable result of a snare of relations into which the advanced-capitalist state fumbles and in which its contradictory activities must become more and more muddled.

To sum up the last part of the discussion, we can conclude that the attempts of the corporatist, or any other, state to introduce a planned order into the intrinsically chaotic, corporations-dominated market, with the purpose of setting the capitalist economy on a steady course, are bound to remain fidgety and half-hearted. Because of the 'split personalities' of the classes, because of the lack of a permanent social basis in the form of at least one class firmly committed to the cause of the state-dominated, administered economy, the development of planning with or without a corporatist tendency must proceed in fits and starts. What is, moreover, at stake, is not just the temporary ups and downs of a fixed trend, but the very continuation of the tendency. The paradox of a state-administered capitalist economy consists in its propensity to generate a reaction to every action, to strengthen resistance by following the dominant pressures, to lose followers because of faithfully implementing their demands. The venture into a corporatist administration of the capitalist system may well collapse under the weight of its contradictions, and prove in retrospect to be either a false start, or (without clear knowledge of its actors) a temporary stage on the road to a perhaps better integrated, but different, system.

This latter supposition stems partly from the observation that the state administration, by reason of its corporatist tendency, but also for other, more general reasons, tends systematically to antagonise the social forces whose interests it is expected to serve, and arouse their resentment to the measures necessary for this service. In Habermas's terms, the state administration systematically fails to generate 'mass loyalty' sufficient to support vigorous 'steering performance' on which an effective 'fiscal skim-off' depends, necessary to finance 'social welfare performance', without which no 'mass loyalty' is possible; the vicious circle is thereby closed, and what emerges as a result is a positive feedback loop which makes a constant

deterioration of state performance on all fronts a strong tendency of the system. But the possibility of the state administration exploding because of its own internal tensions may be
hypothesized on other grounds as well: above all, on the
grounds that the state administration seems to be organically
unable to reproduce capitalist relations without simultaneously
weakening the pressures and mass motivations necessary for
their continuous existence. According to an extreme formulation of this contradiction by Offe and Rouge,[27]

> since, in a capitalist society, all exchange relationships
> depend upon the willingness of owners of money capital
> to invest, i.e., to exchange money capital for constant
> capital and variable capital; since this willingness depends
> upon the expected profitability of investment; and since
> all observable state policies of recommodification do have
> the side-effect of depriving capital of either capital or
> labour power or the freedom to use both in profitable
> ways, the cure turns out to be worse than the illness.

The most important source of this contradiction seems to
lie in the very logic of the state-administered salvage operation.
It starts from the awareness that market mechanisms, lubricated
solely by pursuit of profit, would fail to reproduce conditions
necessary for their continuous operation when left alone. A
force able to take care of such conditions must therefore be
exempt from regulation by market mechanisms. And its activity
must consist in subjecting certain processes vital for the
reproduction of the capitalist system to rules other than the
laws of the market; in other words, it must consist in exempt-
ing these processes and their products, at least temporarily,
from commodity form. Schools, hospitals, youth training,
rehabilitation centres, housing authorities, etc., are effective
only in so far as they are kept free from market rules. Therefore, they erode the commodity form of capital and labour as
much as they help to reproduce them.

This situation has numerous consequences. Some of them are
directly economic. Since the processes considered crucial for
the recommodisation of capital and labour and their political
stability for their mutual relations have been sheltered from
the vagaries of market-defined supply and demand, they
become relatively immune to the market cycles supposed (by
classical theory at least) to balance prices and perpetuate their
market-clearing capacity. They tend to remain, therefore, a
fixed factor in production costs (through taxation), and because
of the dominant position of big corporations in the markets,
also a fixed factor of prices. William Krehm dubbed the phenomenon 'social lien'. Another of Krehm's terminological novelties
is 'social revalorisation' - a factor in price arising from the
levelling-out of wages, legislated equality of pay aimed against
sex or race discrimination, and the general political pressure

towards the autonomy of wages in relation to the age, skill,
and productivity of individual employees. Finally, the whole
of the public sector can be considered to some extent to be
free from market domination as a sector of the economy where
prices are subject to deliberate political purposes of the competition between political, rather than economic, forces. The
three factors taken together are to a large degree responsible
for a constant inflationary pressure; prices tend to rise in a
depressed economy as much as they do in a prosperous one.
Having an inflating effect on production costs, they reduce the
incentive to invest. But attempts to reduce inflation through
squeezing excess money from the system and making credit
more expensive works in an exactly identical direction, only
with yet more vigour. Perhaps the worst impact of the inflationary tendency is that it releases political forces, dragging
the state periodically towards a deflationary flurry. But, in
Krehm's words, 'deflationary policy - whether to stabilize
prices, currency or what not' results in 'imposing idleness on
people who wish to work', and 'having productive capacity
under-employed'; in 'creating on the one hand a growing army
of unemployed, inadequately trained workers, and, on the
other hand, a huge backlog of neglected maintenance in our
cities, not least of all in the very districts where the unemployed
live'.[28]

Other consequences are less obviously economic, however
powerful their mediated impact on economic activity. More
directly, they are related to the structure of motivations
which are indispensable to stimulate individuals to a kind of
behaviour able to reproduce relations to the capitalist type.
Creation of a large sphere of production and distribution inside
which market pressures are mitigated or suspended, exemption
of a growing part of the individual's life conditions from non-
political market forces, transforming the norm of individual
survival into a politically founded, legitimate expectation
unrelated to individual productivity, are bound to erode the
twin motivational foundations of the capitalist system: the civil
privatism and the familial-vocational privatism based on the
ideology of 'achievement principle' and possessive individualism.
Civil privatism is the name given by Habermas to the attitudes
grounded in a merely formal legitimation of systemic authority:
it is assumed that the type of authority currently in existence
is an instrument of promoting the universally accepted end
of the constant life improvement; as long as the end seems to
be promoted, no active participation in the procedures of the
government is required of the individual. Civil privatism is,
therefore, a condition of this degree of autonomy without which
the simulated debate of corporatism, role of the experts and
administrative muscle of the economically active state are hard
to conceive. Familial-vocational privatism is an attitudinal manifestation of the achievement orientation, which counterfactually
relates the quality of individual life to individual performance

in market competition. This kind of privatism channels the
aspirations of individuals into the commodity sphere, thereby
lubricating the market-based economy. Erosion of the two
forms of privatism acts, therefore, against the efforts of state
and administration. The weakening of the familial-vocational
privatism (with the achievement principle losing fast its credibility both in its original, 'the fair judgment of the market',
and its vicarious, 'achievement-through-education', forms) is
bound to re-politicise aspirations and to subject the political
system to the pressures and demands with which it is ill-
prepared to cope without biting deeper into the areas still
left to the autonomy of private capital, and without claiming
yet more sovereignty from social and economic forces. The erosion of civil privatism, on the other hand, makes precisely
this sovereignty exceedingly difficult to maintain, much more
to expand. It forces the issue of legitimation out of its formal
shell. It exposes the contingency of any strategy the state
administration may adopt; it makes the claim to 'objective
rationality' of decisions vulnerable to criticism aimed at their
substance rather than instrumental efficiency. In short, the
weakening of civil privatism augurs the crisis of the 'legal-
rational' legitimation in so far as it requires that the ends
of authority be no longer problematic, and be removed from
the agenda of public debate.
   The deepest roots of trouble lie in the gradual transformation
of the issue of social integration of the capitalist society into
the problem of political legitimation. In the heyday of laissez-
faire capitalism the task of social integration was achieved
matter-of-factly, by the economy which served as its own ideology. Requiring no conscious intervention for its functioning,
it could remove the issue of its own validity or usefulness from
public debate. By the same token, its historicity appeared in
the guise of quasi-natural necessity. In moments of reflection,
it referred its explanation to the timeless attributes of universal man. The memory of historical choices which led to its
ascendancy were suppressed by the overwhelming evidence of
ubiquitous reality. In comparison with the solidly entrenched
'this is how things are', the vexing question 'is it necessary?'
faded into insignificance, and any discussion of the 'oughts'
and 'shoulds' of human purposes could be safely derided.
'Harsh realities' continually demonstrated their invincibility, the
weak were advised to try harder to become stronger, and the
unemployed were burdened with the obligation 'of preparing
themselves better for job markets as defined by potential
employers'.[29] The unquestioned presented itself as unquestion-
able. The market, enthroned as the ultimate judge of the value
of human achievement, implied 'not only the repression of those
practical desires which cannot demonstrate any functional
contribution to the overall system of achievement, but also
discrimination against any attempt to challenge the criteria of
achievement and efficiency through the framework of concepts

of use value'.[30] The laissez-faire economy was self-sufficient
in a most perfect and effective way: it repressed its own
alternatives. Once its battle with the aristocratic regime had
been won, it could do without political legitimation.

This situation is now gone, and the fault lies entirely with
the 'free competitive market', which proved to be efficient not
only in repressing its own alternatives, but also in gradually
destroying free competition. The involvement of an economically
active state as a necessary prerequisite of the capitalist system
is a consequence of the essential inability of the market to
sustain for long the conditions of its own existence. Once the
state stepped in, however, the alternatives are no longer
easily repressed. History cannot parade the mark of nature.
The economic necessities of yesterday have become the political
choices of today.

At first, the state entered the economic scene mistaking itself
for a new director bringing more invention and liveliness into
the performance of an old play. The plot still seemed to be
ordained once for all and not a subject of free choice. The
corporatist network emerged in a piecemeal way, in a series of
attempts to do collectively what private capitalists failed to do
singly, or big firms severally. It was rather the unanticipated
side-effect of the state administration in general, and its corporatist form in particular, which forced the substantive issues
of the ends into the political agenda. Were the corporatist tendency and the state insurance of capitalist economy free of
internal contradictions and interpretative ambiguities, perhaps
their authority would be able to do with a formal legitimation
only. Because of the contradictions and ambiguities, however,
this does not seem plausible.

The various political forces combined in the corporatist network have interests in halting the decline of formal legitimation.
The consensus supporting the fiction of simulated debate is
naturally backward-looking and singularly ill-suited to establish
and defend its grounds by self-assertion. In self-defence it
can only point to a consensus reached in the public debate of
the past, from which the simulated debate of the present
claims to have received its mandate. Renegotiating the ends
would be tantamount to the cutting of its own political roots.
Declaring the ends conclusive and unchallengeable, on the
other hand, requires that the simulated version must retain
the monopoly of public debate. Hence the partners of the
corporatist arrangements are united in their instinctive mistrust
and dislike of all unincorporated articulations of policies, but
above all else they fear the challenge to the finality and irre-
vocability of substantive consensus which legitimises administration by experts. Indeed, the corporatist network may be seen
as the last stronghold of 'efficiency', 'achievement' and
'instrumental rationality' conceived as the sole criteria of
political legitimacy. But the stronghold is under siege.

The sufficiency of instrumental legitimacy is defended with

three major weapons. First, the battered meritocratic ideology
is resurrected as the one reliable orientation point in the sea
of chaos: let the best man be rewarded. The invocation is convenient on several counts. It leaves comfortably aside the question of the exact meaning of virtue - who is to know who the
best men are? It allows every person with a grievance to
applaud - hardly anybody would complain that a reward missed
him in spite of him being the worst man. It supplies a non-
antagonistic interpretation of the existing inequality. Last but
not least, it admits of no alternative - what would the alternative be like? By the same token, it implies that the only
meaningful subject-matter still to be debated is how best to
implement what has been agreed. The second weapon is the
promotion of a 'conception of political action as just another of
the various steps individuals and groups take to secure and
advance their own interests and advantages'.[31] Politics, according to this interpretation, is always about who gets how much
of what all desire. In this view politics is just a special case
of the general rule of competition and self-preference. The
bargaining content of politics is thereby simultaneously
legitimised and fixed within the field of the distribution of
scarce resources between groups similar in their egoism and
greed. The third weapon, in Bob Jessop's convincing description, is the 'authoritarian populism' - a call to rally behind
authority as the bulwark of law and order. The slogan of law,
apart from being inherently conservative and backward-looking,
reinforces what the conception of politics as the play of selfish
interests implied. It suggests a vision of society as an aggregate of self-oriented individuals who need (and have the right
to demand) from the authority a guarantee that their social
environment will remain safe for the pursuit of their interests.
The social contract which self-interested individuals may enter
must remain formal, i.e. limit itself to the rules of the game.
The questions of the nature of the game, the chances it gives
to the players, justice of its results, etc., are therefore out
of order as they violate the rules.

   This rhetoric of defence of the legitimation limited to instrumental rationality is addressed to the deeply entrenched inclination to blame the medicine for the illness: in this perspective,
attempts to renegotiate the ends and values of society are
responsible for the very ailments which prompted them. The
defence is purely negative in character. It offers no positive
programme, feeding, as it were, on the widespread resentment
to the economic malfunctions, easily linked to the latest in the
long succession of causes. Like many a religious revival,
preaching 'return' to Primitive christianity, this defence
enjoins a 'return' to the 'primitive capitalism' (Milton Friedman
insists that Adam Smith solved all theoretical problems of
economy, past and future), conveniently glossing over the
fact that state-management of the economy evolved as an effort
to save society from its dysfunctions. The call is sent in an

unaddressed envelope, to society at large; again like in many
a revivalist movement, the ostensible conservatism of its recom-
mendation does not necessarily represent the interest of the
dominant and the privileged. It is, rather, populist in its
origins and intentions, seeking resonance in the anxieties of
all those who feel their hopes dashed and prospects uncertain.

SPLIT CLASSES, OR SPLIT SOULS?

People with anxieties are not confined to any of the traditional
classes. We have seen already that the 'economically responsible
state' ceased to be a class issue. Classes are split, or ambiguous, or both, regarding the desirability of a further expansion of the state management. In most cases, the attitudes
alternate, with calls for more individual independence following
the demands for more social services, and vice versa; or,
rather, the inconsistent attitudes co-exist, when stipulation
of more state intervention in a whole series of specific cases
is voiced in the same breath as remonstrations against obtru-
sive and all-powerful bureaucrats. Most of the measures initiated
and financed by the state can be interpreted as serving the
interests of more than one class: like bailing out a firm or an
industry threatened with bankruptcy, or redeveloping the
inner cities, or expanding the educational system. The workers,
in their dual capacity of hired labour and consumers, find
themselves often drawn in opposite directions in responding
to the vagaries of successive governments' policies. The middle-
class, as explained above, is similarly in two minds because
of its complex composition and, again, the contradictory effects
of the state economic interventions. As to the managerial
part of this class, Neil W. Chamberlain in his recent comprehensive compilation of the available information about attitudes
and inclinations has come to the conclusion that the one-
dimensional cult of private initiative as manifested and rewarded
in rising profits, and the belief that 'what is good for the
General Motors, is good for the US', both allegedly integral
constituents of the capitalist world-view, are in no way
dominant.[32] The managers, to start with, are split along two
lines. The first division is between old and young managers;
the old remember the time of autocratic rule, regard the
legislation protecting the rights of the employees and their
unions as an assault against their rights, and view the necessity of soliciting the permission of state authorities and consent
of trade union representatives as personal insult. The young
have been 'born' into a new regime and see it as natural,
easily learn their way through it and find in it virtues which
the old would not admit. The second division Chamberlain
found was between the managers of, respectively, big and
small firms. It seems that big firms, expectedly, find the new
arrangement useful and perhaps even indispensable; after all,

the corporatist network is on something of a scale roughly
comparable to their own. They can hope to influence it and
turn it to their own benefit; the mechanism is transparent and
certainly not uncontrollable. This, however, does not apply
to the small firms. They are overwhelmed by big state bureau-
cracies and big unions. Moreover, more often than not they
find the decisions emanating from the corporatist bargaining
to be adjusted to the needs of big business and neglecting
their own. Finally, in Chamberlain's view, there is the intellectual conditioning unmitigated, within the narrow perspective
of a small enterprise, by a sense of history - which may in
part - but only in part - explain the much greater conservatism
of small businessmen compared with the managements of the
large corporations throughout Western Europe. The small
proprietors are unsure of their class position, insecure with
respect to the future. They are opposed to socialism and
dislike the bureaucratic state, but they are also opposed to
the large private corporations, which they regard as oppressive.[33]

The above differences mean varying proclivities rather than
true divisions; the real distribution of attitudes defies any
simple classification - 'for every reformist-minded executive
there is probably a hard-liner'. There is no single set of
beliefs and attitudes which can be described, in an empirical
sense, as the 'managerial', much less a 'capitalist', ideology.
At the same time, one can name a number of significant beliefs
which have become elements of a broad agreement of sorts,
which accommodates organised representations of both business
and labour; much publicised swings of the policy pendulum,
and divergences of opinion, rarely move beyond this broad
framework of consent; even the sections of capital or labour
which are not particularly enthused with one or another of the
joint principles, normally consider them as inescapable, as
parts of the new reality which cannot be dismantled, and to
which one should better adjust his strategy.

Among the tacitly accepted elements of the situation, one
can name above all the changed meaning of property. The latter
does not comprise today the classic right of 'use and abuse'.
The owner is not supposed to be the sole judge of whether,
and how, his property is to be used or neglected. If he leaves
his property idle, or uses it below its capacity, or uses it in
a way which some other parts of community may consider as
harmful, his property may become a matter of public concern
and intervention. The property is some times mortgaged to
the state, and loans and subsidies rarely come without strings
attached. The owner gradually grows used to the idea that his
property is also a public concern; this has its bright side,
as it gives the owner the title to claim state help to back his
investment plans or to stave off the threat of insolvency.

Another, closely related, element of the broad agreement is
concerned with a widened notion of the firm's responsibility.

It has been accepted that company closures, structural changes, pursuit of rationalisation, have social costs in addition to the profit aspect. Social costs must be met for fear of political consequences potentially disastrous for the system's stability. How exactly these costs are to be met is of course a highly contentious issue, subject to short-term changes in policy fashions. They can be met by subsidising the ailing company and keeping it artificially alive until more prosperous times return, or financing its modernisation from the public purse; the wages become in part hidden unemployment benefits. Or, on the contrary, the firm may be allowed to follow its own calculation and disregard the social cost of engendered redundancies - in which case the state bears the burden of social expenditure directly, adding, however, to the production costs of firms through taxation. There is considerable argument about the virtues and vices of each of these policies and the alleged opposition between them is often strongly exaggerated. Whatever policy is currently the dominant fashion, the swings hardly ever reach beyond the boundary assumption of the systemic responsibility for the undesirable (and politically intolerable) consequences of profit calculations.

The third element worth emphasising is the acceptance of the positive role played by trade union officials in stabilising conditions of economic activity and particularly in conflict-management. To an extent, big business as well as public enterprises develop vested interests in reinforcing the power and prestige of trade union leadership. It is better under the circumstances to contain conflicts within the safer framework of simulated debate, but the containment, to be effective, requires complacency and quietism on the part of the rank-and-file unionists, which in its turn cannot be maintained unless the union leadership tangibly manifests its efficiency. For the sake of such an effect, it pays to comply with union-imposed limitations of managerial power; unrestrained nostalgia for lost autonomy may well cost much more. The entrenchment of this principle might sometimes be lost from sight, over-shadowed by dramatised contests between unions and management (particularly spectacular in the public sector, because of the unclarity of power relations in a field prominent for the most advanced erosion of commodity form). With all the inflamed passions such a contest often brings in its wake, it is difficult to conceive of a situation in which business will be able and willing to dispose of the function played already for several decades by the institutionalised spokesman for labour.

As far as the partners in the corporatist arrangement are concerned, all these elements of the new situation are here to stay. The elements combine into a fairly broad foundation, on which many quite distinct policies may be erected. Indeed, every reader of 'Forces of Change in Western Europe', or 'The State in Western Europe', or 'Trends toward Corporatist Intermediation', or 'Government, Business and Labour in

European Capitalism', or 'Pluralism and Corporatism', or any
of the comparative studies of the political systems of highly
industrialised countries, will find a picture of a wide range of
arrangements from highly authoritative central planning in
Norway, through close 'concerted action' in Germany to the
periodically assembled and dismantled corporatist institutions
of Britain. It is all too easy to overlook the forest behind the
trees and to take policy proclamations for reversals of history.
It is, however, no less easy to see that outwardly dramatic
changes of political fortune and bold declarations of intentions
which have accompanied party cabinet changes (Sweden and
Denmark being prominent examples) have failed thus far to
arrest, more still to redirect the development which for the last
half a century or more erased the boundaries between the
economic, politic and cultural sub-systems of society and incorporated into the process of government the hierarchies once
founded on great antagonistic classes. The corporatist tendency
was, and still remains, the institutional product of this development. For its continuation, it requires consensus limited to
broad issues only (of the kind of the elements of broad agreement briefly discussed above); indeed, broad enough to
accommodate wide divergences of opinion and withstand relatively far-reaching shifts of policy without weakening the
partners' determination to continue their simulation of public
debate. Hence its considerable surviving potential. As long
as the network of welfare provisions lasts, 'hard' and 'soft'
policies, expansions and constrictions of the public financing
of the social costs of market competition may alternate. Their
effects held in check and so prevented from pushing the plight
of potential rebels below the tolerable level, they may still
avoid provoking outside pressures powerful enough to undermine the conditions of the corporatist arrangement.

All these considerations lead to a conclusion that the probability
of an initiative to dismantle completely the corporatist arrangement coming from inside the corporatist partnership is low.
All the contradictions and incurable frictions notwithstanding,
each partner seems on balance to benefit more than he loses:
but even if this was not the case, he would certainly be
worse off alone. The perpetuation of a simulated debate of
the corporatist type is possible, however, only on condition
that the formal legitimation of authority in terms of growth by
rational means remains sufficient; that, in other words, the
non-participants of the simulated debate are not prompted to
disavow the corporatist articulation of their interests.

They may be so prompted in two cases. First, if the corporatist arrangement palpably fails to cope with the internal contradictions of the state management of the capitalist economy;
we have seen before that the contradictions are considerable
and the prospects of their solution far from certain. Second,
if for the reason of its own ineptitude, or for reasons external
to its mechanism, the state management of the capitalist economy

fails, i.e. if economic disturbances grow deeper and uncontrollable, if economic growth grinds to a halt and the standard of life, both in its narrow, 'familial privatism', sense, and in the wider sense of the quality of life, falls. In each of the two cases the problem of legitimation may become activated and forces heretofore quiescent and de-politicised may force the public controversy on to a level which the corporatist arrangement may find difficult to assimilate.

All of this venture in forecasting makes sense, of course, only on the assumption that all partners of the political game behave according to the 'systemic logic' of their interests; to wit, that all partners set their strategies in line with interests as defined by the constraints imposed by their mutual systemic dependencies. This, obviously, need not be the case. A successive swing of policy may well go out of control, that means beyond the endurance of one of the partners; radical forces may capture the dominant position of one or other side of the network and fall victim of their own rhetoric of confrontation. How much of this is sufficient to set the corporatist network permanently out of joint is impossible to predict. The balance of the whole arrangement is dynamic and precarious, dependent on all sides observing the conditions of broad consent: far from being pre-determined by an impersonal 'historic law', it needs to be continually reproduced with an active participation of all entailed organised forces. The process of reproduction may well collapse because of too much bull-headedness or simply human mistakes. If this happens, the lines of confrontation now blurred and de-activated may come to life again. The organised representations of capital and labour may be forced back to their pre-corporatist positions and functions. An attempt by the state to force the sides into an armistice, once peaceful debate has proved impossible - with the state gaining, as a result, domination in what used to be a triumvirate arrangement, will be then a distinct possibility.

The very contingency of such developments warns against advance sociological theorising; if pursued, such a theorising would create a false impression of historical determination of sorts where, in fact, the development is shaped by miscalculations and lost opportunities. One is bound, therefore, to focus on such tendencies as are implanted in the system under analysis by its integral contradictions. Not that these tendencies are a more reliable guide to events as they will occur in the future; they are preferred solely because they alone are amenable to analysis by available sociological tools.

Among such tendencies, none points towards the reappearance of the two traditional classes, capital and labour, as the major actors in the historical process; to wit, classes acting as subjects (setting collective goals of action and behaving like a 'collective individual' in their pursuit). The tendencies analysed in this chapter do generate class-type relations, but they do not produce foci around which the bearers of opposite interests may crystallise. On the contrary, objects generated within the structure of the present system are, when considered from the traditional class perspectives, intrinsically ambiguous; they tend to blur, not to sharpen, the traditional class boundaries. The logic of the system is such that the interests of various groups within the industrial core of the society become increasingly intertangled; any consistent opposition soon begins to hurt the interests of the opposer. The rhetoric of historically created class parties still vying for access to office confuses the situation; but any analysis of their conduct when in office reveals it.

Institutionalised memories of the great class divide turn into a major obstacle to the understanding of the real working of the highly industrialised system. They impede the sighting of the new types of conflict for the simple reason that these conflicts do not lend themselves to an articulation in traditional class language. But these conflicts nevertheless exist; and it is in these conflicts that the possibility of a true 'legitimation crisis' of the system resides.

The conflicts in question are spawned by the growing concentration of disposition over the uses of resources crucial for the well-being of the population at large. It has been said before that under the conditions of such centralisation the public discourse of ends and means of utilisation of societal resources is replaced by a simulated debate between hypothesised group claims; and that a chasm tends to deepen between the interests simulated in the hypothetical debate and those which remain inarticulate and unrepresented. For these reasons, the conflicts which the said system cannot help but generate and intensify are related to the problem of the extent of state penetration of society, and the question of representation of neglected interests and of the redress of deprivation lacking institutionalised channels of expression.

At the beginning of the last decade, Alain Touraine concluded that thinking of classes as groups, and of class conflicts as group antagonisms, was no more adequate to the task of the understanding of modern society.

> The definition of a dominant class cannot any more consist in the identification of a concrete group of individuals or families which transform an achieved into a hereditary status. To a greater degree still than in the industrial society, one has to consider the functioning of the system rather than concrete and stable groups.

It would not do to attempt a 'modernisation' of the images of traditional classes, allowing for the technologically generated changes in the nature of jobs and organisational hierarchies. Because of the systemic nature of social dependencies in what Touraine calls the 'post-industrial society', the equivalent of old conflict between class groups is one 'which opposes the

centres of decision to the social categories which are dominated
and exploited by the technocratic apparatuses'. The major
opposition of this kind of society is one between 'technocratic
management and the will to re-appropriate collectively the
direction of global change'.[34]

In his later works, Touraine further radicalised his criticism
of the traditional class imagery: 'As the labour movement has
no more the force to challenge the social order in its totality,
as it has turned, in a large part of the world, into an agent
of order, the stage of history seems empty to those who can
think only with their memory.' The stage, Touraine repeatedly
insists, is not empty. But in order to notice its actors, one
has to stop thinking of society as a building and start to visua-
lise it as a work of construction. The latter derives its dynamism from the pressures to expand the social participation in
the management of history.[35] Touraine is not particularly
explicit about the specific meaning of his suggestion, leaving
the identification of new historical forces to further research.
But one can interpret the suggested methodology as one pointing towards groups and categories left outside the oligarchy
of order, and above all towards a diffuse, class-unspecific
pressure for open participation in a discursive redemption of
ends and values of society. One can postulate a convergence
between the direction of Touraine's analysis and Habermas's
study of the tendency towards the 'ideal discourse' as the
horizon of present social struggles.

Numerous cases of grass-roots articulation of interests
heretofore silent may be seen as the evidence of the tendency
gaining force. With the public debate reduced to the mass
reproduction of expert versions of hypothetical interests, and
with a variety of minority interests, or neglected areas of
life, pushed into the margins of the simulated surrogate of
public debate, the sociological significance of such articulation
is best interpreted as a movement towards new procedures of
validating social consensus or legitimating authoritative decisions. It is much too early to consider them as a decisive movement away from the formal legitimation and the fiction of the
finality of value-consensus. They constitute, rather, a 'meta-
debate', an exploration of the new ways in which the legitimated
debate may be conducted, a practical test of the extent to
which the corporatist monopoly of interest-articulation may be
dented. Naturally, they assume in most cases a form emulating
the established modes of interest representation; ostensibly,
they are no more than another series of group interests clamour-
ing to be admitted to the selective decision-making club. If
they undermine the very principle of selectivity, of simulated
representation, of formality of legitimation - they do it all
only indirectly, in as far as the range of issues they force into
the public agenda and the type of interests they want to be
heeded to is too wide to be contained in the limited space of
corporatist arrangement. They may go a long way before this

happens; and there is no certainty that it will.

One task sociology can perform at this stage is to take stock of the major areas of deprivation left unattended, or generated by the analysed system. It is these areas which, as suggested by the analysis, will grow in importance as the major sources of conflict, dynamism and change.

6 New contradictions, new victims

The current preference for market mechanisms voiced in an increasing number of political circles, and seeking legitimation in a recent resurge of 'neoclassical' economic theories, can well be seen as a manifestation of a 'second degree pessimism'. In the course of several decades, the trust in the wisdom of the market seemed on the wane. Even to those who retained their faith in the long-term ability of the market to get proportions right, it had become clear that short-term consequences of disequilibria might reach an intolerable, nay disastrous, scale. And yet this realisation did not necessarily require the abandonment of hope in the orderly and progressive economy, or the belief that the manifestations of its notorious afflictions can be kept from becoming excessive. The optimism of yesteryear could still be salvaged; a new haven, however, had to be found where it could safely be anchored.

In Keynes's response to the traumatic experience of the economic collapse and mass unemployment, the market had its credits withdrawn, but optimism was offered a new lease of life. Left to itself, the market is a shambles; it is a bustle without inherent logic, in which decisions on a scale capable of devastating results are taken as if they were still the 'small and inconsequential' decisions of minute economic units. There is no innate wisdom in the market. Society cannot rely on the market for the provision of the basic conditions of its existence. Rather, it has to defend itself against the disasters which the chaotic reality of the market can inflict. Such basic conditions can be still provided; not, however, without an active and positive economic programme adopted and consistently pursued by the (traditionally seen as non-economic) powers of the state. Contrary to the old optimism, hoping that the supply will always create its own demand, the market cannot guarantee the balancing of the total output with the total demand; unemployment is, therefore, its organic and ineradicable proclivity. The market can well be capable, in spite of this, of reproducing itself in the 'purely economic' sense; but the economic conditions of such a reproduction will be politically intolerable. Hence the state, a political institution, has the right and the duty to intervene. Its first task is to contain unemployment. That is, to finance the demand which the market as such is unable to generate.

In Keynes's call to action, the sagging optimism received a new fillip. Its intellectual impact reached far beyond the technical message aimed at the economic policy proper. A new foundation of hope and optimism had been found. It was laid on the rock of political authority with the tools of scientific expertise. With such a foundation, one could perhaps erect a model of the future not only foolproof against the most irritating fits of economic fever, but cleansed of practically all, major and minor, social ailments. Rightly or wrongly, in tune with or against Keynes's own intentions, his recipe was widely read as an invitation to social engineering on a grand scale.

Today, almost half a century later, the social engineering animus looks much like a spent force. Optimism has been evicted from its last stronghold, and thus far remains homeless; it can only move from one shelter to another, each time, however, as an illegitimate squatter. There is no room left for it in the corridors of power. In Heilbroner's words,[1]

> there is now a recrudescence of an intellectual conservatism that looks askance at the possibilities for large-scale social engineering, stressing the innumerable cases - for example, the institutionalisation of poverty through the welfare system, or the exacerbation of racial friction through efforts to promote racial equality - in which the consequences of well-intentioned acts have only given rise to other, some-times more formidable problems than they had set out to cure.

But the retreat from social engineering does not mean a revival of faith in the natural wisdom of the market. It means, rather, a resignation to the market's recognised faults. The hopes have faded that these faults could be repaired by a concerted and deliberate intervention. The magnitude of unintended consequences of such intervention has somehow reduced the once frightening size of market-generated problems. The 'recrudescence of intellectual conservatism' should not be read as a return to nineteenth-century optimism. It ought to be interpreted instead as a 'last resort', desperate, straw-clutch-ing measure: since through trying to meddle with market-generated troubles more problems have been created than solved, better allow the market to take its course - and pay the price. As we will see later, this decision has been made particularly easy by the fact that those who are likely to pay the highest price of market vagaries are in no position to refuse the payment.

THE LIMITS OF SOCIAL ENGINEERING

The fast fading of the short-lived glory of social engineering in general, and the Keynes-style role of the state in particular, can be ascribed to two broad groups of factors. One group is related to the intrinsic limitations of the piecemeal strategy as

such. The second is connected with the appearance of new
phenomena which transcend the capacity of traditional social
engineering and the powers of its institutional basis.

The most salient weakness of most social-engineering precepts is their non-systemic character. Within a complex society
they select from a dense network of manifold dependencies a
single pair of variables; a multi-dimensional space of dialectical
interaction they try to reduce, optimally, to a straight cause-
and-effect sequence. They are guided by purpose; purpose
is always a specific problem to which a selective, paramount
relevance has been attached at the time. The resulting solution is, in Gregory Bateson's pungent characterisation,[2]

> a short-cut device to enable you to get quickly at what
> you want; not to act with maximum wisdom in order to live,
> but to follow the shortest logical or causal path to get what
> you next want, which may be dinner; it may be a Beethoven
> sonata; it may be sex. Above all, it may be money or power.

The collection of such recipes is a 'bag of tricks'. Each trick
may be quite effective in performing one, isolated 'economic
miracle'. Inevitably, it interferes on its way with innumerable,
unknown or neglected, relations of the system and may destroy
conditions for the self-regulation of other systemic requirements. Once, for example, the state takes the responsibility
for full employment, and the obligation to guarantee life minimum of the remaining unemployed, a large politically explosive
load is removed from the market, and a lot of morally abominable human suffering is prevented, but in addition two unde-
sired (sometimes unanticipated) economic consequences also
occur. First, the organised (and employed) labour pressure on
the wages refuses to subside, however slack the demand; if
not coupled with the increase of output, it can only be absorbed through increased prices. Second,[3]

> the employers are no longer entirely quit of labour costs
> when they shut down their plants for the lack of orders....
> The unemployed and the problems they develop during
> their forced unemployment are a burden on the state, and
> that ultimately, through taxes, finds its way back to the
> private sector as an added cost.

In addition, according to the so called 'Harrod dichotomy',
when the state attempts to countervail the economically undesirable effects of well-entrenched, care-free unions by squeezing the aggregate demand - the effect of any fall of demand
already below the supply potential (and this is normally the
case during any recession) will be exactly a further rise in
prices. Attempts to deal with unemployment as a separate
phenomenon, without regard to its fundamental systemic inter-
connections, may be therefore more or less successful when

measured by the immediate purpose, but will soon create a
situation when even more massive unemployment than the one
originally responsible for the state action will be unable to eliminate endemic inflation from the system. Benefits brought by
the technique of 'tricks' are normally short-run; but the harm
done on the way can rarely be undone.

The hope to pacify and hence solidify the power patterns
identified as social order, attached to the corrective action of
social engineering, tend to fade in the longer run not just
because of the unanticipated side-effects of each measure. Even
if the dramatic success along the main line of attack far out-
weighed minor frustrations on other fronts, there would still
accumulate an experience of the essential inconclusiveness of
the whole strategy of dissolving the power conflict in a succession of distributive adjustments. Social engineering focused
entirely on the division of surplus and leaving basic human
dependencies as regulated by the power control in production
intact, and completely unconcerned with the oppressive power
relations as such, is bound to remain, after all, a makeshift
expedient, which at best may alleviate the symptoms of the
disease but will not remove its causes. Frustration constantly
replenished by these causes, but barred from turning against
them, will tend, therefore, to boost distributive claims well
beyond the capacity of social engineering in its Keynes-inspired
interpretation. Each successive act of 'redistributive justice'
will more strongly yet commit the social disaffections to the
channel of consumer hopes and demands which the extant power
structure is incapable of satisfying. This general incapacity
of a distributive social policy to solve by proxy the problems
which the unchanging power patterns keep generating, may
well remain unnoticed, or be dismissed as a minor irritant,
as long as continuing economic growth allows current expendi-
tures to be met without an immediate danger of overdraft. But
this situation is not to last.

There is, as well, another natural limit to the attractiveness
of social engineering. Phenomena of economic life are seen as
problems (as something which requires an urgent remedial
action) only if they are defined as such by a social force which
suffers as a result of their effect and which, in addition, is
powerful enough to make its definition hold. In order to do so,
this force must first be admitted to public discourse; then it
must display enough pressure power to impose its definition of
the situation upon the debate. Unless these two conditions are
met, phenomena, no less real, are likely to remain inarticulate,
and 'nonexistent' in consequence. It is, therefore, a rule that
even if proper technical means are found and applied, the urge
to deal with problems weakens with the progress in their solution - as the phenomena in question gradually lose their relevance for the force which insisted on their rectification. As a
general rule, one can say that the technical conditions having
been met, the solution of a problem will tend to go as far, and

only as far, as the pressure of politically effective social force
will push it; the latter, however, tends to ease off well before
the problem has been fully solved. On occasions, the pressure
of a group may even change direction and attempt to 'depro-
blematise' the phenomenon not any more seen as threatening
to its interests. A good example of this general rule has been
provided by the long lapses of time between successive Reform
Bills, enfranchising first property owners, then craftsmen and
'established' workers, then all the male population, and finally
women. Successive steps along seemingly the same line were
taken under the pressure of different social forces. Each force
opted out once the public discourse had been altered in line
with its perception of the problem. The time lapse before a next
step could become a realistic possibility was as lengthy as it
took for the next, heretofore inarticulate, social force to organise itself and to develop a sufficient political muscle.

It seems that the current low popularity of social engineering is at least in part explicable by the absence of a politically
articulate force willing and able to promote its further extension. The post-war period of social engineering, changing the
rules of the game in favour of previously handicapped groups
and introducing a series of redistributive measures, was carried through under a continuous pressure of well-organised
and politically articulate labour. It failed to solve problems
as they may be defined by the radical extreme of the political
spectrum; but then the solution of problems so defined was
never the goal pursued by the real forces which gave the
reform its urgency and impetus. The motive which inspired
organised labour to lend its force to the movement of social
engineering was the right to fight for the rising income of
its members, not equality; the guaranteed standard of living
for the same members, not elimination of poverty, security of
jobs, not elimination of unemployment; and most certainly racial
or sex equality were not among these motives. As far as organised labour is concerned, the motives which forced upon the
state the concern with the public administration of 'distributive justice' have all been, for the time being, satisfied.

Any further extension would serve, again from this perspective,
no clear purpose. Instead of strengthening the position of
organised labour and guarding the privileges it won, any
extension would dilute them by admitting an equality of interests which organised labour, at least in its unionist sector,
does not represent. To the unions, admission of new targets
into the social policy would bring palpable benefits, but would
certainly increase the cost of the caring state to the individuals
(hence, for example, the unions' hostile reaction to 'affirmative
action' for the benefit of racial minorities). Once the basic
rights and safety cushions have become parts of reality and
thus 'deproblematised', labour more and more often think of
themselves as 'taxpayers' rather than as a deprived category
needing a powerful authority to redress the injustices it

suffers. They more eagerly lend their ears to the remonstrations against the excessive power of the state and the hypertrophy of central bureaucracy.

This development can in no way be seen as irreversible. The interest in social engineering may well reappear, perhaps even on a magnified scale, if the framework of social rights surrounding the successful defence of the current form of 'closure' is eroded or, worse still, put in question and therefore re-problematised by action from above, or if the terms of the precarious armistice or the fundamental level of power relations were unilaterally changed and hence a new lease of energy were given to the search for distributive compensation (this is why Andrew Tylecote predicts inflationary, in the long run, effects of the strategy to alter the balance of power nicknamed 'monetarism'). In so far as this does not happen, however, the vindications and demands of organised labour are unlikely to be articulated as a call for more social engineering, and particularly not for a wider, more accommodating definition of its objectives. Such a call could be backed, promoted and forced on to public discourse only by politically effective groups which are thus far only weakly articulated - a point which John Rex has emphasised repeatedly and convincingly.

Part of the explanation of the current cooling of enthusiasm for further social engineering is, therefore, provided by the realisation of the inefficiency of partial, purpose-oriented reform in achieving more ambitious aims, as well as by the fact that some of the most potent pressures behind the post-war upsurge of social engineering activity have run out of steam.

The historically created institutions of organised labour, however powerful and effective in their primary functions, are hardly adequate to the kind of action one would expect of a 'historical class', which cannot defend its own interests without fighting deprivation in all its forms. They represent the corporative interests of their members. More importantly, there is little evidence that these interests are attuned to the needs of other categories of population, who are with equal or still greater justice complaining of the iniquity of their depressed social standing. There is no evidence either that the successes of labour organisations bring the society anywhere near the redress of its most acute wrongs or the remedy for its malfunctions. If anything, the power-related principle of distribution, which the present labour organisations embody and promote adds considerably to the difficulty which any attempt to further equality and to resuscitate the areas of poverty and deprivation must encounter.

There is a wide area in which the interests of big and powerful unions coincide with the interests of big and powerful firms, in a way which deepens rather than mollifies the deprivation of the weaker sectors of the labour force. Oligopolistic firms, burdened with huge capital investments and able to dictate their conditions to the market, need a stable, experienced labour

force and actively discourage labour turnover - for reasons
hardly related to the old ideas of paternalism. They offer their
employees both high wages and job security; union demands
in this respect fall on fertile ground and more often than not
bring the desired fruits. The minimum wage, redundancy
payments and pension facilities are here relatively easily
enforced - effectively preventing the influx of intruders and,
if anything, leaving the remaining labour force to the mercy
of the peripheral, weak firms with little capital, market power,
and resistance to the vagaries of economic cycles. In such
firms labour turnover is high; their employees are first to pay
the costs of the falling economic fortune. They are first to
become unemployed - and last to find jobs when the pace of
economic life quickens again. The black, women, the young,
the old - all sorts of notoriously socially powerless and politically underprotected people - are least likely to be offered
better paid and more secure positions. They are more than
others exposed to the threat of unemployment; their discrimination becomes, so to speak, self-perpetuating. There is no
connection (at least no positive connection) between the prestige and power of successful labour organisations and the
plight of these, weaker, categories. The bargaining triumphs
of organised labour do not save them from poverty. As Lawson
and George recently found out,[4]

> the population groups in poverty are directly related to
> the working class but they are not seen as such, nor do
> they form a unified social group wielding substantial
> political power. So far, the trade unions have not treated
> such groups as part of the working class meriting their
> support in the political and industrial arena. Each group
> has had to fight its own battles, often in open conflict
> with the demands of other groups. If and when such
> groups act in unison and with the support of the trade
> unions, the battle for a guaranteed minimum income for
> all will be won, and easily at that. The prospects of this
> happening in the immediate future, however, appear
> negligible.

In recent years increasing attention is being paid to the
possible consequences the slowing rate of growth may have
on the strategy of organised labour. It has been indicated
that the dissolution of the potential capital-labour all-out
conflict in a multitude of relatively small-scale, trade-oriented,
localised, peaceful or militant bargainings could last only as
long as the rapid and continuous increase of national wealth;
vindications of contending groups may then be satisfied
simultaneously, with nobody's welfare decreasing as a result.
'The awkward moment', says Frank Parkin 'arrives when
increased appetites must be satisfied from a cake that, for
whatever reason, has failed to get bigger. At this point,

expectations can only be met by the net transfer of resources
from one group to another.[5] Heilbroner, similarly, warns of the
imminent 'removal of the safety valve by which the deep tension between the claims of labour and property has been les-
sened in the past'; 'A stationary capitalism is thus forced to
confront the explosive issue of income distribution in a way
that an expanding capitalism is spared.'[6] A number of authors
conclude that the end of economic expansion will render the
established 'piecemeal' method of handling labour grievances
unworkable, and that at least some degree of labour unity,
and perhaps also the thus far avoided head-on confrontation
between classes, will belatedly materialise. Thanks to constant
growth, capitalism could buy social peace without sacrificing
the profits of the privileged. Without growth, the two ingred-
ients of the successful formula will become demonstrably
incompatible, and an overt class conflict will be unavoidable.

This is, however, only one of the possible outcomes of the
end to economic growth; and one which the structure of
organised labour, with its subordination to the power principle
of distribution, does not make the most likely. Another outcome, perhaps more probable, is a further deepening of divisions within labour; widening of differentials between powerful unions and the interests backed neither by strong bargaining assets nor by proficient organisation; and, most of all,
the restoration of the great divide between people able to
derive their income from jobs and those forced to rely on
secondary transfers. However vague and ambiguous the idea
of welfare as the reward for performance has become, it remains
the structural principle of labour organisation and its well-
nigh sole legitimation. In Arthur M. Okun's succinct summary,
'getting paid is "belonging" in the minds of most citizens'.[7]
The trade-unionist form of labour organisation, for better or
worse, is structurally committed to the defence of work ethics,
the performance principle and welfare derived from the contribution to market exchange. It is ill fitted to face the challenge
arising from the failure of the market to provide sustenance
for an ever-growing part of the population. The crisis of the
capitalist market may, therefore, become as well a crisis of the
form in which labour historically constituted itself as a class.
Instead of bringing an intensified capital-labour conflict into
the focus of societal change, the end of growth may well render
the fortunes of the two traditional antagonists increasingly
irrelevant to the most urgent and critical tasks the society
confronts.

THE RISE AND FALL OF ECONOMIC GROWTH

There have been, however, factors of a different category,
which seriously sapped the belief in the feasibility of an administrative solution to social and economic problems. These other

factors emerged outside the original social-engineering discourse. They are related to the articulation of a number of new
problems, only recently assigned high relevance in the public
debate; problems of a kind which administrative action was
never before meant to tackle, and had not developed the institutional basis nor cognitive horizons to deal with. The inadequacy of tried and available practical means is perceived as a
super-human magnitude of the new problems. They seem overwhelming, transcending by far the existing capacity for remedial action. As must happen before the bases and methods
adjusted to problems of new quality are designed, the conviction that the difficulties are just so many temporary irritants
which - with due care - sooner or later will be removed from
the system, is all but gone.

The pride of place among the new problems belongs to the
self-assertion of the Third World. It is truly impossible to
exaggerate the impact exerted by this by far the most seminal
of the post-war developments upon the totality of Western
mentality. It amounts to the general collapse of self-confidence
and has manifold manifestations. On the intellectual level,
the feverish search for the sources of Western uniqueness,
defined as either an exclusive technological genius or incomparable scientific aptitude, alternates with gnawing uncertainty about the possible legitimation of its superiority. On the
moral level, the mood vacillates between new paroxysms of
national insularity and xenophobia and outbursts of remorse
for the imperialist past and fits of inferiority complex. On the
political level, cries and whispers to close ranks in defence of
the 'civilisation as we know it' cohabit with the currying of
favours from the up-and-coming world powers by, first and
foremost, supplying them with the most sublime masterpieces
of Western military inventiveness. The bewildering inconsis-
tency of reactions on all levels is symptomatic of the situation
of acute uncertainty and ambiguity.

Underlying all this uncertainty is a fear, too formidable to
be often voiced in public: the spectre of the wars of redistribution - a repetition on a grandiose, mind-rending scale of
the great civil wars of the past which look puny and cosy in
comparison. The global wars of redistribution, if they ever
materialise, will be an event to which past history can offer
no guidance. We live, after all, in the era of the nuclear weapon;
not only the first weapon capable of destroying the earth as
the human habitat, but the first weapon which can be applied
by a small group of experts without the need to mobilise public
support and to 'educate' the masses in the hatred of the enemy
and the readiness to die for the country, which previous wars
required. In a nuclear war, the traditional factors of military
strength like the size of the population, diffusion of technological know-how and the degree of moral commitment and
political unity are reduced to only secondary importance. The
outcome is therefore hard to predict, as rationality becomes

a poor guide in this context, with too many unknown variables; a situation ideally fit for both gamble and blackmail.

There is a widespread feeling that the necessity of redistribution is only a question of time; and that the length of this time depends solely on the speed with which the poor of the world will muster the powers to make its claims audible, which in the nuclear era may be quite amazing. On the other hand, it is difficult to conceive of a peaceful solution to the problem of redistribution. A most careful scrutiny fails to reveal a single social force in the affluent West able and willing to take the lead in the search and application of such a solution. The almost total indifference with which the Brandt Commission's report was received by all political camps and denominations was a vivid testimony to this incapacity. A party which dared to inscribe a slogan of affluence-sharing on its electoral banners could be certain of losing support regardless of its class basis. The suspicion that the defusion of the redistribution time-bomb is most probably not feasible adds substance to the anxiety born of the endemic uncontrollability of the situation.

Another newly articulated problem, apparently beyond control, is the limit imposed on the improvement of life by the scarcity of natural resources. This problem is not entirely unconnected with the first; the perception of the earth as, for all practical intents and purposes, an empty territory open to unlimited expansion, held back only by temporary and rectifiable scientific ignorance or technological retardation, has been irreparably shattered by the assertion of property rights over resources by new sovereign powers; and the hysterical tone of most doomsday prophecies can be, at least in part, explained by the subconscious urge to invalidate the demands for a universal sharing of Western standards, and by a somewhat more conscious fear of being robbed of what has come to be seen as a natural right. This is not, however, the whole explanation. With all the allowances one can make on the inevitable political distortion of what is at bottom an economic-technological debate, the sudden concern with the shrinking earth resources contains more than just a kernel of truth.

The exact calculation of the remaining supplies of resources is a notoriously contentious matter and posits questions which only future development of science and technology can provide with a definite answer. One issue, for example, which cannot conclusively be clarified ahead of events, is whether the currently crucial scarce materials can be in time replaced without bringing economic activity to a halt. However great the technological ingenuity, it seems nevertheless that the current rate of economic growth (and most of our political and social institutions, as well as culturally supported patterns of conduct and expectations, have adjusted to this rate) cannot be maintained for long. The sheer magnitude of required resources make it implausible. If the growth of 7 per cent per annum is sustained,

thirty-two times more resources than today will be required
fifty years from now. Even if the blood-curdling forecasts of
the Club of Rome could be dismissed as merely reflecting the
arbitrarily selected assumptions of the model, a considerable
doubt would remain whether the organisation of the social
system as a whole should remain oriented to the prospect of
continually growing production of goods; and whether it could
remain such without an ever-increasing risk of the general
collapse of fundamental social institutions.

The seriousness of the problem derives from the fact that in
the course of many decades all major developments in the
organisation of the Western society used continuous economic
growth as an opportunity to by-pass redistributive claims
through the route of a steady improvement of living standards,
measured by the volume of material possessions. Such was the
function of the industrial expansion, which multiplied the number of jobs and spread the phenomenon of the multi-earner
family; or the impact of the expansion of public administration
and service industry, which created a visibility of intense
upward social mobility; or the effects of expanding education
facilities, which - sustaining the appearance of widely available
opportunities of individual advance - developed on all levels
of society a degree of interest in the maintenance of social
hierarchy; or the strategy of 'buying off' potentially incen-
diary antagonisms through transfer payments acceptable to
the rest of the society because partly financed by the increments of output without affecting the existing standards of
living; or the consumer economy, blurring the perception of
class distinctions through the general availability of mass copies
of the coveted goods; or the new 'simulated' version of democracy, possible only on the conditions of political indifference
of the population at large - the latter achieved thanks to the
reduction of political contention to the technical issue of better
fostering further economic growth. All these basic ways
and means of present-day Western society hang on the plausi-
bility of continuous growth; all of them, practically the whole
fabric of society, are at risk once the prospects of further
growth at the present rate have become doubtful. No wonder
that the mere doubt has been enough to sap the confidence
of the industrial world.

The spreading realisation of the implausibility of continuous
growth has been added an extra dimension by the increasing
unpopularity of the growth as an end worth pursuing. The
last decade or two brought a spate of iconoclastic literature
questioning tenet by tenet the formula of human happiness
measured by the volume of material possessions. The hippies
and other radicals of the 1960s caused perhaps the deepest
shock because of the practical form of their criticism; they
actually embarked, though most of them only temporarily, on an
alternative way of life of a kind whose elimination the culture
of capitalism declared as its greatest achievement. The hippies

were, however, only a symptom of the approaching crisis of
the market-oriented and market-promoted pattern of affluence.
Since the brief though spectacular hippy adventure, the crisis
has been articulated in countless indictments of the hopelessly
inconclusive commodity chase and of the exorbitant psychological and moral price which a life of technologically supported
comfort demands. The anti-growth literature has grown
increasingly moralistic. The condemnation of commodity-
oriented affluence focused, at the deepest level, on the philosophical distinction between 'being' and 'having': external
wealth brings internal impoverishment; work, leisure, life
itself are emptied of their meaning; human relations are reduced
to the acts of buying and selling; human identity is dissolved
in so many mass produced symbols of uniformity. The practical
suggestions range from a deliberate slow-down in economic
activity with an emphasis on collective consumption, to the
slogans of a 'great simplification' and return to the small-scale
community and a 'convivial technology' of do-it-yourself and
get-together.

So far the denunciation of economic growth has not been
heard from working-class quarters, still less from the areas of
modern poverty. Neither was there a mass middle-class movement against growth which was remotely comparable in range
or commitment to, say, the activities of a Consumer Defence
Association. Perhaps the most telling to an ordinary ear was
the anti-pollution argument of the stop-growth campaign. But
even this argument failed to goad its massive audience beyond
the protest against true or imaginary conspiracy of big firms
and big governments; if its purpose was to bring home the
necessary connection between destruction of nature and all
commodity production - even this, by far the most popular
among the anti-growth arguments, has failed to make much
headway. It is difficult to gauge the degree to which the campaign has made the continuing support of the growth-extrolling
and growth-promising politicians and parties more psychologically controversial (perhaps even qualmish) now than a decade
or two before. But the support shows no signs of significant
erosion. The situation has been well summed up by Hans
Arndt:[8]

> Ordinary mortals, even in affluent American suburbia,
> remained unconvinced that Galbraith and Schumacher
> knew what was enough for them, if only because for
> most of them the goods and services offered by 'con-
> sumerism' provided some of the sources of social status
> and self-respect which men like Galbraith and Schumacher
> found more easily in their intellectual pursuits and public
> standing.

This perceptive observation goes a long way towards solving the mystery of the sudden outburst of anti-affluence

feelings among book writers and of the highly selective popularity of their books. The late C.A.R. Crosland went further
still in his terse comment that '(a)ffluence is obviously more
agreeable when it is a minority condition'.[9] Like few other
criticisms of present-day society, the anti-affluence platform
is unambiguously a class ideology; it represents, only thinly
veiled, the specific worries of the affluent middle class; the
class of people rich enough to enjoy everything the market is
able to offer them as the satisfaction of their needs as defined
by the same market, but who, unlike the upper class further
up in social hierarchy, are not so rich or influential as to
guard for long their 'minority position' and keep the crowd
from the gate. Perhaps inadvertently, Fred Hirsch let the cat
out of the bag by choosing as a leading motif of his book on
social limit to growth the adage 'if everyone stands on tiptoe,
no one sees better'.[10] In the view of the author, the logic of
the above proposition is universal; a moment of thought shows,
however, that its cogency is selective. No one whose view is
disturbed by other people standing on their toes will be hor-
rified by the social consequences of his doing the same, while
the complaint is natural and understandable when it comes
from the people who have already enjoyed a clear view for some
time but now are worried by so many others following their
example and spoiling the fun.

   The concern with the deterioration of a once-privileged position is not, however, the only fuel which keeps the anti-growth
fire raging. The sour experience with 'disutilities of scale'
rendered visible, also from the bourgeois perspective, a
phenomenon long commented upon by those who criticised
capitalism rather than growth as such: that the plums and
carrots with which the capitalist culture attempted to attract
mass support for a market-centred society was not so much the
promise to get rich (or comfortable, or having one's needs
satisfied), as the exhortation to get richer than one's fellow.
That this recipe cannot apply to all should have been clear
from the outset; but the capitalist ideology, for natural reasons, was never too eager to make this necessarily anti-egali-
tarian aspect of its message particularly conspicuous. Now
that the middle class itself begins to experience that some
goods are goods only in so far as others do not have them,
the limits to equality set by the cultural forms required for
the continuous reproduction of the capitalist system cannot
remain overlooked for much longer. Hence the discovery of
'positional goods', the utility-value of which depends on 'con-
gestion' or 'crowding' in their use. Hence also the discovery
that the market, commodity-oriented economy gave rise to
'false hopes', by 'promising to satisfy individuals' demand for
what only some among them can have'. What has been discovered is an artefact of the increased, and ever more difficult
to contain politically, pressure towards more equitable distribution, which under the conditions of considerable slow-

down in economic growth cannot but bite at the inner and most
coveted regions of capitalist wealth. Consistently pressed
demands cannot be met, like before, from increments in output
- the truth expressed by Hirsch in a rather convoluted phrase:
'The means by which positional goods are allocated make it
impossible to separate relative apportionment of resources -
distribution - from additions to the supply available of
resources - growth.'[11] Again, as so many times in the past,
the inability of the existing social hierarchy to accommodate
the volume of political pressure on resources is reflected intellectually as the discovery of 'economic laws'. Economic limits,
contributing to the general feeling of confinement, are a different name for the fear of an imminent confrontation over
resources.

'Positional goods', according to Hirsch, bring happiness but
cannot be obtained by all who wish them. But there are other
goods, which an increased number of people must obtain in an
increased quantity, which are a 'must', a necessary condition
of survival, but which, once possessed, bring happiness to
nobody. These are 'technological', or - better still - 'density'
goods. They add to the bill of survival, but not to the standard
of living; a true standard of living, not the one artificially
produced by the accepted method of computing GNP. If, because
of the spread of modern conurbations, the distance to the place
of work grows twice as long as before, a second pair of shoes
does not make their owner any richer. According to Leopold
Kohr, among biological, cultural and density necessities, the
latter tend to grow faster than the other two, consuming an
ever-larger part of the surplus income allegedly reserved for
the luxuries. In Kohr's view, once the size and density of an
economic unit steps byond a critical size, increased consumption ceases to reflect changes in living standards.[12] This intrinsic frustrating capacity of growing output and consumption is
often overlooked, at least during the initial period of each successive technological breakthrough, as most density goods,
which end up as necessities everybody must have but nobody
particularly enjoys, start as luxuries before they turn into
headaches. Nevertheless, economic growth is never capable
of supporting a stable and growing margin of luxuries; this
margin is continually eroded, and perhaps completely eaten
up, by the expanding volume of density necessities. This growing realisation of the self-defeating nature of the wealth race
induced Reginald Harrison recently to conclude that 'the development from primitive, hunting society to contemporary industrial society, considered in terms of human satisfaction, has
not been a "progress", it has been argued, but a maintaining
of place'.[13] Looking back from the perspective of recent experience, what tended to be seen a century ago as economic progress looks increasingly like, merely, the growing complexity
of the business of life conducted under the stress of growing
dependency on expanding societies.

In a sense, the notions of 'positional' and 'density' goods articulate the same intuition. They both stand, in the last account, for a complaint that the 'social crowding' (in itself, undoubtedly, a by-product of the egalitarian pressures of the modern era) takes enjoyment out of the possession. 'Density commodity' is, so to speak, the fate of a 'positional commodity' once the latter surrendered to the egalitarian pressures; 'density necessities' are the very pressures which would not let the 'positional goods' retain their quality for long. The intuition articulated by both notions is an old one, familiar at least since the times of Ortega y Gasset and, perhaps, even Gabriel Tarde or Friedrich Nietzsche. One could interpret them as an economic variant of the elitist lament of the 'mass society' encroaching upon the territory heretofore reserved for the enjoyment of the few, and by the same token vulgarising the sublime. (The territorial metaphor is one particularly widely used in the economic writings in Ortega y Gasset's style. Hirsch discussed extensively the access to scenic landscape, the plight of the people who wish 'to recapture the original attractions which newcomers have degraded',[14] while E.J. Mishan, in his passionate and closely argued analysis of the true costs of economic growth, wrote of 'once dreamy resorts and semi-tropical islands' which 'in the attempt to cater for the growing millions of tourists by building hotels, villas, lidos, arcades, casinos, roads, airfields', 'are transmogrified into neon-lit Meccas, agape with jostling crowds and swarming transistorised automobiles'.[15])

Much as the case against growth as the technology of happiness seems convincing, Arndt's word of caution remains in force. The age-old wisdom of the rich, 'money does not bring happiness', had always a hollow ring for the poor. It must sound particularly hollow in a society where social place and meaning, status and identity, escape from the humiliation of defeat and the dignity-bestowing success are all channelled into the chase for consumer goods. The natural human ambition of improvement deflected as the greed of positional goods; the natural desire for meaningful life reduced to the excitement of supermarket sales; the natural need for experience and challenge caricatured as the motorised crowd congesting the coastal motorways; they are all effusions of the capitalist market, which cannot secure its own perpetuation without suppressing all non-marketable alternatives to human improvement, life-meaning and challenging experience. It is the very profit-motivated economy which renders all alternatives to itself irrealistic. It is the pressure of such an economy which makes all critique of itself sound hollow - if not callous and inhuman.

...AND SOME POSSIBLE CONSEQUENCES

In this country, the critical state of the society which had shifted onto the consumer chase all the burdens of the power struggle has been brought dramatically into relief by the recent
spate of urban riots. They have been variously interpreted
in familiar terms of race disturbances (in spite of the obvious
fact that most of them have been, if anything, first genuine
exercises in racial co-operation), or - more naively still, in
terms of shrewd conspirators feeding on the disorientation
of inexperienced youth or parents failing in their police duty
of keeping children at home after school hours (and thus,
presumably, undermining the whole entertainment industry
aimed at the pocket-happy teenagers). There have been
elements of all these factors in the riots; but a longer look will
perhaps reveal their deeper nature as the consumer society's
equivalent of the luddites' quixotic attempt to stem the tide
of industrial revolution. The original luddites turned their
wrath against the contents of factories which epitomised the
demise of the whole way of life associated with the craftsman
shop. The Brixton or Toxteth luddites unloaded their desperation in an attack against the department stores; not against
the temples of ostentatious luxury meant for the rich, but
against their poor replicas stood in the middle of poverty-
stricken districts as the garrisons of the consumer society,
the life-pattern setters, generators of dreams and deflectors
of ambitions. The instinct of appropriation, whipped up by
the distribution-centred society, turned wild and found its
unanticipated expression in the massive looting; but there
was as well plenty of sheer destructive rage, when the symbols
of consumer dreams were torn in pieces, burnt and trampled
underfoot.

The young people who did it belonged to the first generation
about to be squeezed finally out of the role of producers and
goaded into a status determined by the consumption alone; the
first generation not to undergo the body-and-mind drill
administered by the factory-located disciplining powers, but
trained solely in the new consumer discipline, aimed at elicit-
ing proper responses to proper offers. The consumer orientation, first developed as a by-product, and an outlet, of the
industrial pattern of control, has been finally prised from the
original stem and transformed into a self-sustained and self-
perpetuating pattern of life. This transformation certainly calls
for a new type of power, in many respects sharply different
from the disciplining power specialising in the bodily drill,
which made possible the advent of industrial society. The new
power cannot be, unlike its predecessor, thematised as the
opposition between reason and passion, prudence and self-
indulgence, work and idleness. If one accepts Norbert Elias's
name of 'civilising process' for the emergence and establishment of disciplining power, the spread of new powers, those

typical of consumer society which the triumph of industrial pattern of control made inevitable, is, so to speak, a 'de-civilising process'. Passions, self-indulgence, entertainment are cleansed of disgrace into which the surveillance power of early modern society cast them. Moreover, they are no more conceptualised as such, except for a few nostalgic and increasingly irrelevant ritual incantations of industrial gospel. The new powers are articulated in terms of self-identity, authenticity, fullness of life, etc., and none of these articulations has a room for the traditional oppositions.

The demise of an old power and the advent of a new one must be a traumatic experience and a turbulent time. We analysed one such period in the earlier chapters. It is a plausible hypothesis that our own society is going at present through another period of this kind, when the rapidly obsolescing powers are too weak to uphold social order, while the new powers, which may take over the task in the future, have failed so far to develop sufficient means of control of their own.

Whatever the value of this hypothesis, the fact remains that the growing pressures of the consumer role, coupled with the slow disappearance of the producer roles, still remembered as the sole entry to the game of distribution, must put an unbearable psychological burden on the generation which experience the gap to the extent never experienced before (either because the disappearance of producer roles was not so drastic, or because consumer pressures, and the definition of social identity almost fully in consumer terms, were not so intense). The resulting 'social disorder', due to its evident consumer connection, renders the issue of economic growth more acute yet.

The probable outcome of the cessation of growth could perhaps be illuminated by Max Scheler's idea of 'ressentiment' which, in Lewis A. Coser's succinct description,[16]

> denotes an attitude which arises from a cumulative repression of feelings of hatred, revenge, envy and the like. When such feelings can be acted out, no ressentiment results. But when a person is unable to release these feelings against the persons or groups evoking them, thus developing a sense of impotence, and when these feelings are continuously re-experienced over time, then ressentiment arises....As distinct from rebellion, ressentiment does not lead to an affirmation of counter-values since ressentiment-imbued persons secretly crave the values they publicly denounce.

In Max Scheler's view, our society has in all times a high ressentiment-generating potential because of the in-built hypocrisy of more or less equal political and other rights coexisting with wide factual differences in power, property and education.[17]

The hypocrisy has always been a fertile ground for feelings
and attitudes of revenge, envy, the impulse to detract, spite,
Schadenfreude and malice. In most cases, however, these feelings stopped short of the stage of ressentiment; well before
this stage they could be deflated through the succession of
victories evidenced by the rising access to the coveted values.
According to Scheler, only impotence which prevents the feelings of disaffection from being released through the channel
of rebellion makes these feelings rankle and clot into the state
of ressentiment. The continuous adverse pressures are then
experienced as a fatality. Bloody-mindedness, generalised
aversion and indiscriminate, diffuse criticism replace the search
for alternative positive aims. Discontent is reforged into distrust of all ideas and all promises.

The gist of Scheler's concept is a supposition later cor-
roborated in a number of micro-sociological as well as historical
studies: that rallying under the banners of alternative Utopias,
and resulting attempts to revolutionise social conditions and
break the existing network of dependencies are occurring on a
rising tide. They feed on the experience of improvement and
drink from the climate of optimism. Desperation and accumulated
disappointment, on the other hand, is essentially a conservative
force. It suppresses the potential forces of transformation. It
breeds impotence and passivity broken only by the short flashes
of anger.

All these factors taken together explain why the capitalist
countries of the West (which, embracing a mere 18 per cent of
the world population, already consume 90 per cent of its non-
ferrous metals, 80 per cent of petroleum and natural rubber,
50 per cent of raw cotton, vegetable oil and sugar[18]) can hardly
view the possibility of the end to growth as anything but catastrophe. Shrinking resources (both in absolute terms and in terms
of diminished availability) are watched with terror mostly
because of the not at all illusory misgiving that the usurpatory
claims (in Frank Parkin's terms) bound to be set off will rend
the already overstrung fabric of the unequal society. Usurpatory claims are, after all, the rational behaviour in a society
which promotes the bargaining for the share in surplus as the
only legitimate substitute for individual autonomy and self-
management. Personal improvement and dignity, self-definition,
attaining the respectable social standard and all other dimensions of satisfactory life having been articulated, by the consumer stage of the late industrial society, as possession and
use of consumer goods - claims on the social surplus tend,
for the first time, to be prompted by the search of advancement rather than the defence of some equivalent of Rechtsgewohnenheiten. This is the real force which renders growth
so vital to the preservation of the entire power structure ('law
and order') of late industrial society. One would expect that the
slackening of the pace of growth will trigger off, as its immediate outcome, a reconsideration and renegotiation of some

crucial values on which the legitimation of industrial society
has rested so far.

A regular or partisan war against the principle of equality
is one outcome which one would anticipate. In more than a
marginal way, the Utopia of equality played a useful role in
the context of expanding capitalism. As an 'equality of universal man' it was an indispensable ingredient of the capitalist
culture. But even in its class-controversial, vindicatory form
of the equality of life-standards and social position, it was not
pure and simple anti-capitalist ideology. Capitalism could not
preserve its essential power pattern without turning the attention of its underdog to material compensations for lost autonomy, without fomenting desire of 'catching up with the
Joneses', getting richer, acquiring more of the material comforts of life. As long as one could indeed get richer without
making those already rich poorer, the egalitarian spur made
the wheels of expanding economy rotate faster, without unduly
straining their capitalist axis. For almost a century, the prizes
in the great egalitarian race were paid in the small change of
Samuel Gompers's 'more' ideology. As long as the ethics of
equality could be bought off with such small change, the
stability of capitalist power was undoubtedly its beneficiary.
Fearless of the exposure of its hypocrisy, it could - and it did
- cast itself in the role of great patron of equality.

All this has changed, of course, with egalitarian appetites
whetted to an unprecedented height and - as it were - in
unanticipated quarters, but the volume of goods to satisfy
them failing to grow. The Utopia of equality can now show its
other face, which it had neither time nor need to display
before. The old face was agreeable. The moral injunction 'it
is unjust that I have so little' could be used to lubricate the
mechanisms of the mass consumption economy. The other face
has another injunction written on it: 'it is unjust that they
have so much'. With the moment of truth round the corner,
and the bluff about to be called, the capitalist economy may
defend its right to exist only when rallying to the cause of
inequality.

The strategy likely to be adopted in the declared or undeclared war against equality seems predictable. It will probably
include the deployment of historical memory in galvanising the
virtues of achievement and insisting that the belief that the
industrious are rewarded (and, more to the point - that it is
the industrious who are rewarded or, still better, that one
recognises the industrious by their rewards) has been unjustly
discarded. It will have to include blowing the dust off the old
recriminations against the poor as indolent, dishonest, impro-
vident, indifferent to the 'needs of society', naively following
unscrupulous agitators and otherwise responsible for their
own miserable plight - accusations only barely concealed in the
vituperations against welfare scroungers, unemployed basking
in the Spanish sunshine and the denizens of 'dangerous

quarters' preferring mugging to work. It will have to include, finally, an effort to revive the idea that more poverty is the only cure against the innate sloth of the poor, and that only by making their social security less secure will they be forced to do something useful. What it is unlikely to entail is new, unrehearsed, forward- rather than backward-looking ideas. To use Parkin's terms again, one can say that the strategy is likely to be aimed at the reinforcement of the 'exclusion' aspect in the organised labour's 'closure'.

The strategy must be, therefore, supplemented by preventive measures against the 'usurpatory' aspects getting out of control. This is best done by yet further strengthening of the 'relative' aspects of the deprivation as articulated in and by the institutionalised power of labour organisations. The union-generated concern with differentials is likely to be given an additional boost by the government-sponsored exercises in 'comparability'. The exercises of this kind promote and further entrench the idea that equality of 'comparable' jobs and skills is just; by the same token they imply that some other jobs or skills are not comparable and should not be rewarded equally. Like the idea of differentials, the comparability exercises are thoroughly conservative in their effects. If they are resorted to by business interests, or actively backed by the more far-sighted among capitalists, it is for their potential to contain the usurpatory aspiration in a social space still at a safe distance from the defended territory.

Another complementary strategy could be the already mentioned denigration of growth and attempt to dissociate the idea of the good life from the desire to possess more techno-logically produced and marketed goods. This trend, however, is likely to remain the property of intellectual fringes of the middle class. It can hardly be embraced whole-heartedly by either of the two great class adversaries of the past. Capital cannot survive without a search for an ever-increased profit, and within the existing economic structure profit cannot be sought in any other way than extensive and intensive expansion of the markets. The growth of surplus remains the only means of defence of the power structure underlying its production which the capitalist society has historically developed. Capitalist ears will certainly be deaf to Mishan's reasoning, that:

if it is believed that over the last two centuries, during which workers were transformed from artisans and crafts-men to machine-hands and dial-watchers, a decline has taken place in the satisfactions that men once derived from their daily tasks, who is to say that the loss has been fully compensated by the consequent proliferation of goods and gadgetry and the transformation to a mechanised environment?

As to the other side, the argument is no more convincing.
Mishan, as it were, has few doubts as to the lack of resonance:
'once people's satisfactions come to depend almost wholly on
relative income or on some other index of status, a sustained
rise in the level of consumption...yields little additional satisfaction to society'.[19] The latter part of the sentence may well
be true, but its truth does not invalidate the poignant message
contained in the first. Indeed, people's satisfactions depend
almost wholly on income, and indices of status which are almost
without exception purchasable through the market; however
unsatisfactory these satisfactions could appear in the long
run, they have no substitute. There is no alternative to income
as the measure of the good life; and in our status-conscious
society, there is no alternative to the pursuit of status through
acquisition of wealth. It may be that people now search the
department stores for things their ancestors made themselves,
but they have forgotten how to make them; it may be that
this change brought spiritual impoverishment, by depriving
people of the joy of creation and by making them, instead,
dependent on others. Yet the contemplation of the true or
imaginary delights of the craftsman's life is of little avail to
people for whom the volume of their possessions is the only
evidence of their self-worth.

The short-term effects of arrested growth and falling labour
income (tantamount in the market-stimulated culture to a falling
standard of living) are likely to be more fissures and disaccord
within the labour movement. Insistence on differentials, on
keeping 'one's place in the league', on salvaging one's, however puny, privileges, is likely to draw unions apart and possibly make also more difficult a united stand of the many trades
within one union. Trade and organisational differences, often
criss-crossing and thereby adding yet more strength to the
force of cleavage, will in all probability move nearer to the
centre of the stage. When global output is falling, unemployment rising and prospects of general improvement fading,
group advantages seem a more rational strategy than solidarity
with the underdog. Refusal to embark on solidarity strikes,
inter-union and intra-union litigations, cases when two-thirds
of the factory staff vote the remaining third out of a job,
dwindling fortunes for militant shop-stewards - may become the
order of the day. Individual wage-packets may be seen as
security more reliable than the less tangible and less easy to
control social wages or goods of collective consumption. Guarding one's position in the pecking order may become the supreme
rationality, complete with its reverse side: devil takes the hind-
most.

THE PHENOMENON OF CUMULATIVE DEPRIVATION

In his seminal article of 1969[20] Claus Offe defined the principal
function of the 'late capitalist' state as 'cautious crisis management and long-term avoidance strategy'. Offe's argument was
that this function guides the allocation of relevance to various
competing articulations of the system's problems. Selective
state responses are determined by the evaluation of the relative 'crisis-generating' capacity of a problem, 'the greater
share always being directed to those groups which are able to
make most effective contribution toward the reduction of risk
under the circumstances' - in other words, to the groups which
have to be most urgently placated.
   The reverse side of the same tendency is the likelihood that
'certain vital areas of society will have slight prospects of
state intervention or state subvention when they find themselves in a crisis, simply because the consequences of such a
crisis would have no important relevance for the stability of
the system as a whole'. This relevance, however, cannot be,
within the administrative horizon, assessed by any other means
than anticipated extent of political disturbances, and sometimes
- of adverse economic consequences. Hence a 'concentric system
of priorities':

   the more gravely the violation of any claim or principle of
   intervention compromises the basic prerequisites for stability, the higher the level of priority that will be assigned
   to the corresponding problem area. Conversely, social
   needs that cannot present a credible case for the dangerous
   consequences that would ensue (or that they could precipi-
   tate) if their claim were ignored lie on the periphery of the
   sphere of state action.

   This system of priorities tends at all times to create disparities between better and weaker institutionalised areas of social
life. But when the resources standing at the state's disposal
become scarcer, disparities lead to an outright neglect of wide
areas of society. Resources tend to be fully concentrated on
the apparently crucial function of the state management of the
capitalist economy: maintenance of the rate of profit, of foreign
trade relations, of law and order. Vital areas somewhat remote
from the central function, or seen as of no immediate import for
its fulfilment, are starved.
   The overall effect of all these tendencies is the 'disturbance
capacity' turning into the main asset in the fight for resources.
A neglected group can make its claim audible only by making
manifest its ability to generate disorder; a showmanship of
militancy tends to replace argued persuasion. If a group is
incapable of significantly contributing to the market economy
either as producers or consumers, and, in addition, dispersed
and atomised by nature and hence not easily organisable - this

way out from the sordid predicament is not available. It is even
more difficult to envisage ways of overcoming the neglect of
functional areas which affect various groups in a rather diffuse
manner.

In Claus Offe's view, it is precisely the depressed functional
areas which are left behind by the system of priorities. His
argument to this effect deserves to be quoted in full:[21]

> the pauperism of the early capitalist proletariat has given
> way to the modern pauperism of depressed areas: educa-
> tion, transportation, housing, and health, which affect the
> *entire population*, are obvious cases in point. Institutions
> that are marginal to the mainstream of life, such as the
> preschool socialising phase, unemployment, old age after
> retirement, the mentally ill, and criminals, are further
> examples, as are the exceptional situations of ethnic minori-
> ties, branches of the economy with no future, slums, and
> structural poverty areas. A concept that traces a certain
> parallel to the strata and class conflicts accentuated by the
> vertical pattern of social inequality would perhaps be the
> notion of different *'situational groupings'* - a notion that
> emphasises the disparity between vital areas. These would
> be groups that were exposed to situationally dependent
> deprivations and frustrations without the individuals'
> status on the income scale being able to do much to allev-
> iate problems and crises. The examples alluded to tend to
> confirm the view that under *state-regulated capitalism,
> all-out class conflict is no longer the driving force of social
> change. A horizontal pattern of inequality, that is, dis-
> parities between vital areas, is emerging increasingly into
> the foreground.*

It has been shown in the preceding chapter that the social
costs of market competition are met in highly industrialised
societies by the state-administered redistribution of resources.
As Galbraith has emphasised, there are no market mechanisms
able to replace the state in this task; left to themselves, public
services would permanently fall behind the demand. Demand
for public services, however, is a political, rather than economic, phenomenon. It can be promoted only by political means
and by politically organised forces. While group-based political
claims on state-administered resources have been, at least to
a degree, institutionalised in the corporatist arrangement, the
area-based needs have developed no institutionalised means of
expression and representation. In consequence, the system is
biased against them. There is a permanent predisposition built
into the corporatist arrangement to favour privately appropriated shares of national product and to accord lesser importance
to collective consumption without a clear address, and consequently without specific interest basis.

As a result of this bias, income from labour or capital may

still, also under conditions of arrested growth, remain effective safeguards against pauperisation. On the other hand, pauperisation becomes the fate of the groups which are to a larger
degree, if not fully, dependent on the increasingly depressed
areas of social life. The unemployed will not be sheltered
against the rising costs of life which the employed will be unwilling to balance at their own expense. People who are ill
will be exposed to the poor quality health facilities abandoned
by the better-off, who are buying the services of private
medicine. The children of the poor will be offered overcrowded
classrooms but no meals or textbooks in the schools in which
the better-off parents, who can afford to pay for the education of their offspring, have lost interest. Mothers without
husbands will be definitely cut off from the labour market by
the disappearance of nursery schools or creches. Old people
will become the main victims of the shrinking welfare offices.
Ethnic minorities, first to lose their jobs in rising unemployment,
will in all probability suffer a cumulative impact of the bias
with all its ramifications. Families with incomes too small or
too irregular to deserve a mortgage loan will be easy prey
for the cruelty and greed of slum landlords.

All these are, so to speak, examples of a 'mediated' deprivation. Pauperisation of groups or categories of people is a
secondary effect of the pauperisation of specific areas of public
life. This pauperisation, as it were, affects the life standards
of groups receiving regular income from capital or labour in a
less decisive manner. Hence the pauperised groups tend to
be abandoned to their own fate, and defended only by relatively
weak associations of well-wishers, speaking in a low voice in
comparison to the resounding claims of the well-entrenched
partners of the corporatist arrangement. What makes the case
of such groups still weaker is the fact that their grievances
have no specific culprit, nor a concrete adversary. Demon-
stration of the 'disturbance capacity' is a poor guide, if it is
not clear whose interests could be jeopardised by the actions
undertaken by the destitute. Trade unions won long ago the
exemption of their militant measures from criminal responsibility
and, on the whole, public liability. The new pauperised groups,
because of the mediated nature of their deprivation, and no
contractually defined adversary, have no access to the legally
provided forms of self-defence. Their actions have little economic effect; but very easily they acquire a political meaning,
as the state-guarded 'law and order' is the area to which this
kind of disturbance is immediately assigned. These groups
cannot effectively pursue their interests without coming into
conflict with the legal or political system.

The plight of the pauperised groups caught in the net of
'multiple depression' is self-perpetuating for yet another reason. The cuts in collective consumption, social wages and
public services in general are often presented as results of a
temporary re-allocation of resources necessary in the lean

years; 'We cannot pay what we cannot afford' is the usual con-
science-comforting explanation, implying that once the nation
can afford it, the standards of public assistance will be
restored. In fact, building up employment costs much more
than preventing unemployment in the first place. Exacerbation
of neglect is, among other factors, also a function of time.
The costs of its redress rise out of proportion with the sums
temporarily 'saved'. The longer it lasts, the more difficult is
the neglect to repair.

Gunnar Myrdal was one of the first to warn about this tendency of social problems to self-intensification, also (or rather,
above all) in highly industrialised, and therefore potentially
affluent, societies. 'Every year, indeed every month, that a
high level of unemployment is tolerated, makes full employment
more difficult to obtain as a policy goal'.[22] The reason is, again,
the cumulative effect of deprivation. Prolonged unemployment
tends to arrest educational achievement among the young and
occupational re-adjustment among adults, and gradually transforms the unemployed into the unemployable. Their skills and
education records are out of tune with the requirements of an
economy back in a high gear. A rationalising tendency in the
economy renders the jobs such people would be able to perform
obsolete; while another economic expansion would require
occupational specifications which these people cannot meet. On
the one hand, therefore, the pool of unemployed becomes
stagnant and virtually impossible to drain. On the other hand,
any attempt at economic expansion quickly grinds to a halt for
the lack of necessary labour. Myrdal wrote of a 'structural
unemployment': unemployment which is no more a transitory
lack of employment, but a social phenomenon in its own right,
which no 'Phillips curve' can reduce to employment with a
minus mark. Such unemployment is not a tool of adjusting
supply and demand and restoring economy to health, but a
permanent and self-expanding liability placing a heavy fiscal
burden on the national output. The growing gap between the
type of labour demanded and the type the unemployed can
supply, makes the phenomenon of unemployment less and less
sensitive to market stimuli. In Myrdal's view, the inevitable
result is an 'underclass' of unemployed and gradually unemployable persons and families at the bottom of a society....It is
almost as difficult for them to get and hold a good job as it
long ago became for a boot-black to end as president of a great
corporation.[23]

Searching the American political scene for the forces able to
promote a social effort likely to rectify what is simultaneously
the source of human suffering and the case of conspicuous
economic wastage, Myrdal came to the conclusion that trade
unions were 'in danger of becoming protective organisations
for a number of separate groups of job-holders'. If one heeds
the previously quoted conclusion of Lawson and George's survey
of contemporary Europe, the danger seems to have materialised.

The spectacular achievements of the post-war decades in the
field of social security did little to improve the lot of the modern
paupers. In most highly industrialised countries, 'the bulk of
the post-war expansion of social welfare has not been aimed
at low-income groups. It has been much more concerned with
maintaining acquired social status and protecting the capacities
and incentives of ordinary workers for gainful employment.'[24]
In the new situation of arrested growth, organised labour is
even less likely than it had been in fatter years to play the
knight of equality. The great divide between the job-holders
and the unemployable may well become in time the most closely
guarded frontier of the trade union domain.

The social significance of unemployment is not, of course,
reducible to the often abject poverty to which it leads - but
poverty is one of its most sinister effects. Against this poverty
the regularly employed worker has won a degree of protection
which is much more than one could say for the unemployed.
A century and a half later, Harriet Martineau's contention that
except 'the distinction between sovereign and subject, there
is no social difference in England so wide as that between the
independent laborer and the pauper',[25] seems to have been
eroded more in its first part than in the second.

Poverty is today, as it was before, a faithful companion of
national wealth. Unemployment is one of its causes. According
to almost universal agreement, old age and ill health are most
persistent among the rest. The twentieth-century venture into
the 'caring', 'distributing', or 'welfare' state, apparently has
done little to shift income and wealth from the very rich to the
less so; but it has done close to nothing for the elimination of
poverty. Richard Titmuss's summary of the first two decades
of the post-war welfare state in Britain - that those who bene-
fited from it most were those who needed it least - has not
since lost much of its veracity.

Who exactly may be defined as living in poverty, is a matter
of hotly argued and far from conclusive debate among the
experts - economists, social administrators, and sociologists
alike. Even more contentious is the problem of operationalising
the definition - of making poverty measurable. Disagreement
is likely to persist, as each of the suggested solution carries
inevitably far-reaching political consequences. With all the
divisions, however, the debate seems to be based on a broad
consensus entailing several crucial assumptions. The most
important among them is the idea that poverty is always relative. Poverty means insufficient (below socially acceptable
standards) satisfaction of needs; but needs themselves are
changeable and relative to cultural expectations and modes of
life, social pressures on the 'levelling up' uniformity, and the
technological or 'density' necessities as determined by the
infrastructure of the life process. Relativity of poverty is,
therefore, two-fold: the boundaries of poverty vary depending on socially produced needs and socially produced standards

of what is an 'acceptable gap' between the need and its satisfaction. At any time, poverty is socially defined in relation to
whatever passes as 'adequate social functioning'.[26] Peter Townsend, easily the most determined and effective student of
poverty in Britain in the grand tradition of Seebohm Rowntree,
from his first pamphlet, published in 1965 with Abel-Smith,
up to his most recent, comprehensive and conclusive mono-
graph,[27] consistently promotes the idea of poverty as relative
to the style of life prevailing in a given social environment. In
order to remain a member of the community, a social being, one
has to do more than satisfy one's physiological needs - to be
fed, clad, and sheltered. One has to be able as well to invite
friends to tea or meet them at the local pub, or send Christmas
and birthday cards, or to engage in the numerous other little
functions of which the web of community and social interaction
is woven. By this reckoning, almost a third of the British
population can be described as living on, or below the poverty
line. These include above all old people whose pensions, even
when supplemented by welfare care, prove inadequate; persons
afflicted with prolonged illness and their families; the unemployed and their 'dependants'; but also families of low-paid
workers. As it happens, this is simultaneously a list of the
categories most atomised and least articulate; categories with
little 'disturbance potential', without regular representation or
powerful pressure groups, categories with problems unlikely
to be adopted as their own by any of the corporatist partners,
who tend to see these problems as placing too heavy a burden
on other, more important tasks. In short, these are categories
of economically, socially and politically weak people. And, as
Robert Lekachman aptly observed, 'the tendency of government
is to insist where its citizens are weak that rights are surrendered in return for benefits. Few groups are weaker than
welfare families.[28] For the poor of today, the early nineteenth-
century choice between civil and social rights is not just a
matter of a sombre episode of history. As for the poor of that
time, virtually the only way of forcing their plight on to the
agenda of public concerns is, to employ Eric Hobsbawm's pointed
expression, 'bargaining by riot'. By definition, riot is an out-
break (usually sudden) of lawlessness on the part of a crowd.
The most deprived are on the whole the most atomised and
hence crowd-like. The modern form of multiple, cumulative
destitution is, like the one of the end of the eighteenth century
and the beginning of the nineteenth, likely to prompt violent
forms of political struggle. The formidable inflammability of
accumulated social grievances generated by the consumer society
and left to fester by its increasingly inadequate political institutions is often mistakenly explained away by reference to
racial tension by the simple reason that racial and ethnic
groups are the only categories of the 'cumulatively deprived'
who have the backing of community bonds and hence are
quicker to reforge their desperation into one form or another

of collective action.

As a summary of this chapter's argument, one can say that the field of the most drastic inequalities, conflicts and unresolved problems has shifted in late capitalist society from the disputed 'no-man's land' between the two powerful industrial class protagonists towards the deprived sectors of social life. The latter are causally related to the functioning of the system as a whole, to the persistent and perhaps incurable disturbances in the exchange and mutual accommodation between the sub-systems - but they are not directly linked to the traditional repartition conflict between the industrial classes; if anything, they are more likely to be exacerbated rather than cured by the contestation arising from this conflict. Whether the disprivilege of the dispossessed groups (women, racial minorities, the chronically unemployed, old and sick, homeless, residents of the depressed areas) consists of legal or cultural deprivation or a straightforward pauperisation, their disaffection, despair, alienation, even their overt dissent, however significant an effect they may indirectly exert on the range of options as articulated by the partners of the corporatist network, are unlikely to cause a substantive transformation of structures as fundamental as those traditionally associated with the class struggle; they are unlikely, in other words, to destroy or bridle the factors responsible for their continuing existence. In Habermas's assessment, their struggle 'lacks the chances of revolutionary success', as it does not affect the way in which the goods being the object of contention are produced.

Moreover, areas of deprivation from which a most critical challenge arises for the system which can only manage the necessary 'loyalty input' through the substitution of material gratification for the discursive grounding of its legitimacy, cannot be often expressed in terms of clearly defined groups and their interests. One can speak, for example, of such areas of deprivation as health, education, housing, public transport, etc., which normally designate some categories of people as the victims most painfully hurt, but which have also a diffuse impact on the quality of life which cannot be readily localised as 'class interest'. But it is in these areas precisely that the crises and the critical tests for the system tend to arise and must be confronted. Rather than to speak of the industrial infrastructure determining the policies of the state and the dominant cultural pattern of the society, one would be well advised to shift the focus of investigation towards the politically operated repartition, and the institutionalised forces and procedures which determine its course, as the location where systemic crises are born and where the search for their solution can be conducted.

RE-POLITICISATION OF POLITICS

Concepts tend to outlive the historical configurations which
gave them birth and infused them with meaning. This tendency
is rooted in the natural propensity to absorb and accommodate
new experience into the familiar picture of the world; habitual
categories are the main tools of this absorption. New experience
does not fit the categories easily. In order to be reduced to
the familiar and therefore 'understandable', its protruding
edges must be trimmed, its uncustomary colours dulled, and
everything genuinely novel must be explained away or dismissed as an aberration. If all these 'domesticating' expedients
have been successful, much of the truly unprecedented quality
of the new experience may have passed unnoticed for a considerable time, until the volume of 'aberrations' exceeds some
critical size and bursts into public awareness with a sudden-
ness befitting crises and revolutions. Obviously this universal
affliction of common sense cannot be blamed on sociologists.
But sociologists do often assist common sense to be caught
unawares, by reinforcing its natural tendencies with scholarly
sophistication and authority. Their corrections of popular,
'naive' notions amount sometimes to the stretching or trimming
operations which prolong the illusion of their continuing
adequacy and, as it were, their life after death. The bankruptcy of old categories is thereby postponed, and the imminent crisis, once it arrives, is yet more shocking.
   The artificial extension of the natural life of concepts has
consequences more serious than purely academic misinterpre-
tations. As long as the concepts remain embedded in common
sense and used as resources with which historical actors
account for their actions, design their strategies and assess
their results, they must be seen as powerful factors which
co-determine the behaviour of large groups of people, and
perhaps also developmental trends of whole societies. These
factors may remain powerful beyond the time when the strategies they legitimised were bringing intended results. Objec-
tively available evidence of the growing inadequacy of concepts
need not be a reason (at least not a sufficient reason) for their
abandonment. Two circumstances make concepts immune. First,
all cognitive categories employed by common sense have,
thanks to their intimate relation with social practices, an in-
built capacity for self-affirmation, first noticed in the famous
assertion of W.I. Thomas ('when people define a situation as
real, it tends to become real in its consequences'), and then
described by many sociologists in reference to Merton's notion
of the 'self-fulfilling prophecy'. The above capacity is vividly,
though crudely revealed in a common observation (many times
confirmed in psychological experiments), that if people define
a group as their enemy, they embark on antagonistic gambits
which quickly release a 'schismogenetic chain' (Gregory Bateson) of interaction and force the designated group to recipro-

cate aggression. Second, in their 'primitive accumulation of
authority' stage, commonsensical categories spawn institutions
which assume the management of their collective applications.
The institutions, like the categories themselves (albeit with
yet more force), develop a self-perpetuating proclivity, which
further strengthens the resilience of associated categories.
Long after any tangible link with experience has been lost,
the categories may then retain their usefulness, as ritualistic
safeguards of institutional cohesion, linguistic symbols of
institutional identity, or ostensible proofs of the institutions's
uninterrupted legitimacy.

What has been said above about concepts' astonishing capacity
for deferring their demise and outliving the reality they once
connoted, applies in full to the case of 'class'. We saw before
how the notion of class emerged in the first three decades of
British industrial history as an articulation of new social practices and a tool of construction new social bonds in the wake of
the dismantling of the networks of patronage and the emergence
of a new type of social power. We saw the role performed by the
intellectuals as the 'centres' of new formations, whose 'periphery' was annexed and held through institutional allegiance
rather than participation in political discourse. We saw how
the perpetration of the new power structure was institutionalised in a way which inescapably led to the creation of social
pressures which this structure could not accommodate. We saw
how institutions thus created reached in the end the limit of
their dynamic potential, thereby turning into additional causes
of societal malfunctions rather than the forces of their rectification.

I have argued in this chapter that the historically conditioned
tendency to perceive the structure and dynamic tendencies of
the late capitalist society through the prism of the struggle
between the two great classes which confronted each other
inside the ascendant capitalist industry clouds rather than
clarifies vision. Issues which once catalysed class oppositions
embody today the contradictory nature of joint interests.
Contradictions which haunt the socio-political system are
explicable as the incongruence of the state-managed defence
of the production-oriented power structure, rather than as a
reflection of the antagonistic class interests. Most importantly,
perhaps, the sharpest inequalities and deprivations of the
present-day highly industrialised societies cannot be properly
interpreted as the manifestations of class exploitation.

Coming to grips with the tensions and conflicts of these
societies is difficult because of the present chasm between
historically institutionalised interest-representation and the
systemic needs vainly seeking their articulation and practical
means of satisfaction. None of the great institutionalised class
forces may be expected to funnel the diffuse grievances which
articulate the malfunctions of the corporatist arrangement.
These malfunctions arise, as it were (1) from the internal

contradictions of the market economy dominated by big organisations, (2) from the internal incongruencies of the attempt
to solve these contradictions through state management of the
economy, and (3) from the contradictions of the corporatist
form in which this state management tends to be carried out.
Above all, they arise from the essential impossibility of 'rectify-
ing industrial output in such a way that the power patterns
can go on to be sheltered, as this generates the incessantly
growing volume of pressures put on the distribution of surplus.
These malfunctions, therefore, materialise in the persistent
tendency to produce depressed areas of life as side effects of
the crisis-avoidance strategy and in the sedimentation of
marginal categories of population which suffer their cumulative
burden.

Any realistic attempt to grapple with the problems of present-
day society will have to address itself to the systemic contradictions listed above, rather than, following the traditional
model, trace the origins and the solution of problems to the
interests and policies of classes conceived as supra-individual
subjects.

A major obstacle which any such attempt is likely to encounter is the location of a social force answering the description
of the 'historical class' – a group which, when rallying to the
support of its own particular interest, cannot but promote the
historical needs of the society as a whole. Neither capital nor
labour seem to fit the model. On the one hand, their interests
are increasingly self-contradictory; on the other hand (or,
rather, in consequence), when pursued, they seem to generate
grave systemic problems rather than rectify them.

In general, one could say that at the later stage of industrial
society, the stage we live in now, there is no group, or assem-
bly of groups, whose interests could withstand a discursive
scrutiny as the 'universal' interests of the society as a whole.
This is the main reason why the analysis of the present afflictions of this society and their conceivable solution in terms of
the traditional theory of class struggle is misleading and can
generate, however pursued, merely extrapolations of particular
interests, which cannot but further exacerbate the malfunctions
which they promise to rectify. That this is so is the outcome of,
so to speak, the very historical success of the pattern of power
characteristic of industrial society, and the correlated shift of
articulated interests and associated conflicts into the field of
the distribution of surplus. With the latter issue acquiring
increasingly the features of a zero-sum game, no 'conflict
to end all conflicts', postulated by the traditional class theory,
is feasible. Its historical chance seems to have been lost with
the 'economisation' of the power struggle at the early stage of
industrial society.

The belief in the continuing topicality of class theory is ultimately based on the assignment of centrality to the conflict over
control of labour and its products, located within the production

of surplus. This is manifested in the virtually axiomatic selection of capital and labour as major classes of the modern society - and in viewing industry as the central location of their conflict (a habitualised thinking shared by sociologists and the public at large - consider how automatically any action for a higher share of national income is labelled 'industrial'). But it is exactly this habit, supported by historical memory and its institutionalised infrastructure, which is to be questioned in view of the very different character of power struggle typical of the present stage of industrial society.

The formation of class society was the outcome of the submission of the vast masses of expropriated and unemployed poor to a new type of work discipline, which entailed control over their bodies and denial of their personal autonomy as producers. As we have seen in earlier chapters, this essentially power struggle was soon 'economised', and social classes had been identified as factors of industrial production; class conflict has been subsequently institutionalised as the bargaining over the price of control pattern which the productive process now involved - in view of the deroutinisation of distribution patterns.

The present issue, however, is not any more the question of the share in surplus as a compensation for (and the cost of the acceptance of) the power over the producers. The issue fast assuming centrality among the systemic problems is that of the progressive dissociation of distributive entitlements from the participation in the production of surplus. First, the efforts to supplement the market in its function of the reproduction of conditions of continuing production, led to the gradual, but steady increase of the distributive role of non-productive agents (and thus to the politicisation of the division of surplus), but also to the direct intervention of political agents into the production itself, guided by distributive objectives. Later on, the efforts of the managers of production to shed the growing costs of politicised distribution led to the squeezing of an increasing number of producers out of the productive roles. In opposition to the early stages of industrial society, with its tendency to subordinate the distributive entitlements to the productive roles, the problem consists now in the growing independence of the right to participate in the consumption of surplus from the possibility of partaking in its production.

This means that at the present time the distribution of surplus and hence also the provision of conditions for continuing reproduction of society has become a directly political problem, which extends far beyond the confines of the 'economy proper'. But this means also that the power control aimed at the maintenance of public order cannot be operated (as it was hoped at the early stages of industrial society) mainly through the productive roles - as an increasing volume of distributive needs are provided for outside, and in no connection with, such roles. The joint result is an immediately political character for the previously economised issues of control and personal autonomy.

Ours seems to be, therefore, a time of transition. Much as in the era of industrial revolution, ascendancy of a new type of power tends to be seen, interpreted, and criticised in terms of the old type, now largely defunct and at any rate increasingly ineffective. What is increasingly evident is that the control over the bodies of producers is increasingly inadequate as a major vehicle of social integration and the reproduction of society. What is much less evident from the perspective moulded by historical memory, is the nature of the social power which is likely to replace it.

What seems, however, inevitable is that the new grounds of social organisation would eventually involve revision of the principles of social integration promoted and established by industrial revolution and the consequent development. The latter buttressed the security of the power structure on the 'positive feedback loop' between ever-increasing surplus and rising distributive claims. For reasons listed before, progress along this road seems to be nearing the end. The outcome may be only a direct, unconcealed and explicit politicisation of the issue of power structure and social organisation in general. The pressure on social surplus can be relieved only if the stiff and highly asymmetrical patterns of control (which generated this pressure as a substitute for the re-negotiation of power relations) are replaced by a pattern of interdependence, allowing for a direct confrontation (as distinct from one mediated by distributive status) with the issues of personal autonomy and fulfilment. In other words, what seems to stand in the way of the resolution of the present crisis is not merely the capitalist ownership of the means of control but the industrial pattern of control as such.

This pattern is characterised chiefly by the sharp division between the agents and the objects of action; and, on the whole, by the kind of action the success of which depends on the trained passivity of its objects. The inherent and ineradicable activity of the latter is then let loose in another area – that of consumer maximisation. People deprived of control over a wide area of their life are, so to speak, forced to become maximisers instead. Much as the factory system used and deployed the already developed patterns of disciplining power, modern merchandising industry used and deployed the already developed maximising tendency and brought it to new extremes, having invented and refined sophisticated agencies of promoting, advertising and otherwise creating and intensifying new appetites for marketable goods, together with the belief that personal problems consist in the lack of specific commodities and may be resolved by their acquisition. In the long run, the production of social surplus itself came to depend on constant exacerbation of the so-deployed maximising tendency. Once the reasonable satisfaction of this tendency has become problematic, the whole system of social production and satisfaction of needs seems to be in an acute crisis. But this is ultimately a crisis of the vicious circle generated by concrete patterns of control, and not the crisis of the productive potential of the society, as it is often presented. Maximisation of commodity possessions is not a viable solution to the problems arising from the deployment of disciplining power as the means of social integration. But then the disciplining power is itself a historical development and need not be the only means through which society can be organised. The maximising tendency is intimately associated with the specific powers of control which redefined the problem of personal unfreedom as the lack of access to marketable goods, and personal emancipation as the broadening of such an access. It need not survive the disintegration of the type of powers responsible for these definitions.

In the long run, the present crisis, often described as economic or technological, seems to be mostly political in character; it concerns above all the type and the distribution of social power and the way it affects the life patterns of people forced to seek the improvement of their lives through the maximisation of their - purchasable - possessions. The prospect of a solution to such a crisis seems to be associated with the re-negotiation of the problems of unfreedom and emancipation; shifting them away from the field of the market and the distribution of social surplus in general and directly into the field of organisation and administration of social life.

This means, among other things, that the field of politics would come into its own; it would cease to be - as it has been increasingly throughout the history of industrial society - 'economics by proxy', i.e. a set of activities reducible virtually in full to the competition between groups claiming their share in allocation of goods and the making of authoritative decisions about this allocation. Politics would become instead more directly political - i.e. concerned with the organisation of social life, self-management, restitution and preservation of human control over the ways in which human bodily and spiritual potential is developed and deployed.

What the crisis of late industrial society puts on the agenda is, in other words, not just a further extension of political franchise to allow the remainder of handicapped categories or groups to employ the extant political institutions, complete with their inherent 'corporatist bias', in the pursuit of an increased share in the national surplus (these institutions, by their very constitution, cannot be so universalised). Instead, it puts on the agenda the emancipation of politics from its subordination to economics. More concretely, it posits the question of the re-possession by politics of the right to validate, re-negotiate and transform discursively the basic structure of power heretofore left to the discretion of economic institutions and only defended and reinforced by politics through its generalised concern with 'law and order'. The scope of involvement in active politics is one element of such a re-possession; another is a radical shift in the topics and objectives of political

discourse - the redefinition of democracy in terms of the substance of political discourse, the extensiveness of its agenda
and the scope of issues open to discursive renegotiation, and
not merely in terms of the numbers formally admitted to political
participation. Such a qualitative, as distinct from merely
numerical, transformation of politics has been sketched by
Tom Bottomore in his comments on Schumpeter's classic characterisation of democracy:[29]

> Competition for political leadership makes it possible for
> those social groups which are dissatisfied with their posi-
> tion in society, or with the general direction of social
> policy, to express their criticism and to bring some influ-
> ence to bear upon those who are political leaders for the
> time being. But this is still not the only important means
> of ensuring that a society is open to criticism and change,
> and that decisions are not made in an arbitrary way or in
> the service of particular interests. For the effective work-
> ing of a thoroughly democratic society at least two other
> things are essential: first, that as many citizens as possible
> should share in making decisions, that is to say, should
> have the opportunity and experience, in diverse spheres
> and for some part of their lives, of exercising political
> leadership; and second, that there should exist a consider-
> able variety of relatively autonomous associations (includ-
> ing publicly owned business enterprises) in which such
> self-government can be practised, and which provides a
> basis for a permanent, unimpeded critisim and reform of
> social arrangements.

Notes

1 CLASS: BEFORE AND AFTER. A PREVIEW

1 W. Barrington Moore, Jr, 'Injustice, The Social Basis of Obedience and Revolt', London, Macmillan, 1978, p. 135.
2 Harold Perkin, The Social Causes of the Industrial Revolution, in 'The Structured Crowd', Hassocks, Harvester, 1981, p. 37.
3 Cf. Richard Burn, 'The History of the Poor Laws with Observations (1764)', Augustus M. Kelley, Clifton, N.J., 1973, pp. 60-103.
4 Ernest Barker, 'The Development of Public Services in Western Europe 1660-1930', Oxford University Press, 1944, p. 69.
5 Olwen H. Hufton, 'Europe: Privilege and Protest 1730-1789', Hassocks, Harvester, 1980, p. 348.
6 E.P. Thompson, 'The Making of the English Working Class', London, Methuen, 1963, pp. 357, 832.
7 John Rule, 'The Experience of Labour in Eighteenth-Century Industry', London, Croom Helm, 1981, p. 212.
8 Moore Jr, op. cit., pp. 143, 147.
9 Rule, op. cit., p. 209.
10 In M.W. Flint and T.C. Smout (eds), 'Essays in Social History', Oxford, Clarendon, 1974.
11 Cf, for example, Herbert G. Gutman's portrayal of the factory drill applied to East European immigrants in twentieth-century industrial America 'Work, Culture, and Community in Industrialising America', Oxford, Blackwell, 1976, pp. 4-6.
12 Max Weber, 'The Protestant Ethic and the Spirit of Capitalism', trans. Talcott Parsons, London, George Allen & Unwin, 1976, p. 181.
13 Michel Foucault, 'Power and Knowledge', ed. Colin Gordon, Hassocks, Harvester, 1980, p. 41.
14 Cf. Anton Menger, 'The Right to the Whole Product of Labour', trans. M.E. Tanner, London, Macmillan, 1899, p. 28.
15 Claus Offe and Helmuth Wiesenthal, Two Logics of Collective Action, in G.M. Zeitlin (ed.), 'Political Power and Society Theory', vol. I, Greenwich Conn., IAI Press, 1980, p. 104.
16 Ibid., p. 73.
17 Ibid., pp. 71, 79.
18 Cf. Daniel Bell, 'The Coming of the Post-Industrial Society', London, Basic Books 1973.
19 Cf. H.D. Lasswell, The World Revolution of Our Time, in H.D. Lasswell and Daniel Lerner (eds), 'World Revolutionary Elites', MIT Press, 1965, pp. 86, 87, 92.
20 Cf. 'The Intellectuals on the Road to Class Power', trans. Andrew Arato and Richard E. Allen, Hassocks, Harvester, 1979, pp. 14, 53, 224.
21 Cf. 'The Future of Intellectuals and the Rise of the New Class', London, Macmillan, 1979, pp. 1-8.
22 Cf. Jürgen Habermas, 'Legitimation Crisis', trans. Thomas McCarthy, London, Heinemann, 1976.
23 James O'Connor, 'The Fiscal Crisis of the State', St Martin's Press, New York, 1973.
24 Cf. Claus Offe, Political Authority and Class Structures, trans.

Michael Vale, 'International Journal of Sociology', 1972, vol. II,
pp. 73-108.
25 Cf. Lasswell, op. cit., p. 80.
26 Cf. for instance, 'Production de la Société', Paris, Seuil, 1973;
   'La Voix et le Regard', Paris, Seuil 1978.

2 FROM RANK TO CLASS

1 In M.W. Flinn and T.C. Smout (eds), 'Essays in Social History', Oxford,
   Clarendon, 1974, p. 157.
2 Harold Perkin, 'The Origins of Modern English Society 1780-1880',
   London, Routledge & Kegan Paul, 1969, p. 26.
3 Ibid., p. 218.
4 Conditions of the Labouring Classes, 'Quarterly Review', vol. 46,
   1832, pp. 363 ff.
5 'Gorgon', 8 May 1818; 'Address on the Reform Bill', 1831. Both quoted
   from Patricia Hollis (ed.), 'Class and Conflict in Nineteenth-Century
   England 1815-1850', London, Routledge & Kegan Paul, 1973, pp. 10 and 78.
6 Quoted from Asa Briggs, in Flinn and Smout, op. cit., p. 156.
7 R.J. Morris, 'Class and Class Consciousness in the Industrial Revolution
   1780-1850', London, Macmillan, 1979, p. 18.
8 Michel Foucault, 'Power/Knowledge', ed. Colin Gordon, Hassocks,
   Harvester, 1980, p. 39.
9 Cf. Georges Duby, 'L'économie rurale et la vie des campagnards dans
   l'occident médiéval', Paris, Presses Universitaires Françaises, 1962,
   p. 98.
10 Robert Muchembled, 'Culture populaire et culture des élites dans la
   France moderne (XVe-XVIIe siècles)', Paris, Flammarion, 1978.
11 Cf. Frances Fox Piven and Richard A. Cloward, Social Policy and the
   Formation of Political Consensus, in G.M. Zeitlin (ed.), 'Political Power
   and Society Theory', vol. I, Greenwich, Conn., IAI Press, 1980.
12 Cf. 'Civilisation, le mot et l'idée, exposés par Lucien Febvre et al.',
   La Renaissance de Livre, Paris, 1930, p. 9-10 and the footnote on p. 48.
13 Foucault, op. cit., p. 101.
14 Dorothy Marshall, 'The English Poor Law in the 18th Century', London,
   Routledge & Son, 1926, pp. 247, 248.
15 Alexis de Tocqueville, 'The Ancien Régime and the French Revolution',
   trans. Stuart Gilbert, London, Collins, 1966, pp. 51 and 69.
16 Olwen H. Hufton, 'Europe: Privilege and Protest 1730-1789', Hassocks,
   Harvester, 1980, p. 37.
17 Quoted from Henry C. Payne, 'The Philosophers and the People', Yale
   University Press, 1976, p. 29.
18 Alan Forrest, 'The French Revolution and the Poor', Oxford, Blackwell,
   1981, p. 19.
19 Witt Bowden, 'Industrial Society in England towards the end of the
   Eighteenth Century', London, Macmillan, 1925, p. 215-6.
20 Foucault, op. cit., p. 148.
21 Cf. Alexandrian, 'Le socialisme romantique', Paris, Seuil, 1979, pp. 98-9.
22 Foucault, op. cit., p. 155.
23 Maurice Manston, 'Sir Edwin Chadwick', London, Parsons, 1925, p. 51.
24 J.L. Hammond and Barbara Hammond, 'The Town Labourer 1760-1832',
   (1917), London, Longmans, 1966, p. 101.
25 'The Labouring Classes of England, in a series of letters by an English-
   man' (William Dodd), (2nd edn 1848), Clifton, N.J., Augustus M. Kelley,
   1976, pp. 70-1.
26 John Fielden, 'The Curse of the Factory System' (1836), London,
   Frank Cass, 1969, pp. 5-6.
27 Cf. J.L. Hammond and Barbara Hammond, 'The Rise of Modern
   Industry' (1925), London, Methuen, 1951, pp. 196-7.
28 Forrest, op. cit., p. 26.

29 Hufton, op. cit., p. 348.
30 J.L. and B. Hammond, 'The Rise...', pp. 206, 207.
31 Hufton, op. cit., p. 348.
32 Barrington Moore, Jr, 'Injustice, The Social Basis of Obedience and Revolt', London, Macmillan, 1978, p. 143.
33 William H. Sewell Jr, 'Work and Revolution in France', Cambridge University Press, 1980, p. 1.
34 Cf. John Foster, 'Class Struggle and the Industrial Revolution', London, Weidenfeld and Nicolson, 1974, p. 21.
35 Ibid., p. 25.
36 Barrington Moore Jr, op. cit., p. 155.
37 Quoted from Sewell Jr, op. cit., p. 23.
38 Barrington Moore Jr, op. cit., p. 160.
39 John Rule, 'The Experience of Labour in Eighteenth-Century Industry', London, Croom Helm, 1981, pp. 211-12.
40 John Stuart Mill, 'Principles of Political Economy', vol. II (4th edn), London, John W. Parker & Son, p. 337.
41 Cf. Claus Offe, 'Industry and Inequality', trans. James Wickham, London, Arnold, 1976, p. 40 ff.
42 Sidney Pollard, Factory discipline in the Industrial Revolution, 'The Economic History Review', Second series, vol. XVI, 1963-4, pp. 254-71.
43 J.L. and B. Hammond, 'The Rise...', p. 208.
44 E.P. Thompson, Time, Work Discipline, and Industrial Capitalism, 'Past and Present', 38, December 1967, pp. 56-97.
45 Foucault, op. cit., p. 163.
46 John Fielden, op. cit., p. 68.
47 Adam Smith, 'Wealth of Nations', vol. I, London, Gollancz, p. 141.
48 David Roberts, 'Paternalism in Early Victorian England', London, Croom Helm, 1979, p. 85.
49 Ibid., p. 4.
50 Rev. Richard Parkinson, 'On the Present Condition of the Labouring Poor in Manchester', London, Simpkin, Marshall & Co., 1841, pp. 13, 17, 18-19.
51 Roberts, op. cit., p. 172.
52 Pollard, op. cit., pp. 267, 268.
53 Revolt of the Workers, 'Blackwood's Magazine', vol. 52, 1842, pp. 646-7.
54 The Claim of Labour, 'Edinburgh Review', vol. 81, 1845, pp. 304-5.
55 P. Gaskell, 'Artisans and Machinery' (1836), London, Frank Cass, 1968, p. 78.
56 Ibid., p. 111.
57 Ibid., p. 96.
58 Ibid., pp. 289-90.
59 Cf. Fielden, op. cit., pp. 29-30.
60 Quoted from D.G. Paz, 'The Politics of Working-Class Education in Britain 1830-50', Manchester University Press, 1980, p. 51.
61 Ibid.
62 Cf. A.P. Wadsworth, The First Manchester Sunday Schools, 'Bulletin of John Rylands Library', 33, 1951, pp. 299-326.
63 H. Brougham, 'Practical Observations upon the Education of the People, Addressed to the Working Classes and Their Employers', (13th edn), London, 1825, p. 31.
64 Piven and Cloward, op. cit., pp. 135-6.

3 THE SELF-ASSEMBLY OF CLASS

1 R.S. Neale, 'Class in English Society 1680-1850', Oxford, Blackwell, 1981, p. 98.
2 Francis Hearn, 'Domination, Legitimation, and Resistance', Greenwood Press, London, 1978, p. 242.

3 J.S. Mill, 'Principles of Political Economy', (4th edn), vol. IV, London, John W. Parker & Son, ch. 7.
4 Guy Fourquin, 'The Anatomy of Popular Rebellion in the Middle Ages', trans. Anne Chester, Amsterdam, North Holland Publishing Co., 1978, p. 163.
5 Dorothy Marshall, 'Industrial England 1776-1851', London, Routledge & Kegan Paul, 1973, p. 118.
6 Ibid., pp. 115, 120.
7 John Foster, 'Class Struggle and the Industrial Revolution', London, Weidenfeld & Nicolson, 1974, p. 33.
8 Peter N. Stearns, 'Paths to Authority', University of Illinois Press, 1978, p. 119.
9 Foster, op. cit., p. 26.
10 Witt Bowden, 'Industrial Society in England towards the end of the Eighteenth Century'. London, Macmillan, 1925, pp. 274-5.
11 Ibid., p. 293.
12 J.L. Hammond and Barbara Hammond, 'The Town Labourer 1760-1832' (1917), London, Longmans, 1966, pp. 239, 307.
13 Quoted from Patricia Hollis (ed.), 'Class and Conflict in Nineteenth-Century England 1815-1850', London, Routledge & Kegan Paul, 1973, pp. 332-3.
14 Present Condition of the People, 'Fraser's Magazine', vol. 9, 1834, pp. 74-5 and 78.
15 Bowden, op. cit., pp. 293 and 294.
16 G. Howell, Trade Unionism - New and Old, in H. de B. Gibbins (ed.), 'Social Questions of Today', London, Methuen, 1891, pp. 1-2.
17 J.M. Ludlow, Trade Societies and the Social Science Association, 'Macmillan's Magazine', February-March 1861, p. 316.
18 Cf. L. Brentano, On the History and Development of Guilds, in Toulmin Smith (ed.), 'English Guilds', London, Early English Text Society, 1870.
19 G. Unwin, 'Industrial Organisation in the Sixteenth and Seventeenth Centuries', Oxford University Press, 1904, p. 200.
20 Cf. A.E. Musson, 'The Typographical Association', Oxford University Press, 1954, p. 14.
21 Cf. A. Howe and H.E. Waite, 'The London Society of Compositors', London, Cassell, 1948, p. 82.
22 Cf. W. Kiddier, 'The Old Trade Unions', London, Allen & Unwin, 1930, p. 66.
23 Cf. G.C. Holland, 'The Vital Statistics of Sheffield', Sheffield, Greaves, 1843, pp. 182-3.
24 Cf. W.H. Warburton, 'The History of Trade Union Organisation in the North Staffordshire Potteries', London, Allen & Unwin, 1931, pp. 11-12.
25 Cf. Unwin, op. cit., p. 214 ff.
26 Cf. Howe and Waite, op. cit., p. 53.
27 Selig Perlman, 'A Theory of the Labour Movement', London, Macmillan, 1928, pp. 242-3.
28 Cf. W. Ross Ashby, 'An Introduction to Cybernetics', London, Chapman & Hall, 1958.
29 John Rule, 'The Experience of Labour in the Eighteenth Century', London, Croom Helm, 1981, p. 157.
30 Ibid., pp. 163-4.
31 Trades Unions and Strikes, 'Edinburgh Review', vol. 67, 1838, pp. 209-59.
32 Cf. Foster, op. cit., pp. 228-9.
33 P.J. Armstrong, J.F.B. Goodman and J.D. Hyman, 'Ideology and Shop-floor Industrial Relations', London, Croom Helm, 1981, pp. 43, 53-4, 74, 61.
34 Foster, op. cit., pp. 42-3.
35 Bowden, op. cit., pp. 289-90.
36 Cf. Claims of Labour, 'Westminster Review', vol. 43, 1845, pp. 445-60.

37 The Claims of Labour, 'Edinburgh Review', vol. 81, 1845, pp. 498-523.
38 Paul J. McNulty, 'The Origins and Development of Labour Economics', MIT Press, 1980, p. 24.
39 Ibid., p. 64-5.
40 Ellen Frankel Paul, 'Moral Revolution and Economic Science', London, Greenwood Press, 1979, p. 157.
41 Anton Menger, 'The Right to the Whole Product of Labour', trans. M.E. Tanner, London, Macmillan, 1899, pp. 53, 56.
42 Thomas Hodgskin, 'Labour Defended against the Claims of Capital' (1825), London, Hammersmith Bookshop, 1924, pp. 62, 83, 99.
43 Ibid., p. 70.
44 William Thompson, 'An Inquiry into the Principles of the Distribution of Wealth Most Conducive to Human Happiness', London, S. Orr & Co., 1850, pp. 67-8.
45 Cf. Claus Offe and Herbert Wiesenthal, Two Logics of Collective Action, in Maurice Zeitlin (ed.), 'Political Power and Social Theory', Greenwich, Conn., IAI Press, vol. I, 1980, pp. 75, 78-9, 74, 79.

4 THE TENDENCY OF INDUSTRIAL SOCIETY: AN INTERIM SUMMARY

1 Patricia Hollis (ed.), 'Class and Conflict in Nineteenth-Century England 1815-1850', London, Routledge & Kegan Paul, 1973, p. 35.
2 Allan Flanders, 'Trade Unions', London, Hutchinson, 1965, p. 76.
3 Ellen Frankel Paul, 'Moral Revolution and Economic Science', London, Greenwood Press, 1979, p. 185.
4 J.S. Mill, 'The Principles of Political Economy', Clifton, N.J., Augustus Kelley (17th edn), p. 977.
5 W. Arthur Lewis, 'The Principles of Economic Planning', Dickson, Chicago, 1949, p. 423.
6 P. Samuelson, 'Economics', New York, McGraw Hill, 1948, p. 16.

5 CORPORATISM AND ITS DISCONTENTS

1 John Dunn, 'Western Political Theory in the Face of the Future', Cambridge University Press, 1979, p. 30.
2 Cf. J.F. Clarke, 'The Pattern of Expectations 1644-2001', London, Jonathan Cape, 1979, pp. 276-9.
3 Stephen Rousseas, 'Capitalism and Catastrophe', Cambridge University Press, 1979, p. 98.
4 William Krehm, 'Babel's Tower, The Dynamic Economic Breakdown', Toronto, Thornwood Publishers, 1977, p. 2.
5 Gardiner C. Means, The Problems and Prospects of Collective Capitalism, in Warren J. Samuels (ed.), 'The Economy as a System of Power', vol. 1, New Brunswick, Transaction Books, 1978, p. 124.
6 Philip A. Klein, Economics: Allocation or Valuation? in ibid., p. 13.
7 Cf. A. Shonfield, 'Modern Capitalism', Oxford University Press, 1965.
8 J.F. Wright, 'Britain in the Age of Economic Management', Oxford University Press, 1979, p. 67.
9 Leopold Kohr, 'The Overdeveloped Nations, The Diseconomics of Scale', Swansea, Christopher Davies, n.d., p. 65.
10 Fred Emery, 'Futures We Are In', Leiden, Martinus Nijhoff, 1977, pp. 9-12.
11 Robert L. Heilbroner, 'Business Civilisation in Decline', New York, W.W. Norton, 1976, p. 35.
12 Keith Midd' nas, 'Politics in Industrial Society, The Experience of the British System since 1911', London, André Deutsch, 1979, p. 433.
13 Claus Offe and Volker Rouge, Theses on the Theory of the State, in J.W. Freidberg (ed.), 'Critical Theory - European Perspectives', New York, Irvington Publishers, 1979, p. 349.
14 Robert Lekachman, 'Economist at Bay', New York, McGraw Hill,

1976, p. 137.
15 Offe and Rouge, op. cit., p. 349.
16 Bob Jessop, The Transformation of the State in Post-War Britain, in Richard Scase (ed.), 'The State in Western Europe', London, Croom Helm, 1980, p. 58.
17 Middlemas, op. cit., p. 391.
18 Ibid., p. 383.
19 Introduction 'The State in Western Europe', p. 16.
20 Middlemas, op. cit., p. 377.
21 Norbert Elias, 'The Civilising Process', trans. Edmund Jephcott, Oxford, Blackwell, 1978, p. 238.
22 James O'Connor, 'The Corporations and the State', New York, Harper, 1974, p. 114.
23 Ibid., p. 142.
24 Alain Touraine, Eight Ways to Eliminate the Sociology of Action, in 'Critical Theory - European Perspectives', p. 187.
25 Jürgen Habermas, 'Legitimation Crisis', trans. Thomas McCarthy, Heinemann, 1976, p. 63.
26 Ibid., pp. 62-3.
27 Offe and Rouge, op. cit., p. 353.
28 Krehm, op. cit., pp. 78 and 91.
29 Lekachman, op. cit., p. 57.
30 Claus Offe, 'Industry and Inequality', trans. James Wickam, Arnold, 1976, p. 12.
31 John H. Schaar, Equality of Opportunity and Beyond, in Anthony de Crespigny and Alan Wertheimer (eds), 'Contemporary Political Theory', New York, Nelson, 1970, p. 147.
32 Cf. Neil W. Chamberlain, 'Forces of Change in Western Europe', New York, McGraw Hill, 1980, ch. 6.
33 Ibid., p. 254.
34 Alain Touraine, 'Production de la société', Paris, Seuil, 1973, pp. 190, 196, 157.
35 Alain Touraine, 'Le voix et le regard', Paris, Seuil, 1978, pp. 72-3, 111.

6 NEW CONTRADICTIONS, NEW VICTIMS

1 Robert L. Heilbroner, 'An Inquiry into the Human Prospect', New York, W.W. Norton, 1974, p. 18.
2 Gregory Bateson, 'Steps to an Ecology of Mind', London, Paladin, 1973, p. 409.
3 William Krehm, 'Babel's Tower, The Dynamic Economic Breakdown', Toronto, Thornwood Publishers, 1977, p. 16.
4 Vic George and Roger Lawson (eds), 'Poverty and Inequality in Common Market Countries', London, Routledge & Kegan Paul, 1980, pp. 241-2.
5 Frank Parkin, 'Marxism and Class Theory', London, Tavistock, 1979, p. 83.
6 Robert L. Heilbroner, 'Business Civilisation in Decline', New York, W.W. Norton, 1976, p. 109.
7 Arthur M. Okun, Equality and Efficiency, Colin D. Campbell (ed.), 'Income Distribution', Washington, American Enterprise Institute for Public Policy Research, 1977, p. 29.
8 H.W. Arndt, 'The Rise and Fall of Economic Growth', London, Longman, 1978, p. 146.
9 C.A.R. Crosland, 'Socialism Now and Other Essays', London, Jonathan Cape, 1974, p. 79.
10 Fred Hirsch, 'Social Limits to Growth', London, Routledge & Kegan Paul, 1978, p. 5 and many other pages throughout the book.
11 Ibid., p. 32.
12 Cf. Leopold Kohr, 'The Overdeveloped Nations, The Diseconomies of

Scale', Swansea, Christopher Davies, n.d., pp. 39–42.

13 Reginald J. Harrison, 'Pluralism and Corporatism', London, George Allen & Unwin, 1980, p. 73.

14 Hirsch, op. cit., p. 38.

15 E.J. Mishan, Ills, Bads and Disamenities: The Wages of Growth, in Mancur Olson and Hans H. Landesberg (eds), 'The No-Growth Society', London, Woburn Press, 1975, pp. 74, 84.

16 Max Scheler, 'Ressentiment', trans. William W. Holdheim, Chicago, Free Press, 1961, pp. 23-4.

17 Ibid., p. 50.

18 Stephen Rousseas, 'Capitalism and Catastrophe', Cambridge University Press, 1979, p. 82.

19 E.J. Mishan, 'The Costs of Economic Growth', Harmondsworth, Penguin, 1969, p. 177.

20 Claus Offe, Political Authority and Class Structures, trans. Michel Vale, 'International Journal of Sociology' 1972, vol. II, no. 1, pp. 73-108.

21 Ibid., p. 102.

22 Gunnar Myrdal, 'Challenge of Affluence', London, Gollancz, 1964, p. 29.

23 Ibid., pp. 40, 43.

24 Lawson & George, op. cit., p. 240.

25 Harriet Martineau, 'The Parish', 1833: quoted in Karl Polanyi, 'The Great Transformation', Boston, Beacon Press, 1957, p. 100.

26 Dudley Jackson, 'Poverty', London, Macmillan, 1972, p. 13. Also cf. G.P. Marshall, 'Social Goals and Economic Perspectives', Harmondsworth, Penguin, 1980, pp. 128 ff.

27 Cf. B. Abel-Smith and P. Townsend, 'The Poor and the Poorest', London, Bell, 1965; P. Townsend, Poverty as Relative Deprivation, in Dorothy Wedderburn (ed.), 'Poverty, Inequality and Class Structure', Cambridge University Press, 1974; P. Townsend, 'Poverty in the United Kingdom', London, Allan Lane, 1979.

28 Robert Lekachman, ' Economists at Bay', New York, McGraw Hill, 1976, p. 138.

29 In Joseph A. Schumpeter, 'Capitalism, Socialism, and Democracy', London, George Allen & Unwin, 1976, p. III.

Index